# COMMITTING JOURNALISM

# COMMITTING JOURNALISM

## THE PRISON WRITINGS OF RED HOG

*By Dannie M. Martin and Peter Y. Sussman*

W.W. NORTON & COMPANY

NEW YORK   LONDON

Excerpt from "Truckin'" by the Grateful Dead. Words by Robert
Hunter. Music by Jerome Garcia, Philip Lesh and Robert Weir.
Copyright © 1971 by Ice Nine Publishing Company, Inc.

The text of this book is composed in 11.5/13.5 Berkeley Old Style Book,
with the display set in Latino Elongated at 180% horizontal scale.
Manufacturing by the Haddon Craftsmen, Inc.
Book design by Margaret M. Wagner.

Library of Congress Cataloging-in-Publication Data
Martin, Dannie M.
Committing journalism : the prison writings of Red Hog / by Dannie
M. Martin and Peter Y. Sussman.
p.    cm.
1. Martin, Dannie M.    2. Prisoners—United States—Biography.
3. Journalists—United States—Biography.    4. Prisons—United
States.    I. Sussman, Peter Y.    II. Title.
HV9468.M3A3    1993
365'.44'092—dc20
[B]                                  93-12569


ISBN 0-393-31322-0


W. W. Norton & Company, Inc.
500 Fifth Avenue, New York, N.Y. 10110
W. W. Norton & Company Ltd.
10 Coptic Street, London WC1A 1PU

1  2  3  4  5  6  7  8  9  0

In memory of
Mrs. Gay K. Eddy, 1920–1991,
a loyal reader, a feisty supporter,
and a true friend to us both

# CONTENTS

I committed bank robbery and they put me in prison, and that was right. Then I committed journalism and they put me in the hole. And that was wrong.

DANNIE M. MARTIN

# COMMITTING JOURNALISM

# INTRODUCTION: A COMMON CRIMINAL

The man they call Red Hog was coming home to a city he'd never lived in, and a television camera followed his progress down the plane ramp.

Three and a half hours out of prison, Dannie Martin walked ponderously, like an astronaut just arrived back on Earth, as he descended from the commercial airliner toward a cluster of well-wishers at San Francisco International Airport. It was shortly after noon. The ruddy-faced former bank robber with the shaggy mustache and the thick thatch of blond-gray hair was wearing prison-issue white golf shirt and blue polyester slacks, handmade leather moccasins, and a grin that stretched from San Francisco to Phoenix.

He was walking into the glare of a television light and a strange new life, yet he had none of the wary, wry reticence I had come to associate with him in prison visiting rooms. Where Dannie had spent the previous eleven years, it was dangerous to betray the kind of open, unalloyed emotion he exhibited that day.

Although he carried only a few possessions off the plane, he brought with him far more baggage than he realized at the time. Life would never be as easy as it looked at that glowing moment.

Dannie's release from a federal prison in Phoenix on October 23, 1991, marked the end of his five-and-a-half-year "career" as a convict-writer, mostly in the pages of the *San Francisco Chronicle*'s "Sunday Punch" section, of which I am the editor. Dannie's was a distinguished career—the first lawful one he had ever had—that won him a national readership, numerous journalism awards, and, along the way, a stretch in solitary confinement. That last episode also made him the focus of an unprecedented First Amendment lawsuit.

Because of him, Kevin Sherbondy, twenty-five, had been freed from an unjust fifteen-year sentence, thirty-two-year-old John Chaffee's prolonged death agony had become the subject of a federal prison investigation, and dozens of formerly anonymous prisoners had regained their individual birthrights.

After greeting his welcomers and answering questions from the journalists who had met his plane, Dannie was walking down the airport corridor when a young woman rushed up to him, handed him a book she had been reading, and requested his autograph.

"My what?" he asked, incredulous.

"Your autograph," replied the young woman.

"Well, I'll be," said Dannie in his characteristic drawl.

For the last year and a half of his prison term, he had not been able to use his own name on his newspaper articles because of a federal court ruling, and now an admirer wanted him to sign his name. It was his first autograph request.

Over the next few days there were to be many other firsts for the self-described "hillbilly" as he settled into a halfway house in a city he was adopting at age fifty-two—but which had long since adopted him *in absentia*. In his first hours and days on the outside, Dannie lived in a swirl of excitement in an utterly new environment. To all appearances, he was a very different person from the heroin addict and lifelong criminal who had last entered prison in 1980.

Like all emerging convicts, Dannie was confronted with a disorienting assault of speed and sensory stimulation, but there was the added excitement of media and public attention. Interview requests had begun stacking up weeks before his release. Letters and phone calls from readers flooded into the *San Francisco Chronicle,* offering good wishes and financial and other assistance and expressing appreciation for his courageous journalism.

At the San Francisco airport, Dannie's initial instinct was to seek out small, familiar certainties. He asked to stop at an airport shop. After eleven years of confinement, his first request was to purchase some legal-size yellow writing tablets like those on which he had hand-printed his prison dispatches. "I feel naked without them," he said.

It didn't take Dannie long to start using those pads. The "convict-writer" whose formal education had ended with a high school diploma that he earned in prison was determined to become a writer without a hyphen.

Simultaneously, he had to deal with the cosmic changes in his personal life. Because of his writing, the man who still called himself a "redneck thug" seemed to have skipped a few rungs in social class. But he was able to see the humor in his incongruous new life:

Two weeks after his release from prison, Dannie and I were honored by the Prison Law Office. Among the many lawyers, elected officials, and other professionals who introduced themselves to Dannie at the reception was a man who passed him a business card on which he had written that he had enjoyed the convict's reports and would like to take him to dinner. Dannie put the card in his pocket with the others that had been thrust at him, and only later, back in the halfway house, did he look at his pocketful of cards and realize that this admirer was a bank operations manager. Dannie told me later, bemusedly, "The last bank manager I talked to, I took him into the vault and told him I was taking all his money. And now here's a bank manager who wants to *take me out to dinner!*"

Dannie walked out of the prison in October 1991, but before slipping into the looser leash of parole, he had to negotiate four months of quasi-captivity in the halfway house—a period that started with drama and goodwill but ended closer to a peculiarly demented theater of the absurd.

As Dannie scrambled to catch up with the world and his new role in it, he and I were also drawn to the past, defining in retrospect our five and a half years as collaborators and long-distance friends. The behind-the-scenes story of that improbable joint venture will be interspersed in the following chapters with the writings through which Dannie made his mark.

■

In August 1986, when I published in the *Chronicle* Dannie Martin's first commentary on prison life, the forty-six-year-old convict had a rap sheet that spanned more than thirty years. He had done about twenty-one years in reform schools, prison camps, jails, prisons, penitentiaries, even a workhouse chain gang, and he was six years into a thirty-three-year sentence for bank robbery at Lompoc penitentiary, a federal prison in central California. He was, as he later wrote, "a criminal by any definition I know of."

I had done twenty-two years as an editor at the *Chronicle*, and I could not then imagine a more unlikely writer, let alone colleague, than this burly convict known to his fellow prisoners as Red Hog.

Yet our unusual journalistic collaboration—though that would have seemed far too grandiose a word for what we began doing that summer—has had a widening national impact. In more than fifty essays, most of them reprinted in this book, the self-educated bank robber has given a human face to his fellow convicts, challenging prevailing American attitudes toward prisons and prisoners during a time when the United States surpassed the former Soviet Union and South Africa to become the nation with the highest percentage of its population behind bars.

It was only later that I learned what a remarkable man I was teaming up with. He is a person of many apparent contradictions. In appearance and manner, he is rough around the edges, with a face that bears the scars of a knockabout life in the seamiest of neighborhoods and a body that sports the forbidding tattoos so dear to the committed outlaw. But in social situations his kindness and sensitivity set at ease people who would otherwise feel instinctively uncomfortable in his company.

He is a powerfully built man, a weight lifter, who has long lived in the company of imprisoned men who respect physical presence; in the words of one old friend, Dannie always gave the appearance of a man "whose plumes can still come up." He is also a closet poet, a writer of fairy tales, and a kitchen-table philosopher who is passionately interested in the works of the nineteenth-century philosopher Arthur Schopenhauer and rarely misses a copy of *The New Yorker*.

An outsider by temperament, he is a loving father and grandfather and the most loyal of friends. He is often happiest in solitary pursuits, yet he is an easygoing, gregarious raconteur.

He is a highly intelligent man who has done the dumbest of things; a stubbornly independent person who has spent his life in abject dependence on heroin and other addicting drugs. He has what one friend calls "a fierce sense of justice," yet he has committed the grossest of injustices.

Dannie has lived in extreme situations and seen others *in extremis*.

Perhaps one needs to see people at their worst to recognize also the best that they are capable of. For whatever reason, Dannie was able to write with compassion and honesty about a world that contained little of either. His revealing free-lance narratives and engaging writing style soon gained him a large readership, both in Northern California and—through wire-service syndication—in newspapers throughout the country.

The response was also enthusiastic among Dannie's fellow convicts; as with all prisoners, their deadening isolation had been reinforced by the stereotyped ways they were regarded by the world outside the walls. Countless correspondents from jails and prisons have told us over the years that they never expected to see their perspective portrayed in the news media. In Dannie they found a voice, someone who did much to "help 'jail people' become 'regular people,' " in the words of one convict letter writer.

In the five-plus years over which these prison essays were written, Dannie and I made few overall assessments of our venture as we shaped each story for publication in the *Chronicle*. Indeed, prison life, like journalism, is notoriously a day-by-day existence, with little room for sweeping evaluations or projections. But in retrospect, ours appears to have become the most sustained attempt in memory to tell the inside story of prison life in a general-circulation newspaper.

Through most of those years, I conferred with Dannie almost daily by phone, living the prison life vicariously (by far the best way to do time). In turn, I was his primary link with the readers and their interests and with the reporters who wanted to tell the world of this compelling writer and the legal stir he had kicked up.

In our collaboration is a useful metaphor. As Dannie gained more of a stake in the society whose values he had ignored all his life, we forged a mutual trust. Dannie and I—a junkie who had spent most of his adult life inside prisons and an editor who had seen prisons only from a car window—were passing figurative messages back and forth between our respective worlds. We were opening the way for dialogue about crime and punishment in this culture that has had too much of each.

It was a heady role for the ne'er-do-well son of migrant workers from California's Central Valley. Dannie never made more than glancing references in his *Chronicle* essays to his own crimes and personal history, so newspaper readers never got a proper introduction to the popular writer. We will correct that deficiency here and then proceed on to Dannie's writings and to the eventful story behind his high-risk journalism career. Although it may not fit in with Americans' upbeat mythology of growing up in this country, in many respects Dannie's life of crime and addiction is an all-American story.

Dannie's history reads like the sequel to a Steinbeck novel; it begins soon after the migration of his mother and father in the great "Okie" influx into California's agricultural heartland.

Zellium (Zell) Rosson and her parents arrived in California in 1937, working their way out from Alabama, from farm to farm. While most of her family labored in the fields on a cotton-and-grain ranch in Dos Palos, California, Zell, then nineteen, cooked in the single farmhands' boardinghouse. There, in the summer of '37, she met ranchhand Roy Martin, twenty, who had arrived with his brother not long before on a boxcar from tiny Silsbee, Texas.

Roy was big and physically tough, a handsome man, a dancer and "a charmer," his family recalls. He worked a hard six-day week in the fields. He was also an alcoholic; it ran in the family. Roy never got into serious trouble with the law, but he acknowledges he "wasn't any angel" and would often get into fights under the influence of the bottle before "the Lord took it away from me" in 1965. He has been a teetotaler and a devout Southern Baptist since then.

Zell was a large woman, a flaming redhead, who is described by everyone in her family as a wise and happy person with an open, tolerant, and gentle manner. She was for most of Dannie's life a deeply religious woman. Everyone agrees that Zell never smoked and never tasted alcohol in her life.

Roy and Zell were married a year after they met on the Dos Palos farm. One year later, in 1939, their first son, Dannie, was born in Stockton, another farm town. The couple later had two more sons, Jerry and Jimmy. Through most of their years together, Zell and Roy worked in fields and ranchhouses throughout California's Central Valley. "We were just a poor family in a poor time," says Roy.

By all accounts, the Martins were a happy, loving family. "We grew up hard, but we were a close family," as Dannie's aunt, Peggy Frost, puts it. But when family members talk of Dannie's younger years, many of their anecdotes center around alcohol.

Peggy, two years older than Dannie and a frequent childhood companion, says that the boy "got the taste of alcohol real early." When he was two years old and still in diapers, family legend has it, Dannie would tag along with the menfolk as they advanced down the rows of cotton, picking and talking. His job was to fetch the wine. Sometimes, by the time he'd catch up with the men, the boy would be staggering drunkenly. The men "got a big kick out of this," his brother Jerry reports, until Zell found out about it and "the wine hit the fan."

A year later, at three, he got into the beer in a closed ballpark concession stand with an older cousin. His aunt Peggy says Dannie was almost lifeless when the boys were found.

Drink also played a major role in what Dannie recalls as perhaps his earliest and certainly his most terrifying childhood memory: the night in 1947 when his mother kicked his father out of the house for good. Roy Martin was a mean, abusive drunk, and he was very drunk that night. Dannie remembers cowering by a coal heater in their wooden shack as his mother and father fought in their small bedroom.

Roy Martin never lived with the family again after that night, and the couple were soon divorced. But he did pass through town on visits over the years, and when Dannie was a delinquent teenager he several times went to stay with his father in Colorado and then Texas.

After the split from Roy Martin, Zell and her sons moved in with her parents, who at the time were running a cafe in Clovis, near Fresno. When the cafe went bankrupt two years later, Zell's father got a job in a cotton gin, and all three generations of the family moved to nearby Pinedale. It was in that hot, flat, godforsaken farm town of two thousand that Dannie spent his teenage years—when he wasn't in reform school or jail. Roy Martin calls the town one of his son's "curses . . . a terrible place for a child to be brought up." Brother Jerry says it was the kind of place that "just followed you through life."

The town's social structure was rigid and easy to understand: "Okies and hillbillies" on one side of Minarets Street, Mexicans on the other— and all of them dirt-poor. For all practical purposes, working meant picking crops. It was a living, and not much more.

Pinedale was a town of dirt roads, shacks, tents, and outdoor toilets. In fact, when Zell and her family first moved there they lived in a tent in a backyard while her father upgraded a one-room shack into what was to become the family home.

Commercial Pinedale consisted of two bars and a small pool hall, along with three small markets, a gas station, a whorehouse, a small movie theater, and a post office.

One of the few public buildings was the modest Pinedale Baptist

Church down the block from the Martin family home. There Zell worshiped and did various volunteer chores through a succession of ministers. Dannie was brought up in the church—"my mom saw to that," says brother Jerry—and relatives still proudly show a certificate attesting to the ten-year-old's "regular attendance and faithful work in the Vacation Bible School" at Pinedale Baptist Church.

It didn't quite take. Dannie now says his mother "put a hell of a conscience in me, though she couldn't get me to be religious." Nevertheless, he retains an intimate knowledge of the Bible and quotes from it frequently. And he has an almost biblical sense of evil and sin.

Dannie unquestionably missed something by being unable to believe in the simple but powerful religion of his mother. Indeed, it sometimes seems as if he grew up with a strong moral code and an equally strong spiritual vacuum—and with enough booze and dope to help him ignore them both.

The picture that relatives give of pre-teen Dannie is of a highly intelligent boy who, perhaps out of boredom with his peers, was always hanging out with and trying to prove himself to older kids, and then getting into scrapes with them, often on a dare. Family members say that in grammar school his IQ was measured as 147. As a three- or four-year-old, he appeared to have a photographic memory. After his mother read a book to him, he would recite it back to her word for word, although he could not yet read. He got by easily in school without ever needing to study.

The scrappy redhead was known in school for his pranks and his smart-ass independence. He was skipped from the sixth to the eighth grade; his family says it was because of his good grades, but Dannie suggests that a fight he had with a teacher might also have had something to do with his rapid elevation—she refused to have him in her class the following year.

Dannie's high school was in Clovis, seven miles from his home and a very different kind of town. It was a snooty place where the kids were more likely to be the children of ranchers than field hands. Clovis people called their neighbors from Pinedale "white trash," and they nicknamed the town "Winedale."

When he thinks back to his high school years, it is not events in the classroom that come most readily to Dannie's mind. He remembers drinking with friends in his first year of high school; they'd get local winos to buy booze for them. The gang of five or six kids, again mostly older than Dannie, would party all weekend and late into the night during the week, often heading to the fig orchards in Dannie's '49 Ford for some heavy-duty drinking, smoking, and fighting. Dannie believes that every one of those buddies ended up in reform school and prison except for one who went on to work in an auto plant in Detroit.

By the age of sixteen, Dannie had stopped putting in even occasional appearances at Clovis High.

The road to reform school and jail began with malicious pranks and neighborhood ruckuses: setting fire to a cotton trailer and taking a potshot at a neighbor's dog that had mauled his cat. No charges were filed for those misadventures.

When, at thirteen, he and an older friend went joyriding in a car stolen from a teacher, Dannie got probation on an auto theft charge, but not before spending about a week in juvenile hall in Modesto, his first taste of incarceration. He does not recall it as a particularly scary experience.

At fifteen, he burglarized a school with four or five friends. It was not a sophisticated crime—the boys were after the contents of the safe, but no matter how hard they beat that safe, they couldn't make a dent in it. When he was caught, in a car in an orchard just after the burglary, his probation on the auto theft was revoked and he was sent to an honor camp in the mountains near Bakersfield.

Camp Owens was run with military discipline. Dannie walked off within a day or two. When he was picked up down the road, hitchhiking, he was returned to juvenile hall and then sent to reform school at Paso Robles for a year. He was just turning sixteen, and there he did get an education—in crime and prisons—that he was to remember the rest of his life.

He calls Paso Robles "one of the meanest places I've ever done time." The staff was brutal and the other delinquents not much better, and Dannie, who never liked violence, felt he had to fight several times a week just to be "left alone." As one writer has said, "For the kids at Paso Robles, there are only two choices of identity: victimizer or victim."

Dannie got back at his captors through smart-aleck games like strutting to a syncopated beat when the young men were marched from place to place.

In many respects, Paso Robles was a classic prison, and Dannie soon learned his way around. There were special dorms for gays and sex criminals. Blacks and Hispanics congregated in their own groups, as did the "stool pigeons." And there was a system of gangs by which one was tested and gained "respect."

The gangs were called the Little Firm and the Big Firm. Dannie felt like a hick when he arrived; he had not been to reform school before, as many of the other kids had, so he was unknown to them. About forty or fifty of the boys sat staring at him when he first arrived. When someone tried to steal his chair, Dannie fought for it until a guard broke up the scuffle. Having passed that first test, Dannie was invited to sit with the members of the Little Firm. Later, when a boy from the Big Firm saw his spunk, he was asked to sit with that group. He had arrived.

At Paso Robles, like all career cons, he also got himself a lifelong nickname. The redhead was dubbed Red Hog after he "got into a fight with a guy over a pork chop. . . . In fact, I went to the hole for it." For all practical purposes it became his name. When, in the mid-'80s, he began earning widespread recognition under the name Dannie M. Martin, many prison buddies did not recognize the byline. His nickname was so much a part of Dannie's own identity that on at least one occasion he even signed a legal paper "Dannie M. Martin AKA 'Red Hog.' "

At seventeen, a year after leaving Paso Robles, Dannie burglarized a wine cellar in an exclusive suburb near his hometown, walking off with most of the wine. He was caught easily when he tried to sell it in Pinedale, and this time he got his first prison sentence, at Deuel Vocational Institution in Tracy, a facility for young offenders and older men.

At Tracy, Dannie fit right in. He met a group of boys from Paso Robles who remembered him as a member of the Big Firm and vouched for him, so he immediately got in with the "regulars," the tough and committed outlaws. He has been in that group ever since.

At Tracy he also perfected the "stuff it" attitude that he was to carry with him into each of the prisons he frequented with little interruption for the next thirty-plus years. He smuggled in marijuana. He taunted his captors. He also began walking the walk of the longtime con. That exaggeratedly slow pace is a wordless way of telling one's keepers: "I may be doing time, but I'm doing it at my own sweet time." After a lifetime of conditioning, he still walks with that shuffling gait.

While at Tracy, with a minimum of exertion, Dannie took several classes, enough to assemble the credits he needed for a high school diploma, the end of his formal education.

Dannie's next scrape with the law—the last of his childhood—was for receiving stolen property. He landed in a road camp. There, after stealing some pills from a guard's house and getting the whole camp loaded, he was placed in the Fresno County Jail drunk tank. Guards shaved off his long hair and threw the bald young rebel into a sunless cell, where he spent about a year "going halfway batty."

However difficult that may have been for Dannie, the succession of prisons also made him something of a hero in the eyes of his home-town buddies. He believes that by the time he got out, he knew prison was to be his life. And, he told himself, he had survived the experience, it wasn't that bad, he could handle it.

■

For all Dannie's substance abuse, by this time in his life he was not yet a heroin addict, and he vigorously rejects the notion that drink or drugs made him a criminal. He believes his own decision to become a criminal was just that—a conscious decision. And he attributes his choice to one major factor: his lifelong abhorrence of work. He recalls watching his grandfather come in from the cotton fields, dirty and tired and "getting nowhere." Subsequently, in Pinedale and in prison and wherever else he lived, Dannie and the people he associated with lived by the same simple credo; as he puts it, "That's the line we won't cross: We ain't carryin' no lunch bucket."

He says, "In my day, it was get a high school education, get a wife, get a bunch of kids, get a TV on credit, get a car and refrigerator on credit. People just sort of drifted through life like that. I never wanted any of it. . . . I rejected the work ethic. If you're lower-class and reject work, there's not much else except crime and prison."

So the young man and his friends started adult life with the most libertine of values—in his own words, "We'll do what we want until we get caught." But that is not to say he observed no values whatso-ever. Both in prison and outside, Dannie lived by the most rigid of ethical rules: the convict code. The strict underworld laws were passed down from one generation of convict to another, and Dannie had them down cold while still a teenager. He cleaves to the code with all the rigor of a Southern Baptist, despite the dwindling number of old-time cons who share his beliefs.

For Dannie's tribe, informing is the deadliest sin. They obey their own laws, they are straight with each other, and they pay their debts. "We live by our word," he says. "If your word's no good, then you're no good. If I tell someone I'm going to pay him some money, that's better than any kind of paper I could sign."

They despise sex crimes and sex criminals, and they despise personal violence—except in self-defense or to punish violators of the code. In the heyday of the code, outlaws stayed out of the way of "squares," but "everything in a uniform was the enemy, and if you got caught, it was name, rank, and serial number. I never pleaded guilty to anything in my life."

■

After his release from the Fresno County Jail in 1959, Dannie, then twenty, went to stay with his father in Silsbee, Texas. Roy Martin says the move was intended "to keep him away from the gang he was hanging out with," but the young man managed to find new gangs to hang out with. When he returned to Fresno a couple of years later he had a young wife and a baby daughter; he also had a few more arrests under his belt and the beginnings of a lifelong drug habit.

In Silsbee and nearby Beaumont and then in Houston, Dannie attracted people, and, again, most of the people he attracted were older and they were troublemakers—with one exception. Linda was a beautiful, quiet Cajun woman who was married to a military man. Her husband was out of the area on duty when she met Dannie at a skating rink in Silsbee.

Linda and Dannie fell in love, and Linda was soon pregnant. Roy Martin's small-town neighbors were scandalized by the relationship, so the young couple left town for Houston. After Linda's divorce, she married Dannie in April 1960, and in November of that year Linda gave birth to Julie, Dannie's only child.

In Houston, Linda found work as a cocktail waitress and Dannie worked briefly as a car salesman, but most of his time was spent in a pool and beer hall, drinking and brawling, and in the company of a legendary Texas con man who befriended him and taught him various elaborate scams.

When Dannie's Houston hangout was the scene of a drunken murder, word went out that the police would like to talk to him as a material witness. At the time, such interrogations often involved a beating and an invitation to inform on a friend, so Dannie packed up a few possessions, cashed out, picked up Linda at her job, and, by day's end, was on the road to Fresno.

Dannie first recognized his opiate addiction while on that drive home.

A year earlier, in Houston, he had begun getting high on paregoric, $1 a bottle in drugstores. He had been introduced to this diversion by a gambling buddy who had picked up his own dependence in the Army. By the time Dannie left Houston, he was taking the over-the-counter opium-based analgesic daily. From then until about the time he began writing for the *Chronicle* twenty-five years later, he used opiates continuously when he was not in prison—and often when he was there, too.

During the drive from Texas with Linda, Dannie became violently ill with diarrhea, stomach cramps, and achy bones. He thought he had the flu. His wife suggested it might have something to do with the paregoric that seemed usually to make him feel better, so they stopped at a drugstore to stock up and were informed that in California, "p.g.," as he called it, was available only by prescription. The couple headed back to the freeway, but on the way Dannie had his wife stop at another drugstore, which he robbed at gunpoint, taking drugs but declining the terrified clerk's offer of money. Thus was established not only a tenacious addiction but also a lifelong link between drugs and crime.

When the young couple reached Fresno, Dannie was not yet well connected in the drug underworld. He got his fixes by burglarizing drugstores throughout the area, taking only the drugs. He was arrested finally after burglarizing about fifteen stores and in February 1962 was convicted of possession of drugstore dope. He spent the next four years in some of California's most notorious maximum-security prisons: Soledad, San Quentin, and Folsom.

Those were turbulent years in the California prison system, and Dannie was in the thick of it. He has called the prisons of that era "a nightmare . . . pure madness." "I've seen some young men get gray hair in ninety days," he says. Dannie was in Soledad and San Quentin during major race riots—"wave upon wave of senseless killings." He knew the people who started such notorious prison gangs as the Mexican Mafia and the Aryan Brotherhood, and he knew many of the prisoners who brought 1960s radical politics to the world behind the bars. If there was any question before, Dannie was now certainly a hard-core convict.

At the beginning of his imprisonment, Linda and Julie, who were living with Dannie's mother, visited him frequently in Soledad. But some time after his transfer to San Quentin, Linda divorced him. She remarried and moved to Nashville with her new husband, a country-and-western singer and songwriter.

The divorce from Linda was shattering for Dannie. He was furious at her both for divorcing him and for taking away his daughter, although he recognizes he "didn't leave her in good shape." He believes that if he ever had a chance to make it outside of prison, the divorce killed it, for Linda and Julie were the last reasons he had to change his destructive behavior.

In the decades following his divorce, Dannie's addiction to heroin—which by now had replaced drugstore dope—reached monstrous proportions. During his years on heroin his thoughts were dominated from the instant he first opened his eyes in the morning by one overwhelming question: Where was he going to get that day's dope? His habit was so bad that during one withdrawal in 1974 he couldn't sleep for twenty-one straight days. A jail doctor watched his ordeal with tears in his eyes and told Dannie that he wouldn't live through another such withdrawal, but when the convict was released a few weeks later, he went right back on heroin.

During the '60s and '70s, Dannie "yo-yoed" to prison, to use his own word. "I was nothing but a bumbling, commonplace crook." Most of the arrests during those decades involved drugs—drugstore burglaries, possession of narcotics, sale of controlled substances, drug smuggling. The word "affray" also recurs with some frequency on his rap sheet. One such middle-of-the-night "affray" in the parking lot of a Texas drive-in restaurant left him with lifelong tinnitus and hearing loss.

There are also numerous parole violations on his rap sheet. As he put it once in a letter to me, "I've never completed a parole or probation. Usually just hang them on the wall and take off." He moved often and with no notice, finally settling for a spell in the early '70s on a farm he bought in Arlington, Washington, north of Seattle. That sojourn in Washington—a total of thirty months—was the longest period he spent out of prison as an adult. He devoted most of his time there to various drug-smuggling enterprises.

One drug-business altercation sent him before a judge in Madera, California, charged with an array of serious felonies. He got off on most of the charges after such courtroom antics as subpoenaing Death Row inmates to testify that he and the victims of the alleged crimes were all friends. The judge summed up: "I've never seen such a bunch of thugs in my life."

He played a similarly inventive game with the legal system in 1976 in Everett, Washington, where he was charged with a two-ounce heroin sale that would have got him a thirteen-year "career criminal" sentence. For well over a year, Dannie fought the rap tooth and nail and tongue in cheek. He peppered the judge with motions. One of his legal pranks was an attempt to subpoena a New York fingerprint expert by citing evidence he said was found at King Tut's tomb. Such legal high jinks cost Snohomish County a small fortune before the charges were finally dropped.

In May 1980, three months out of an Everett halfway house, Dannie dramatically changed his MO. Feeling the heat from the Drug Enforcement Administration and convinced by a former cellmate that he should go for bigger bucks, he robbed a small bank in Silverdale, near Seattle. It is a matter of some perverse pride to Dannie that he "never robbed a teller; I went to the vault and took all of it."

By posing as a businessman making a $400,000 deposit, Dannie stalled the bank's manager and gained his confidence until after closing time, when the alarms were turned off. He walked out of the bank with $105,383 and fled to Los Angeles, but there was soon a warrant out for his arrest. He lent part of the bank take to the untrustworthy friend who had inspired the robbery and blew the rest of it on partying and dope.

His second and last bank job occurred four months later, on September 10, 1980. The elaborate game plan for this one—dreamed up with the same former prison buddies—involved a plane that was standing by to whisk him and his female accomplice to safety. The bank was the Seattle First National branch in Cle Elum, Washington, pop. 1800, located ninety miles east of Seattle in "the heart of the Cascades." The bank, a simple stucco structure on the town's main drag, was chosen because employees at such a remote small-town bank would not expect a robbery; in fact, this was the only attempted robbery in the bank's sixty-year history.

To further allay fears in the bank, his accomplice wheeled Dannie into the building in a wheelchair, again just before closing time. The wheelchair gimmick was an old John Dillinger trick, says Dannie, but it worked for Dillinger. In a three-piece Western-style suit and posing as a Vietnam veteran, Dannie once again discussed large deposits until all the tellers were closed for the day. At a signal from his accomplice— apparently a premature signal—Dannie drew a .357 Magnum and announced to the manager, "I'm not depositing money; I'm taking it all with me." Once again he headed for the vault with the employees, but a teller had already sounded a silent alarm.

The chief of Cle Elum's four-man police department soon arrived at the bank and saw through a window that a robbery was in progress. Dannie dashed out of the bank and yelled at the chief, "Freeze!" Then he retreated inside as a deputy arrived on the scene. That deputy, Sam Krahenbuhl, now the police chief, says the incident could have become very serious at that point if Dannie had taken hostages, and in fact, inside the bank, Dannie's woman friend, who was also a heavy drug user, was suggesting that he do just that. Instead, muttering, "What am I gonna do with hostages once I get out there?" Dannie handed their guns to an assistant manager and said, "Bring them to the cops. I'm giving up."

Two days after the robbery, in an interview room in the Yakima County Jail, Dannie met his court-appointed attorney, thirty-five-year-old Mike Schwab, an earnest and idealistic New Yorker who had come west in the VISTA program. The bank robber was two days into heroin withdrawal, and he was a frightful sight. His hair looked electrified, his demeanor menacing; his eyes were bloodshot and rheumy, with dilated pupils. There was a button on the wall for the attorney to summon guards to the locked interview room, but Schwab was so alarmed by the "wild man" in front of him that he asked sheriff's deputies to leave the door ajar, and he positioned himself close to it in case he had to beat a quick retreat.

The man who had been caught inside the bank then further stunned his attorney by announcing, "We're going to beat this case." It was vintage Dannie. Despite the quixotic nature of some of Dannie's suggested legal tactics, over time he became an active participant in his defense. He soon realized that his idealistic defense attorney, unlike so many of his previous lawyers, was willing to fight against near-impossible odds for his client and force the government to prove its case, point by point.

Schwab says he came to admire his client's "antic mind" and "intriguing" legal ideas. And as Dannie came out of heroin withdrawal, Schwab grew comfortable in his presence. The former antipoverty lawyer began, in fact, to enjoy his unusual client and their challenging "dead loser" of a legal case.

Much to Schwab's surprise, the jury spent four or five hours deliberating the cut-and-dried case, but in the end Dannie was found guilty and sentenced to eighteen years. He was subsequently convicted of robbing the Silverdale bank, and by the time that sentence was added on, he was facing a possible thirty-three years in the pen.

By the end of the trial in Yakima, Dannie and the man who had been afraid to confer with him behind closed doors had developed a mutual respect that blossomed into friendship during the next eleven years of imprisonment. They talked by phone about once a month and established a lengthy correspondence. When Dannie embarked on his career as a published writer, Schwab was a cheerleader and an adviser.

Dannie's hard-core criminal history seems an improbable prelude to a writing career, but along the way this thug developed another addiction that did as much to liberate him as his opiate addiction did to imprison him: He began a serious reading program.

While he was out of prison, Dannie's frenetic daily search for drugs allowed him little leisure to read, but in his various cells, he became, over time, an omnivorous, eclectic reader. The self-directed education that began tentatively in his late teens prepared him for the day decades later when he would call upon a lifetime of prison experiences in explaining to the outside world what prisons look and feel like from the inside—and what they do to the people involuntarily housed there.

Family members say that both Dannie's parents read novels and magazines and other popular publications, and his mother read to her children frequently when they were young. But before his arrival at Tracy, Dannie's reading was limited to newspapers and an occasional magazine.

One day at that prison, a friend gave him a copy of Ayn Rand's *The Fountainhead* and recommended that he read it. Dannie was captivated by the book's emphasis on individuality. When he returned the volume, he inquired about other books that his friend could recommend and was soon on the list for hand-me-down reading. Among the other writers who drew him into regular reading were Steinbeck, Hemingway, and Dostoevsky.

At every prison, Dannie says, there are circles of readers of varied tastes and reading levels. There are, for example, the Stephen King / werewolf / horror readers, the Louis L'Amour western aficionados, and those who like more serious contemporary novelists. When he got to a new prison, Dannie would always seek out the latter group and get onto its distribution chain. He was soon consuming "everything I could get my hands on" by Bellow, Fast, McMurtry, Styron, Fowles, Robertson Davies, and many others. He also loved Shakespeare and remembers asking his mother to bring him a copy of his works.

Dannie says his growing passion for reading was not shared by his "running friends in the joint." They were a separate set entirely from his "book friends," leading to an occasional awkward encounter in the yard. But one prison buddy who often discussed books with Dannie comments that many prisoners were illiterate and that "everyone respected and envied Red Hog's reading." In prison, he adds, "respect like that is mostly earned through being your own man."

In his early twenties, beginning in the unlikeliest of ways, Dannie began reading philosophy. He first dipped into Plato in the Soledad Prison library to check a bit of Socratic folklore he had heard from a Greek underworld friend. In the course of this casual research, Dannie became dazzled by Socrates' formidable displays of logic. From that time on, "I didn't feel right unless I had Plato's dialogues with me in my cell—especially the first three books."

He read other philosophers, too. He found Will Durant's books on philosophy "thrilling." Then, in the mid-'70s, he discovered an apparently unread copy of Schopenhauer's works, covered with cobwebs, in the social worker's office at the county jail in Everett. It became another of his addictions. He read the lengthy book repeatedly.

What was it in the metaphysics of that difficult philosopher that so enthralled the high school dropout? When I first asked him, he replied with characteristic slyness, "Schopenhauer believed in the theory of leisure, and so do I." He elaborated in a letter from prison: "Schopenhauer said the highest goal man can attain is to have plenty of leisure time. He probably didn't think I would take him literally enough to languish in prison."

Of course, there was a great deal more to it than that. Dannie struggled with the issues of Will and Idea that so fascinated Schopenhauer, and he applied them to his own life, especially his heroin addiction. He was also attracted to Schopenhauer's discussion of "purchas[ing] pleasure at the cost of pain." But he did not read Schopenhauer simply as a psychic cookbook. He talks even today of his pleasure at the intellectual daring of Schopenhauer as the philosopher constructed a metaphysical system, rung by rung, over an intellectual void. He says it was the sort of "gutsy" endeavor that "appealed to the outlaw in me."

"Prison life," Dannie says, "teaches convicts to scorn and ridicule feelings. Feelings are viewed as weakness." In a world that "dampens your emotions," he says, "I tried to hang on to mine through reading. It was a way of keeping prison from deforming me."

Dannie has always credited his heavy reading regimen with inspiring him to write, although it took years for him to get beyond the inspiration. As he put it during his trial testimony, "I always had a dream of being a writer. And at some point there, I put the dream aside and picked up the pencil. It was getting late in the game."

His earliest writing, in his twenties, was rooted in oral traditions. He became fascinated with an ancient prison genre—the jailhouse poem. In those days, he says, there were no radios and televisions in the jail tanks, and the convicts would entertain each other after the lights went out at night by reciting jailhouse poems. The elaborate ballads, which were passed around by word of mouth, might go on for as long as an hour. His own facility at the genre gained much from the storytelling talents he picked up from his grandfather. Dannie can still quote from some of his own ballads thirty years later. He is proudest of "Pike Street Lil," the story of a prostitute and her pimp in which the villain was heroin, "the serpent in the silver spoon."

In 1976, Dannie was befriended by a remarkable woman, Diane Osland, a social worker in the county jail in Everett and the first "straight" to encourage him to write. When he met her, he had written little aside from jailhouse poems and occasional letters to family members.

Osland, who got her B.A. in "law and justice" (a major designed for students going into the field of poverty law), was a "prisoner advocate" in the jail as part of a unique federally financed program that allowed her almost unlimited access to the prisoners. The program, which grew out of a court settlement in a jail brutality case, provided a broad range of prisoner services in an attempt to cut both recidivism and abuse of prisoners. To allow the prisoner advocates the kind of access that they needed for their experimental program, the social workers were given keys to the cells—much to the anger of the old-line guards. But the animosity of the guards helped the advocates to gain the trust of some of the more recalcitrant prisoners in that very tough jail.

Osland could not miss the prisoner they called Red Hog. She describes him as a very powerful person in the jail. "He took no shit from anyone," she says, but he exercised his power without being abusive. In fact, he was a protector of the weakest—the frightened younger prisoners and the frail older cons. "He treated people with dignity," she says, "and he expected to be treated with dignity, and not out of fear."

Because of Dannie's leadership role in the prison, the social workers needed his cooperation in order to assist the other prisoners, and Osland chatted with him frequently. She began to appreciate and rely on his unusually perceptive views on prisons and on the psychology of incarceration.

Osland is the daughter of a journalist and a creative writer, and she set great importance on writing. In the prison context, she saw it as "a safe outlet," a way that tough hoods could talk through problems and come to terms with their vulnerabilities. So she encouraged many of them, including Dannie, to write down their feelings and observations.

Those first notes and letters to the "square" social worker were obviously uncomfortable for Dannie. They were sprinkled with comments like "I can't believe I'm writing this shit." And the convict never handed his letters to Osland directly. As she walked down the catwalk to her office in the morning, she would pass Dannie's cell, and there, wedged between the bars, she would find a roll of up to a dozen pages of writings waiting for her that he had composed overnight.

Osland would read them at her leisure during the day and later discuss them with Dannie, although she was never formally his counselor. Instead, she became his friend. "I was someone who actually listened to him and heard him," she says, and there were not many straights of whom that could be said.

As the two grew closer, the convict's writings became increasingly varied, ranging from philosophical meditations to poetry to stories for her to deliver to the four-year-old girl who lived with her. In the letters, he learned self-exploration, too. As he wrote to her once, "I'm figuring now that people should [write letters] more because you can express feelings a lot better like that. I found that out when I first started writing you. I am not afraid of my feelings anymore. I don't hide them as much."

Osland says the convict's writing talent was immediately apparent. He was able to write what he thought and in the way he talked, and she told him so. Once, she told him that he was born to be a writer, that he was very good at it.

"How good?" he asked.

"Good enough so someone would pay for it," she replied.

The seed was planted. From that time on, she says, Dannie talked and dreamed of getting published.

There was another kind of letter-writing that occupied Dannie at

McNeil Island and Lompoc penitentiaries, after he left Osland's jail, and it too taught him much about the writing craft. Dannie was a jailhouse scribe. He helped less literate convicts by writing letters for them to wives and girlfriends as well as to judges and other officials. For some he obtained sentence reductions; for some he settled domestic spats. He says both kinds of letter taught him to use writing for effect, to push emotional buttons.

At the county jail in Everett—and continuing later at other prisons—Dannie also dabbled in fiction. He wrote a funny, irreverent novel-length marijuana fantasy called "The Church of the Unborn Troglodyte" (later lost when he fled from a safe house), and he wrote an extended fairy tale for children called "Sixtoes and the Lonely Isle" while he was at another lonely isle—McNeil Island Penitentiary. "Sixtoes" is the story of a young fairy's battle against an odious opium dragon and other monsters that had taken over his ancestral homeland. The fairy, who was scorned because he had six toes on each foot and refused requests to sweep away any trace of his odd footprints, has always been a favorite of its author.

Dannie began the fairy tale as he was coming off heroin. He says he realized that for him, heroin was a way of perpetuating the magic of childhood, as religion is for some people. He thought that writing a fairy tale might help him to recapture that magic while he sat in a dreary cell twenty-two hours a day.

But most important to the author was his shallowly buried antidrug message for children. Many of his fellow convicts sent copies home to be read to their children. Dannie recently turned the fairy tale into a stage play for children in response to a request from the Young Performers Theatre of San Francisco.

---

After he left Everett, Dannie corresponded with Osland regularly for fifteen years. It was the same kind of wide-ranging, candid, sometimes playful, sometimes serious letter-writing relationship that he developed four or five years later with Mike Schwab, another straight and another veteran of the antipoverty programs of the '70s. As Dannie wrote Osland once, "I exchanged a heroin habit for a letter habit."

He used the letters to polish ideas and writing style in ways that he could not do with fellow convicts. He also talked openly about his search for direction in life, as if trying to write his way out of his self-destructive habits. His search for new goals is evident in a letter to

Osland in which he confessed, "I can't see any honor or justice in this manner of my living now. . . . Time was when I thought I shared a basic outlook with others of my ilk. Now I'm pretty sure all we share is jail."

Osland suggests that Dannie's unlikely friendship with the two young social progressives may have demonstrated to him that it is possible to be anti-establishment without being an outlaw. In any case, he was communicating openly with "squares," and it changed his life. "I would like you to know," he wrote Schwab once, "that meeting you was a good thing for me at that time in my life. I sensed that you held out some hope for me even when I didn't. I suppose I needed that type of feeling that to some folks I was still a human being."

In his correspondence with his square friends, Dannie wrestled repeatedly with his drug and alcohol abuse, but one major shove toward sobriety came from an even more unlikely source: his parole board.

In 1980, Dannie had been told that the parole board didn't even want to see him until 1991, but a technicality got him a hearing in 1985. The convict went to that hearing with no hope whatsoever of getting a target date for parole. He brought to the board an abysmal record that included eleven write-ups for prison infractions, including use of heroin and alcohol, gambling, and even a knife fight.

The chair of his panel, a notoriously hard-nosed man, asked Dannie if he was going to stop robbing banks and taking dope. Dannie guaranteed that he would rob no more banks, but he added, "Don't ask me not to take heroin. I've been taking it all my life and probably will the rest of my life." The astonished chairman told him, "That's what got you in here," and asked if he'd been using heroin in prison. Dannie replied, "Just when I can get it."

For reasons that were unclear, the board responded by giving him a 1991 target parole date. Dannie and his friends were astonished. Not only was it the best outcome he could have hoped for but, according to one jailhouse lawyer, the board had to break its own regulations to give him such a sweet deal.

Back in the privacy of his cell, Dannie responded to this unexpected act of trust by resolving again to give up drugs. Thereafter, his lapses became less frequent. In March 1986, four months before he submitted his first manuscript to the Chronicle, Dannie was caught with a heroin needle. That was his last write-up, or "shot," for drug use in prison.

The parole board's action followed a difficult year for Dannie. The two women he had been closest to in his life, his mother and his former wife, both died. The news devastated him. It was to be a continuing source of regret to him that his mother never lived to see him "do anything constructive" with his life. Increasingly after Linda's and Zell's deaths, his daughter and grandchildren were on his mind. He was driven to show them something they could be proud of, and he dreamed of providing them with financial assistance he was never able to give Julie when she was young.

■

Sometime in the mid-'80s, everything seemed to come together for Dannie. He had honed his craft, he had begun to tame his fierce addiction, and he had established important personal ties in the straight world that he had previously spurned. He had genuine talent and the self-confidence to put it to use. He was ready to go public and make a name for himself. And so he did—until the Bureau of Prisons and a federal court took away his name.

What follows is the double-faceted story of Red Hog's journalism: how it looked from the inside, the prison cell, as first reported in the pages of the *Chronicle,* and how it looked from the outside, the newspaper office, where I became his improbable partner—editor, colleague, friend, and then, when it became necessary, defender.

# I

---

# CASING THE JOINT
# JULY 1986 – MAY 1988

Dear Peter: ... One of the things I fervently want to accomplish is to give readers a true picture of prisons, convicts, and our way of thinking and our way of life in prisons. I want them to know that many of us are just like them only we are doing some time right now.

All the codes and values of convicts have changed so much in the past 20–30 years that a lot of us now feel like dinosaurs. ... In fact, this is one of the things motivating me and giving me the energy to learn to write. Before criminals and convicts as I know them become extinct, I would like for society to know exactly what they are. ... The men and women that society identifies as "criminal," and their ways and methods, are undergoing a metamorphosis that is going to have a devastatingly harmful effect on society.

—*Letter from Lompoc*

In July 1986, a Lompoc penitentiary convict identified on the return address as Dannie M. Martin, #11319-086, sent me an unsolicited manuscript on AIDS in prison. I knew nothing further about the author, not even the crime that had sent him to that maximum-security federal lockup.

As the editor of the *Chronicle*'s "Sunday Punch" section, an eclectic mix of features and commentary, I was always on the lookout for authentic voices from inaccessible places. The submission from this novice writer qualified on both counts—especially inaccessibility.

Over the years, I had received what seemed like more than my share of free-lance submissions from prisoners. Almost invariably, such writings are bitter, self-serving screeds, and they are usually accompanied by a thick packet of legal briefs and other supporting documents. But this submission was different. The writer's "voice" was engaging, humane, refreshingly direct. It had none of the sputtering anger that animates most prison writing, though it was on a subject that he would have every right to feel angry about. Nor was the manuscript in the slightest self-aggrandizing.

And the topic was of great interest to my readership in Northern California, where AIDS had already cut a wide, cruel swath.

In most prisons, all the AIDS risk factors are present, and HIV exposure there is potentially a big killer on both sides of the wall. But at that early date, the threat of HIV infection in prison had not yet engaged the attention of the major media. The convict's feature article seemed a good way to start to tell that important story.

After checking the article with Randy Shilts, the *Chronicle*'s distinguished AIDS expert, and receiving his enthusiastic endorsement, I informed the writer in a letter that I would be publishing his story. The letter set out the usual business terms—$100, payable on publication—and discussed minor editing questions, such as the use of pseudonyms for the prisoners named in his story. I also told him we planned to use his name in the byline and to add a line at the bottom identifying him as "an inmate at the U.S. Prison at Lompoc, California."

In a businesslike reply, he expressed pleasure at my decision, adding that this was the first article he had submitted to a newspaper, and he agreed to my editing changes. He informed me that he wished to be known as a "convict," not an "inmate." I later learned that he associated the word "inmate" with psychiatric hospitals and bristled at the passive institutionalization that the term suggested to him.

Later, the government literally made a federal case out of the format in which I published this and subsequent articles by Dannie, so it is worth underlining here that all were displayed in the customary manner: with a byline and an author ID line labeling the article as the work of a "convict" at Lompoc. Later, when interest in him increased, he was identified on each story as a bank robber. Masking the source of the stories would, I believe, have been journalistically irresponsible—a disservice to the reader.

In his letter, Dannie also revealed that one of his biggest motives for submitting that first article had been to gain name recognition as a writer, to enhance his chances of publishing other of his writings—a reference to his fairy tale, "Sixtoes and the Lonely Isle." He later recited to me a long list of noted novelists whose first published writing had appeared in newspapers.

Dannie says he had been thinking about ways to get something published when "one day I realized that I had material all around me." He told one interviewer he "was reading a story about AIDS in the paper. And I told a guy, 'Man, I could do better than that. They don't even know what's going on in here about AIDS.' "

And, of course, he was appalled—both as a recent IV drug user and as a human being—at the silence surrounding the peril of AIDS in prison.

Dannie was a regular reader of "Sunday Punch" and had noted that I ran some free-lance material, which is why he decided to send his manuscript to me. There is no telling if he would have submitted it elsewhere had I rejected it.

The prospect of compensation provided an added, and continuing, incentive. "It made me feel," he said later, "like what I had to say was valued, was worth something to someone." But most important, telling the straight world about prisons was "a way I could turn a pretty negative life into something positive."

## AIDS: THE VIEW FROM A PRISON CELL

LOMPOC, CALIF. (AUG. 3, 1986)—In the latter months of 1985, one of the most voracious homosexuals in the federal prison system violated parole in Florida and was returned to the men's maximum-security prison at Lompoc to finish his sentence.

This one was so predatory that the cons had long ago nicknamed him "Honey Bear." Honey Bear was known to shoot a load of "crank" and go walking down a tier advertising favors at every cell he passed; he would enter at the beck and call of anyone who was interested. If there happened to be two men in the cell, appropriate adjustments could be made. The Honey Bear was an accommodating soul.

No one seemed to notice the little sores on the back of Honey Bear's neck, although quite a few of his "clients" had an intimate view of them. Early in 1986, the sores got out of hand, and he was having other health problems. Honey Bear went to the doctor and was soon diagnosed as having AIDS. He was immediately transferred to the medical facility at Springfield, Missouri, and isolated from contact with other prisoners.

Honey Bear liked to do a lot of drugs, especially crank, a stimulant he injected by hypodermic needle, or "outfit," as it is called in prison. Outfits are hard to come by in here, and there were only three in the 130-man cellblock where Honey Bear lived.

The men who own these outfits loan them to others in return for a "fix" of the drugs. Sometimes a loaned "rig" will be used by eight or ten people before it is returned to the owner.

After Honey Bear left, a few worried drug users approached the men who owned the outfits, seeking reassurance that Honey Bear had not used them. The news was bad. Honey Bear had not only used them but used all of them several times. This news had a most chilling effect on the future dreams of some of these cons.

The exchange of bodily fluids through sex and the sharing of contaminated needles are the two primary ways that AIDS is spread through a population. In prison or jail, the user of illegal drugs "sterilizes" needles by squirting a little cold water through the needle after using it and before handing it to the next in line. All types of alcohol are contraband.

Some of the cons were relieved when Honey Bear was quarantined in Springfield. The Bureau of Prisons has not yet formulated a firm policy concerning those diagnosed as having or carrying the AIDS virus. Everyone assumed after Honey Bear left that the government intended to at least isolate everyone they determined to have been exposed. Then "The Greek" died here at Lompoc on Father's

Day, and that fond assumption became just another shattered illusion.

The Greek was a homosexual, a likable soul with a sunny disposition and an inclination for a quantity and variety of men. He had been serving time at Lompoc for about five years, and if chronicled and illustrated, The Greek's sexual shenanigans would go a good ways toward filling a book the size of a Sears Roebuck catalog.

The Greek got involved in a pickup game of basketball in the gym on Father's Day and, after playing awhile, became exhausted, went to the sideline, began throwing up, and fell out. After prison authorities got him to the hospital, he was said to have choked to death on his own vomit.

When the prison doctor arrived, he told everyone working around The Greek to put on long rubber gloves, since The Greek was a known HIV carrier. Even the officer who was sent to The Greek's cell to pack his personal belongings was told to wear long rubber gloves.

If The Greek was indeed a "known" HIV carrier, it was a fact known only by the medical staff and/or the administration. None of the convicts, including The Greek's sex partners, and none of the mainline prison guards knew anything about it.

Now the convicts wonder if those diagnosed as having the AIDS virus are going to be allowed to roam the yard with everyone else. The Bureau of Prisons has made no public policy statement on the subject. It looks now as if officials intend to treat AIDS just as they do the common cold, except in obviously terminal stages.

It isn't likely that the canteen will soon be selling condoms for safe sex or alcohol to sterilize needles. The only safe sex and drugs in prison will be no sex and no drugs, and so far no one who indulges in either is considering that option. The attitude in here seems to be that life goes on for the living and that the chances of contracting AIDS are about the same as being hit by gunfire during the commission of a felony or dying of an overdose. So what?

Then there are those who rationalize in lieu of curtailing their behavior. One man who had shared an outfit with Honey Bear on several occasions said he wasn't worried about it at all because he is immune to AIDS in any case. When prompted to explain how he is immune to AIDS, he said that the AIDS virus is similar to the hepatitis virus and that he had shared needles for years outside with people who were infected with hepatitis and he had never caught it.

Therefore, by this man's reasoning, he must also be immune to AIDS. He sounds so sure of himself that he makes one wonder if there has been a study done on the correlation between hepatitis and AIDS.

There are married men in here who have had sex with Honey Bear and The Greek while their wives anxiously wait for the day they are freed. They aren't likely to disclose these potentially volatile indiscretions; most of these long-distance marriages are strained and fragile already.

Those of us who don't indulge in drugs or sex in prison stand around like so many buzzards waiting and watching for the next to fall. These days we speculate about the lovers of Honey Bear and The Greek and which among them is likely to go down.

In a world where all the lies have been told and all the jokes have been heard, it does give us something new to talk about. One thing about AIDS is very reliable: About the time you exhaust the talk and speculation about the latest victim, another is sure to bite the dust. Sometimes it is someone we would never have suspected.

---

Seven months after Dannie's article appeared, *Newsweek* magazine discovered the "growing menace" of AIDS in prison, citing 1,232 inmate cases nationwide as of October 1986. *Newsweek* quoted federal Bureau of Prisons Director Norman Carlson on the lack of routine HIV testing in prison: "We are not going to panic and do things inconsistent with medical advice." But the magazine went on to say, "Others . . . suspect that officials are fearful of a public-relations debacle." The magazine quoted the director of an AIDS support group as saying, "My understanding is that wardens don't want to test [prisoners for HIV infection] because they're afraid of what they're going to find."

In the prison, the reaction to Dannie's story was immediate and positive. Dannie was first alerted to its publication as he was heading for brunch, hours before the convicts' newspapers were delivered. "Hey, that was a good article you had in 'Sunday Punch,' " a guard told him as they passed in a hallway.

Later, convicts began coming up to the author and thanking him. "They were amazed that I had that published in a mainstream paper," he testified later in court, "because there's an attitude among convicts that no matter what happens or what we do, the mainstream press won't tell our side of the story."

The response from the general newspaper readership was also encouraging to the neophyte writer. "I received a number of letters from people in the Bay Area after my article was published . . . nice letters from nice people," he wrote me. "They were all favorable, and the amount of interest surprised me. . . . I knew the public was concerned about AIDS, but I had no idea of the magnitude of that concern."

According to his friend Diane Osland, Dannie "couldn't believe he was getting letters from people he'd never even met." He made it a practice to thank each correspondent who included a return address. He continued to correspond with many of those early letter writers, and over time he developed a large network of "square" friends and contacts.

Letters of praise came to the newspaper, too, but one response was troubling. It was a form letter from the "mail officer" at Lompoc penitentiary, and it provided the first indication that what Dannie and I were doing might be illegal in the eyes of the U.S. Bureau of Prisons. The officer returned the check that the *Chronicle* had routinely sent the author for his article. On the accompanying form, the officer noted that "an inmate may not receive compensation or anything of value for correspondence with the news media."

Dannie, informed by a counselor that the check had been sent back, wrote me that he was "flabbergasted, to say the least." He had been informed that in accepting the check he would be in violation of a BOP regulation prohibiting "conducting a business," a regulation that he said "is traditionally used for people in here who loan cigarettes or money for interest. It takes a long stretch of the imagination to apply it to writing an article for the newspaper."

Dannie said he "was also informed that I had better let my counselor look at any material I decide to send out in the future. They argue they are well within their rights on this, as the paralegal here instructed them. I know better. . . . [Prison officials] were obviously unhappy with the exposure. . . . Other people here have received money for articles which didn't pertain to the prison, and nothing was said about it."

He added, "I will continue to write as I please about anything I please. I believe with all my heart that is an inalienable right I was born with."

By the time I received Dannie's indignant letter I had already done some cursory research on the cited regulation, which also forbade a convict to publish under a byline or to "act as [a] reporter." I then consulted with the *Chronicle*'s law firm. Our consultations were brief; there seemed no need for in-depth investigation because the issue was so obvious. The *Chronicle* attorney said something like "That's non-sense—they can't do that." He confirmed my layman's view that the regulation was a clear violation of the newspaper's First Amendment rights as well as the prisoner's and agreed that we had a right to run the works of a prisoner—and to compensate and credit him—in the same way we did the works of any other free-lance writer.

Because the prison mailroom would not pass checks on to Dannie, the attorney recommended following Dannie's suggestion to send the returned check—and any future checks—to his attorney, Mike Schwab, to hold for him. I then conferred with my superior at the *Chronicle,* and we decided to follow that procedure.

For the next two years, we got no further official word from the prison about the legality of Dannie's high-profile journalism, despite the many indications that prison officials had read most, if not all, of his articles. I assumed that the bureau recognized the regulation in question was constitutionally unenforceable and that there was a tacit understanding we could continue to run Dannie's articles as long as we didn't trumpet our seeming violation of BOP rules. I was, as it later turned out, very, very wrong.

But the issue passed from our minds until two years later, when Dannie wrote critically about his warden and stepped on that long-buried land mine.

■

We had one more indirect indication that the AIDS article—and media exposure of prison issues generally—was causing Lompoc administrators some consternation. After publication of Dannie's article, a local television reporter, Eric Spillman of KSBY, asked for permission to interview him on camera about the AIDS issue. Prison regulations are supposed to facilitate such interviews, with appropriate scheduling and safety precautions, but Spillman was repeatedly denied access by the warden's office. The denials were ostensibly based on unspecified rules and on concerns for the convict's "safety." Spillman also recalls allusions to "the controversial nature of the subject matter."

After months of rejections, Spillman raised the issue of AIDS with

Lompoc Warden Robert Christensen at the prison's annual media open house. The TV journalist says Christensen became visibly angry that he had shattered the "clubby atmosphere" of the warden's public-relations event with such a sensitive question.

Unable to interview Dannie on camera, Spillman ultimately made do with a taped telephone interview.

■

Dannie was eager to capitalize on the interest he found in his writing, and the AIDS article was soon followed by other submissions. I ran some, I sent some back for revisions, and I rejected still others. But the rejections were never devastating to Dannie. He took them as a way of honing his writing skills.

At irregular intervals over the two years covered by this chapter, before prison officials forced him out of Lompoc, I published twenty essays by Dannie. Most were printed in the form I received them, with no more than the usual amount of editing and reorganizing. The untutored author was sometimes ragged on his grammar—"It's the skeleton in my writer's closet," he said. "My muse can't conjugate a verb." But he was a ready student. In any case, his fine storytelling instincts carried him across many a grammatical pothole. And I was reluctant to tamper with his unique voice by smoothing out all the rough spots.

Dannie had two manuscripts on my desk soon after the appearance of the AIDS article. I accepted one, a wildly entertaining true story that, he later told me, he had polished through years of retelling to new generations of prisoners.

# A LEGEND OF LOVE BEHIND BARS
# AND ONE MAN'S TUBA

LOMPOC, CALIF. (SEPT. 21, 1986)—There's a lot of history in prison, and it's the kind of place where history passes quickly into legend, handed down from one convict generation to the next. Clarence Whitely has long been legendary.

It has been almost forty years now, and old Bob the bunco man is walking on a cane in Lompoc penitentiary, back on a new charge (something about some poison pickles, carrier pigeons, and diamonds). But still old Bob loves to retell the story of Clarence Whitely.

Clarence was a con in the Walla Walla, Washington, prison in the late '40s, serving a long sentence for armed robbery. He was a tall, slim, no-nonsense sort of redhead with very little sense of humor. He played the tuba in the prison band, and although not musically inclined, he managed to sound enthusiastic and robust.

Every Friday evening there was a movie in the auditorium—mostly war movies, Roy Rogers westerns and Jimmy Cagney shoot-'em-ups. The women came over from the women's joint next door and sat in the balcony overlooking the men below.

Facing the balcony, the band would play a few tunes before the movie began. Clarence did real good on tunes like "Battle Hymn of the Republic."

One Friday night, a new woman sat in the front row of the balcony. She had a cameo face and long curly hair black as a raven's wing, with a red rose pinned in it. When she moved, the front of her prison smock heaved provocatively. She was a beauty, all right, and Clarence Whitely was in love. The tuba made its presence known that night.

Next morning, Clarence went to see Bunco Bob at the prison library.

Clarence figured that since books went from the library to the women's prison, Bob could get a note to the raven-haired beauty. Bunco Bob, never one to disappoint a man in love, and being short of smokes, allowed as how for a few packs a note he could do just that. Clarence handed over the smokes, along with a sincere, if unimaginative, note telling the fragile beauty how he had loved her at first blush.

The books were carefully screened for messages and Bob didn't even know the girl's name, but he refused to let these details stand in the way of a blossoming love affair.

He sat right down and composed an answer to Clarence. In a girlish hand, he wrote how the young girl, too, was "taken" with Clarence. He even mixed some talcum powder, prison laundry soap, and lemon extract to produce a scent to dust on the letter. He colored his lips red with a crayon and sealed the envelope with a big smack.

The movie the previous Friday had been *To Have and Have Not,* so he signed her "Lauren" after Lauren Bacall.

When Clarence received her missive, he was ecstatic. The love letters began to flow hot and heavy, with Clarence paying postage both ways.

In those bygone days, convicts could keep a secret, and Bob let a couple of friends in on why Clarence was acting so strange. They, in turn, told a few friends, and soon everyone in the yard was giving Bob suggestions to put in her answers to Clarence.

She told him that on Wednesdays she could see the men's yard from an upstairs room in the women's hospital and suggested he wear a baseball cap backward so she could recognize him. On Wednesday, Clarence hit the yard with a red baseball cap jauntily perched bill aft.

Another letter asked him to walk a bit differently from everyone else, because she still couldn't make him out. The next Wednesday Clarence hit the yard with his backward red cap and put on a fine rendition of the Frug, the Monkey, and the Twist all rolled into one. Bunco Bob swears to this day that that's where all those dances originated.

The affair was getting downright interesting. Each Friday she sat up there smiling, and Clarence knew she smiled for him alone. Then Bob got carried away, as he did in all his schemes.

In a poignant letter to Clarence, "Lauren" confessed to certain sexual preferences and wanted to know if they were compatible with his inclinations. Now, this was the era before even *Playboy,* and folks weren't all that liberated. Graphically, she explained the sex she longed for, and it was a long and lurid list, including a passage about tying Clarence up and busting turkey eggs on his forehead. (Obviously, Bob was now taking suggestions from the lunatic fringe.) She told him that if he agreed to all this, he could let her know this on Friday by tooting the tuba three times before the band began to play. If he didn't toot, she would know their fledgling affair was finished.

Clarence was obviously shocked. Until now they had been writing platonic love letters. Things like, "Darling . . . it is lonely enough in this dark pit of despair without you chipping at my heartstrings with hints of losing our love." Now he was walking around in frowns, cap backward, popping his knuckles in an agony of indecision, while the ever-vigilant cons made odds and laid bets.

By Friday, the suspense was palpable, and things grew awfully tense as the inmates took their seats and the bandleader sorted his music. Then Clarence made his move. Frantically grasping the tuba, he put a liplock on the mouthpiece and cut down on it. Barrumph! Barraumph! Barrumph!

Only the warden was more astounded than Clarence when all the men rose and gave him a five-minute standing ovation.

They say old Clarence met his maker at the end of a high-speed chase in Oakland in the late '60s. His love for Lauren was never consummated, but it will long be remembered by convicts everywhere.

---

The story of Clarence Whitely had a distinctively folkloric quality about it, as did a number of Dannie's subsequent stories, and it showed his consummate skills as a storyteller. But he had an ulterior purpose in sending it to me, as he later disclosed.

Dannie was beginning to realize that he could use his new forum to portray prisons and prisoners as he knew them, without the overlay of TV crime-show images. As he put it during the trial that ultimately resulted from his writing:

> Letters I got from people outside made me realize to what extent they don't have any idea what's in a criminal's mind. They see a guy on TV bust someone's head, and he's off the picture. . . . He doesn't have a wife and family. He's just a thug. They see him for a minute, and he's gone. And they wind up with a stereotype of what a criminal is, and it's wrong.

Dannie says he'd never seen anything written from prison that was funny, nor anything that indicated that prisoners relished humor. Yet humor was a big part of the way he and many other convicts survived emotionally. "It would be awfully hard," he said, "to do a long jolt without some humor." So he had chosen to write a funny piece for the most serious of reasons—to illustrate the humanity of his fellow convicts. And he succeeded, as the growing number of letters from readers demonstrated.

Dannie's Lompoc articles played well on both sides of the wall. For most *Chronicle* readers, they were a window on a hidden world; for the residents of that world, the essays were an affirmation of their identity.

The convicts were no longer invisible to the world that had isolated them, and that meant a lot. During our trial, former Lompoc prisoner John Hamlet testified:

> Every time an article came out, it was kind of big news around the institution. Everybody waited for them. And everybody would really think about them. We discussed them in the chow hall and out in the yard. We were proud that Dannie was doing it. . . . We all felt that through Mr. Martin we had a voice going out to the public, telling our side of it.

Some of the prison staff were also supportive. Dannie's counselor urged him to keep writing, and other prison employees periodically stopped him on the mainline to chat about his most recent *Chronicle* article.

Back at the *Chronicle,* there was never a corporate or high-level editorial decision to tell the prison story from a convict's perspective, and we certainly couldn't have dreamed up a Dannie Martin if we'd tried. Nor were there any models for the kind of writing Dannie was doing. Article by article, he and I redefined what we were accomplishing.

We also began a personal and professional correspondence. Dannie felt it was vital for his editor—his go-between with the outside world—to understand both him and the prison world that we were trying to interpret for others. So his letters were often part of what he called "a short course in Penology and Other Assorted Forms of Garbage Disposal," otherwise known as my "education in the art of doing heavy time." He once told me solicitously, "If all this is boring you, let me know. It's been boring me all my life."

Dannie was especially intent on demonstrating to me that his penitentiary was not to be confused with the nearby federal prison camp, often called Club Fed. So I heard about each stabbing, lived through each lockdown, was introduced to each babbling psychotic in a neighboring cell. He would talk about how the ever-present violence warps prisoners, how they become habituated to it, "sort of like the noise" that reverberates incessantly through the cellblocks. And he explained at length the subtleties of outlaw psychology. He persisted in that project despite the great gulf between our backgrounds: "What I am trying to say to you is like communicating with a person of another language. I believe you will get the gist of it, though. I hope so."

Often I'd suggest that Dannie expand into articles some subject that he had touched on in a letter, and in time our dialogue helped to shape the direction of his writing.

Within a few months, that dialogue was expanded to include phone calls—collect calls to my home or office in specific time slots for which he had to sign up in advance. Those phone calls were frustrating, shouted conversations with a hard-of-hearing convict calling from a place of wall-to-wall din. In the background I could hear reverberations of clanking steel and the raucous jeers and yells of pent-up men. But the calls were helpful in solidifying our unusual working relationship; together we edited his stories, discussed new story ideas, and generally mediated between his world and mine.

■

**D**annie's cover letter with his next submission said he was "contemplating making some comments to you about this one, but it should speak for itself." Indeed it did.

## REQUIEM FOR MR. SQUIRREL

*LOMPOC, CALIF. (OCT. 26, 1986)*—Convicts always walk around a track counterclockwise, as if to deny time itself, as represented by the clock. It's a losing battle—time always wins. As the years go by, the exercise walks around the track at the prison's perimeter only get more boring.

Four years ago this month, as my walking boredom threatened to become terminal, I met Mr. Squirrel on the yard here at Lompoc penitentiary. Mr. Squirrel was indeed a squirrel and not the nickname of a bushy-haired convict with an overbite.

He was only one of many squirrels that ventured in between the double prison fences and sat upon hind legs in attitudes of supplication, seemingly praying for a morsel. We did throw them food, but mostly all we had was croutons sneaked out of the mess hall.

Most of the croutons fell short of the first fence, as it is hard to throw a small piece of toasted bread more than fifteen or twenty feet. Especially against the wind; and here at Lompoc if you are facing west, which is where the squirrels were, a brisk ocean breeze will almost always be blowing directly in your face.

The squirrels would watch with chagrin and sometimes chatter furiously as our windblown croutons fell short of the fence, only to be swooped on by the ever-present seagulls and vigilant crows that had no sympathy for squirrels at all. Sometimes those croutons that reached the no-man's-land of rolled razor wire between the fences where the squirrels waited were picked off in the air by diving gulls.

Every day during the noon lunch break, eight or ten of us crouton carriers were beneath the corner gun tower, trying to feed the squirrels. Yet even this diversion was getting boring until the day I met Mr. Squirrel.

Nothing about his looks distinguished him from the others. He looked exactly like a half-grown ground squirrel. His pose was rather striking. While the others ran about frantically chattering at thieving gulls, he sat upright in an attitude of absolute repose.

I chunked a crouton in his direction, and the wind blew it back to a spot about six feet beyond where I stood by a sign that read "Out of Bounds Beyond This Sign," and about twenty feet from where Mr. Squirrel sat between the fences. Three gulls hit the ground in hot pursuit of the crouton, and as I reached for another, a strange and unprecedented tableau unfolded.

Before any of the gulls could snatch the crouton, Mr. Squirrel was right in the middle of them, and they were running in all directions. In my memory it seems that a few feathers flew, but I doubt that; for while gulls are loud, gluttonous, and aggressive, they turn into craven skulking beasts the moment they are confronted by anything larger than a hummingbird.

Mr. Squirrel ate the crouton, and a few more, then left with his jaws stuffed full of the others I had brought. The next day he was waiting, and before I even reached for a crouton, he ran right up to me and sat calmly watching. Before we parted that day, he ate right out of my hand. This squirrel had more nerve than John Dillinger.

Our friendship was born on a note of pure justice. He had rescued me from terminal boredom, and I reciprocated by easing his hunger and teasing his palate with an ever-increasing variety of hoarded edibles.

He was especially fond of peanut butter. I rolled it into little balls, then laughed when he stuffed it in his jaws to save and chattered furiously as it melted in his mouth.

Now that Mr. Squirrel had broken the barriers, most of the squirrels followed his example and sat begging only a few feet from where we walked the track.

Mr. Squirrel would take food from other cons, but he never approached anyone but me. If I had peanut butter or candy-coated almonds, he would sometimes climb up my arm and eat on my shoulder. He left each day with his jaws stuffed. His pantry in the field beyond the fences must have been well stocked.

The day I grabbed him and turned him over to find out if he was a Mr. or a Ms., he clawed me good, bit a chunk out of my arm, jumped down, and chattered at me for a good five minutes. Then forgave and forgot. I never tried that again, but there was no need—he was a Mr.

We met each day at noon for almost a year, except for fifteen days I spent in Isolation for a minor rule infraction. Then he was absent for a while around January.

In early spring that year, he showed up one day followed by two baby squirrels. I don't know if they were his progeny or just admirers, but he led them right up to share my groceries. They never squabbled at all and sat patiently as I fed each in turn. Mr. Squirrel was raising them impeccably, but unfortunately they would never get to grow up.

On a windblown day, as I walked the track to where Mr. Squirrel waited, I noticed outside the fences, at about thirty-foot intervals, a row of little boxes with holes cut in the sides. Squirrels, including Mr. Squirrel's babies, were running in and out of the ominous little boxes and chattering happily.

My heart began to sink as it dawned on me they were being poisoned. Poisoned by a slow-acting agent like arsenic trioxide that would allow them time to crawl to a hole where they would die a slow and agonizing death, thereby leaving the little boxes clear of dead bodies and free of suspicion.

I was a hurt and helpless spectator to the warden's final solution to the squirrel problem. I harbored a dim hope that Mr. Squirrel would be too smart to go for this trick. In the few days that followed I fed him much more than he could eat or carry, and I continually lectured him on the evil that lurked nearby.

The little ones weren't seen again, and after five days Mr. Squirrel was the only one left.

When Mr. Squirrel approached me and pawed listlessly at my peanut butter while looking at me out of reddened and pain-filled eyes, I knew he had been in the box. I knew I would never see him or feed him or play with him again. A most harrowing thought was that he may have wondered if I did it to him.

I walked away knowing that for years to come I would have to pass each day by the place where I fed him, and the justice of our friendship would surely be lost in the bitterness of remembrance.

I haven't seen a squirrel these past three years. Not even on a nearby hill where they used to frolic on good days.

A few gulls were found dead, but all the crows seem to have survived. The vulture population was severely thinned. Two fluffy owls and a beautiful mating pair of red-tailed hawks disappeared about the same time as the squirrels.

The boxes are long gone now, and strange as it seems, not one convict or guard ever said a word about the squirrels or their fate.

Mr. Squirrel was like me in some ways. He disdained the status quo, and gun towers, fences, and razor wire never impressed him much. If he lay in a hole surrounded by peanut butter and croutons while arsenic ate his stomach, I have lain in Isolation strip cells surrounded by vulgar graffiti while the pain of life ate my guts.

My spirit is diminished by the way he died, stunted by the brutal termination of his refulgent soul.

Some days when I walk along by the place I used to feed Mr. Squirrel, I am haunted by a verse from an Oscar Wilde poem, "The Ballad of Reading Gaol," where he wrote:

> The vilest deeds like poison weeds
> Bloom well on prison air.
> It is only what is good in man
> That wastes and withers there. . . .

Of course, he never said a word about squirrels. Neither did anyone in here.

---

After publication of "Mr. Squirrel," Dannie said he was "damn near deluged" with letters from readers, and so was I. Six months and several published stories later, his correspondents "still want to talk about

Squirrel," he wrote me. "That piece had legs, buddy. I mean *legs*. It's still running." To this day, I receive letters from Dannie's admirers who establish their bona fides by writing, "I've been a reader of his since 'Mr. Squirrel.' "

Delighted though Dannie was with the readers' responses, his greatest satisfaction came from the writing itself. He later told me he felt better about writing this story than anything else he's written. His article was a kind of personal memorial: "That story was important to me. . . . I fervently wanted to give Mr. Squirrel some justice."

Although it is not known whether the article affected prison policy in any way, Warden Christensen certainly heard the author's message. He later told a *Los Angeles Times* reporter that the article had brought a flood of irate letters to the prison from all over the world, including Australia and Switzerland. The warden told the *Times* that the prison's squirrels had been a very expensive nuisance, chewing up road and electronic surveillance equipment. He said that poison had been used only after trapping proved ineffective.

A number of convicts approached Dannie to tell him that they had unsuccessfully tried to enclose copies of "Mr. Squirrel" in letters home. Some had the letters returned again and again until they removed the newspaper clipping; others said their letters arrived at their homes but without the enclosure.

Prison officials would later argue that convict writing in the news media under a byline is dangerous to security because of its effects on other prisoners, but in their response to "Mr. Squirrel," as with the AIDS article, they seemed primarily concerned about what outsiders were able to learn of the internal workings of the prison.

■

Meanwhile, our unusual writer-editor relationship surmounted a variety of impediments that could not have been imagined by readers of his essays. One problem was the format in which I received his essays— and the difficulties that created for the author.

Technically, as Dannie told an interviewer, "I'm not allowed to have a typewriter in a federal prison. No telling what kind of evil a typewriter could do if you got one. They won't allow it." But he did arrange for a convict who worked in a prison office to type his manuscripts "on the sneak."

That arrangement worked fine for a while, but there were frequent gaps during the first few months as we waited out his typist's periodic trips to "solitary" for drinking prison hooch. And there were often typos and inexplicable syntactical changes ascribed to the irascible typist's "towering hangovers." ("When I get out," Dannie wrote me, "I'm going to hire my typist at an AA meeting.")

Once, Dannie encountered his "weaving and wobbling" typist in a hallway and told him to get himself together because, "Man, you are interfering with my career." Dannie wrote me that the typist replied, "Fool, I was drunk before you had a career, and I'll be drunk when your career lies in ashes and dust along with Homer and other would-be scribblers." Dannie, although flattered to be put in the company of Homer, chastised the typist further and then spent the next thirty minutes maneuvering him back to his cell.

Finally, he dispensed with the typist's services, which had been costing too much in cigarettes anyhow, and I permitted Dannie to send hand-printed manuscripts.

We also had to cope with mail problems. The regulations on my letters to Dannie seemed contradictory, but on his letters to me there could be no doubt: All mail to public officials, news media, and attorneys is placed sealed in a different ("Special Mail") mailbox and is to go out uncensored and, indeed, unopened. Nevertheless, some of Dannie's letters to me were delayed, or lost, or on several occasions apparently opened surreptitiously. ("It will have a chilling effect on my future letters to you," he wrote. "Sort of like the captain reading over my shoulder as I write.")

We encountered other communication problems, too, such as prison-wide lockdowns that always seemed to occur as we were in the final stages of editing a story. And convict sources were sometimes transferred to other prisons while Dannie was writing stories based on their information.

But in spite of such obstacles, we managed to get Dannie's work into print, story by story, to ever-increasing attention. In fact, whenever three or four weeks passed without an article by Dannie in "Sunday Punch," I'd start getting phone calls and letters from the public asking if anything had happened to him and when the next one would run.

◼

In April 1987, less than a year after I began running Dannie's work, the *Los Angeles Times* published a profile of the convict. The *Times*' initial request for an interview had surprised and flattered us both. It seemed an unusual tribute for a major national newspaper to pay such attention to a writer whose only published works had appeared in a Sunday section of another newspaper. *Times* writer Miles Corwin dubbed Dannie "the unofficial storyteller laureate of the prison system," and he explored some of his views on imprisonment:

> Simply "warehousing" criminals, [Dannie] said, is not the answer. "A lot of people have the attitude: 'The hell with those guys. Lock them up and throw away the key.' But say you take a few thousand guys and lock them all up for fifteen years in the most brutal, violent places. Pretty soon everyone—even the ones who don't deserve that kind of punishment—turn into the kind of monsters it takes to survive in there."
>
> For fifteen years, he said, the "hard-liners" are happy because the criminals are off the streets. But, he asked, what happens when the fifteen years are up?

In the course of the interview, Dannie also revealed to Corwin some of his personal ambitions:

> I don't want you to get the idea that I'm doing this strictly for altruistic reasons. I'm writing to make money, and I want to make a career out of it. And if I can write things that are valuable to me and valuable to society as well, then that's perfect.

The *Chronicle* had published a number of stories by Dannie but none about him; it had seemed too self-promoting to do so. But I arranged to publish the *Los Angeles Times'* revealing profile in "Sunday Punch," and I asked Dannie to write for the first time directly about himself in an accompanying story, or, as journalists call it, a sidebar.

"Here's the one I did on the question you asked me," he wrote in the cover letter. "When I read it, I think to myself, 'Well, this wouldn't fit in "Sunday Punch," no way.' But then when I do that, I also think that I am getting into the realm of the editor and I have no business there. I am supposed to write 'em and send 'em. You are supposed to think about whether they fit or not. Right?"

# TO ANSWER 'THE QUESTION' . . .

*LOMPOC, CALIF. (APRIL 19, 1987)*—After having several articles published in "Sunday Punch," I received a surprising amount of correspondence from readers in all walks of life. I am grateful for all those letters, as I not only needed a forum to express my feelings and views, I needed to know that someone out there heard me.

Yet in most of those welcome envelopes there seemed to be a question, either directly asked or discreetly implied. As a direct question it was: How did a man of your intelligence and writing ability come to be spending so much of his life in jails and prisons?

My initial feeling about that curiosity was probably exactly the same one a prostitute feels when a client inquires: "What's a nice girl like you doing in a place like this?" Somehow I assumed that it wasn't a legitimate question, and when I did respond my answer was generally analogous to a hooker's programmed reply.

The other day I phoned the editor of "Sunday Punch" about some work I had done, and he popped The Question. His asking came on the heels of an interview I did recently with a *Los Angeles Times* reporter, in which he had asked the same thing. I now realize that the verdict is in, and I am guilty of dodging that question. It does deserve an answer, and I will do my best here in a thousand words or less to answer it honestly.

"Honestly" is the key word there, because I am a criminal by any definition I know of—one who has spent over twenty years in jails and prisons. By virtue of those facts, most of my life has been spent attempting to deceive society, always seeking invisibility in what I viewed as hostile surroundings. The long years of jail and prison only serve as evidence that in spite of my supposed intelligence, I was somewhat of a failure even in the underworld.

I failed as a citizen and I failed as a bank robber. I turned to writing. My ever-present intellect informed me that it would be far less onerous to fail as a writer than to botch another bank job.

Writing came naturally to me. I am descended from a long line of hill and mountain folk who were all natural storytellers. Contrary to what most people think, writing is really as simple as telling a story to a sheet of paper. Another advantage for me was that my years in prison added another dimension to my personal experiences. So much for my ability as a writer.

As to my mental acumen, I see that as a big part of the reason that I chose this rocky road in life. That, along with a tendency to abuse drugs and alcohol.

My forebears were migrant farm laborers who came to California from the coal mines of Alabama and the pulpwood forests of East Texas in the dust-bowl era of the early '30s. By the time I reached puberty, the idea of work represented to me a twelve-foot cotton sack or a shovel full of heavy mud. My first rebellion was against manual labor.

The mantle of poverty passed on by my ancestors fit me just fine, but the backbreaking labor was totally alien to my nature. Both my grandfathers worked themselves to death, and I decided very early that I would not do that. They never understood my recalcitrance but loved me nonetheless until they died.

I began cutting school and hanging out with a crowd who drank beer and smoked marijuana. We had a bit of a conspiracy against work and school. We began to develop our little secrets and our own protocols. If you broke wind too loud in that crowd, you could smile at someone and say: "I think I just stepped on a bullfrog." If you did it in the local church congregation, it was much harder to get forgiveness. And you'd better not smile.

I believe that period in my life was when I learned and accepted what I have come to think of in my middle years as "the Phenomenon of Them," or better stated as "the Idea of They." At first they or them were the police, truant officers, and parents—anyone determined to thwart my wayward goals. It was me or us against them or they.

The Idea of They began to grow larger in my mind. If a group of us were on the corner smoking dope and a neighbor like Mrs. Jones happened by, we would conceal the joint and attempt to look innocent. While she was not the police, she would call them if she saw us committing this crime. Now Mrs. Jones was added to the list of theys in my mind. She became one of those I had to deceive and conceal my true nature from. By this progression, it wasn't long before all law-abiding society was the them. The enemy.

I am reminded of a nursery rhyme a gypsy friend once told me he learned from his mother as a small child:

> Prepare a face to greet
> The faces that you meet.
> Become a different person
> Every time you hit the street.

That conscious choice to deceive and the idea of drawing lines, of choosing sides, us against them, is the reason I define myself today as a criminal. "They" represent law-abiding society, the work ethic, and Judeo-Christian values.

My values are outlaw values, the ethics of the us. I have to keep my word because, not having contracts or claims courts, we must live or die by our word. I don't inform because informing delivers us to the enemy. I pay my debts and I collect what is owed me. Those values are the only rigid requirements for membership in the us. Anything else is open to suggestion.

Many of us thought that leisure time was a good and work was an evil. Being stoned on alcohol and drugs was a desirable state of existence as opposed to the cold sober facts of life.

There is much more to the story than that, and I hope no one thinks I attempt to glorify this way of life. I don't recommend it at all. As a matter of fact, now that I'm getting a bit of fame for my writing, I'm a little concerned about some naked pictures I had taken when I was a younger man. I'd sure be embarrassed to find them printed now in the pages of some nudie magazine.

My thousand words now become critical. In spite of what every so-called penologist, psychologist, or any other "ist" has said or written on the matter, I want to say this: I have never met a criminal or self-respecting convict in my life who didn't live by and recognize "the Phenomenon of They" or the idea of us against them.

I have met many men in prison who didn't know this concept or the value system attendant to it. Their crimes were all crimes of passion, crimes of mental illness, total unawareness of sanctions or sheer stupidity. I don't view those types of people as criminals because they never made the conscious choice. I either distrust or pity them. They don't belong in prison and they can't live in society. They are homeless in the world.

Criminals come from all strata of society and all intelligence levels. Some of the smartest people I have ever met were in prison. Their common regret was falling into the clutches of the enemy. Getting caught makes an intelligent person feel stupid.

In the world of the outlaw, the intelligent fall almost as often as the dumb. The two real requirements for success there are cunning and lack of conscience. My road was harder because I possess neither of those qualities. They are as alien to my nature as hard work.

I hope I have taken some of the edge off The Question. I feel I owe a debt of explanation to those who enjoy and encourage my writing. Should anyone feel shortchanged by this response, I urge you to consider one mitigating fact in my behalf: It is an extremely difficult question for a guy like me to answer from a place like this.

---

The Lompoc prisoners saw much of themselves in Dannie's article. "They *really* liked the answer to The Question," Dannie wrote me, "and convicts are *very* harsh critics." And, he added, his fellow convicts told him repeatedly how happy they were to have him writing so that he could "get some of that Jack Abbott sicko heat off all of us."

That was a reference to the convict-author of *In the Belly of the Beast,* a killer whose release from prison in 1981 had been championed by Norman Mailer in the apparent belief that Abbott's vivid writing style and unbroken, if violent, spirit somehow conferred on him a kind of moral redemption. Mailer wrote of him, "I love Jack Abbott for surviving and for having learned to write as well as he does." Abbott killed a waiter in New York not long after the release from prison that Mailer helped him obtain.

The Abbott comparison dogged us both. On the outside, I had to cope with the suspicion of some readers, coworkers, and other journalists who were uncomfortable with the very idea of trusting a prisoner's judgment. "Remember Jack Abbott!" I was warned again and again.

There were two and only two similarities between the criminal but nonviolent Dannie Martin and the explosively angry Jack Abbott: Both were longtime convicts; both wrote well. And there were even fewer similarities between me and Abbott's champion, Norman Mailer.

There was simply no reason to suggest that because Dannie, like Abbott, wrote well about prisons, I should therefore beware of any commitment to him or his writing. But so powerful are the myths and fears surrounding prisoners that Dannie and I could not escape the comparison. "The word 'Abbott' is around my neck like an albatross," he wrote me once.

It's around my neck, too. But if Dannie Martin returns to prison—

and it is certainly a possibility for any man who has spent half his life there—it will be because he is Dannie Martin, not because he is another Jack Abbott.

On June 13, 1987, after eleven months of long-distance collaboration, I finally met my popular writer, but to do so I had to surmount a barrier almost as formidable as the ones surrounding the prison itself— the bureaucratic mentality.

To get on Dannie's visiting list, I had filled out an application identifying my "relationship to the above named individual" as "editor," and I had submitted to a police record search. Once on the list, I purchased airline tickets and made final plans for our visit. But three days before that first visit was to take place, with no warning and no provocation, the prison bureaucracy removed me from Dannie's visiting list because, I was informed, it had "approved me on the wrong list." It was a bitter disappointment for both of us.

During a phone conversation with the warden, I came up with a way around the rejection by accepting the cancellation of the "visit" and requesting instead to "interview" Dannie—same day, same time. It was an almost comical circumnavigation of a capricious prison ruling.

I had one last, ominous phone conversation with an official in the warden's office before that visit. I asked if I was allowed to bring Dannie a gift. Could I, for instance, bring him a *Chronicle* T-shirt or baseball cap? The answer was an emphatic no. In the course of the discussion, I mentioned that Dannie "writes for the paper."

"He's not allowed to do that," the warden's assistant said.

His words hung in the air an uncomfortable moment, and we both quickly dropped the subject.

Although Dannie and I had been working together by phone and letter for nearly a year, because of the great disparity in our backgrounds neither of us knew what to expect in person. Dannie speculated in a letter: "I've been trying to guess what you look like, and no luck at all. Fortyish, button-down, and dark hair is about all I can come up with. Probably wrong on all counts. I do look forward to our visit."

So did I.

Lompoc is a remote town about an hour's drive north of Santa Barbara. Although better known as the home of Vandenberg Air Force Base, the area is also the location of the largest federal prison in the West. It is a colorful five-mile drive from the town to the penitentiary, through a patchwork quilt of flower fields. Lompoc bills itself as the Flower Seed Capital of the World.

The penitentiary, which at the time housed about twelve hundred prisoners, is a large, stark concrete structure of three-tiered cellhouses. The heavily fortified multiwing building stands in a field cleared of vegetation for security reasons. It was approached through the campuslike federal prison camp, a tree-shaded low-security institution where Ivan Boesky used to reside, but there was no confusing the two facilities. The massive penitentiary is the kind of place only a government could build, and the impression is in no way softened by the planter boxes of flowers flanking the front door.

The world behind the double rolls of razor wire was a strange and frightening one to me, and I was sensitized to every sight and sound. Disembodied voices from hidden speakers periodically startled me with demands:

> State your purpose. . . . Secure your car and proceed to the first tower. . . . Do you have any of the following contraband on your person? . . . Place two forms of identification in the pouch on your right.

Heavy, remote-controlled gates, surveillance cameras, squawk boxes, barking voices—but there were no guards in sight until I was inside the first few "lines of defense." It was an intimidating process that I couldn't help but feel was intended to be so—for "free world" guests as well as for convicts. Perhaps, I thought, the tone of intimidation defined the prison and its keepers as much as the physical plant itself.

Although I viewed the crowded, maddeningly noisy prison visiting room as Dannie's "terrain," the convict had only infrequent visits from family members, and the visiting room was, in fact, almost as new to him as it was to me. That room was his "outside world." It was a spare place of linoleum, Formica tables, molded plastic chairs bolted to the floor—and embarrassingly intimate family reunions.

Dannie and I talked haphazardly during that first visit of many things, personal and professional—family, interests, backgrounds, upcoming articles, writing styles, visiting rules. Then, a month later, I was back at the prison, this time to appear before his parole board.

It was very important to Dannie that I attend that hearing—primarily so that he would have an outside witness in case of a bureaucratic ambush—but my testimony that day came only after some soul-searching. It was one thing to publish the writings of a convict and even to develop a professional friendship with him; it was quite another to testify on his behalf.

Until that point, I could hide behind the conviction that our association entailed no endorsement of Dannie's character or criminal history or of his prospects in the "free world." It became a more tenuous self-defense after my appearance before his parole board, but I was careful to inform the members of the panel that I was testifying on what he had accomplished in his writing and on what I had observed of his character and that I was not urging his release. Nor, I told them, was I able to speak to his prospects after release.

The record Dannie brought to his parole board was revealing: three infractions (all for drugs and alcohol) in the eight-month period following his previous board hearing—before he began writing for the newspaper—with no infractions in the next sixteen months.

I showed the panel members copies of Dannie's published articles, which they spent some time scanning. The members nodded appreciatively and made passing comments on the articles. Then they added a lenient four months to his sentence for the serious infractions on his record but praised his work for the *Chronicle* and said that if he kept up the good work and had no new incident reports, they would take time off his sentence when he appeared before them two years later.

After the hearing, several prison officials in the hallway outside the board's hearing room expressed genuine interest in the writer's work. One asked me if I could spare my copy of "Mr. Squirrel," saying he had heard about the article but hadn't had a chance to read it.

---

In April 1987, there had been a change in the prison that proved especially beneficial to Dannie's writing career. He was moved from E Unit, which "always sounded like a gorilla cage at feeding time," to H, an honor unit:

> I moved to a single cell last night! I wish I was writer enough to describe the feeling of luxury. Sleeping alone with no bunk on top of me. First good night's sleep I've had in two years. Now I will try and get to know myself again. No telling how much I've changed.

And, as he settled into his new digs, Dannie got to know the neighbors, too, especially the guy next door.

## RICHARD KEMP: WHITE ON WHITE

*LOMPOC, CALIF. (JUNE 28, 1987)*—In the fall of 1982, Richard Kemp was a liberal-minded freshman at Hartnell College in Salinas. He was twenty years old, an aspiring yuppie with dreams of knights and maidens of old. Today Kemp is a different sort of yuppie. He's a young urban political prisoner doing sixty years in a federal prison.

What began as a young man's idealistic journey in search of his identity ended in gunfire, betrayal, and prison. The remainder of his dreams are tucked away in a sheet-metal locker mounted on the bars of a small prison cell. He now occupies the cell next to mine in H Unit at Lompoc penitentiary. It is here that we talked of his philosophy and of the personal changes that brought him to this place.

As a student at Hartnell, Kemp began his journey by writing a term paper on the white separatist movement. It was a well-written essay that pointed out the flaws in the macabre political philosophy. He received an A on it.

While researching his project, Kemp encountered a fellow student named Bill Soderquist. Soderquist, a white supremacist, was a personable, persuasive man. In time they became friends, and under Soderquist's tutelage, Kemp became a follower of the white separatist movement.

Together they left school and journeyed by Greyhound bus to the tiny hamlet of Metaline Falls, Washington, where they joined Bob Mathews on a small farm. Mathews was a fiery, charismatic man who would later achieve martyrdom in what they call the white racialist cause.

Kemp was receptive to the romance of Mathews's movement. He says he favors a "clan-type government," although "I know I was born eight hundred years too late." A self-described "rural person and a romanticist," Kemp admires what he calls "the chivalrous ways of the past" and guesses that "I probably would've fought in the Crusades if I was born then."

Kemp told me that he became thoroughly indoctrinated under the guidance of Mathews and with him began attending the Christian Identity (also called Aryan Nations) church in Hayden Lake, Idaho, run by the Rev. Richard Girnt Butler. They also began recruiting and training more militant factions of the white separatist movement.

It wasn't long before political rhetoric found expression in sedition and violence. In less than a year's time, Kemp had passed from academic monotony to militaristic chaos.

"Mainly I think we were all frustrated," he says of those days. "We had lost jobs because of affirmative action bringing nonwhites to our community. There was 14 percent unemployment in our area already. Friends were losing small farms to bankruptcy, people being arrested for not sending their children to state-approved schools.

"We harbored delusions of having no voice in our government and passed out literature trying to shake our racial kinsmen out of a boob-tube trance. We never plotted to overthrow this government. It's too powerful and would squash any uprising like a bug. Ours was more a cry for attention. 'Listen to us, dammit! Our race is dying, and no one is doing a frigging thing about it.' "

The government had a less benign view of the group. Members of the "Bruder Schweigen" (Silent Brotherhood) or "The Order," as Mathews and Kemp's group came to be known, were prime suspects in numerous armored-car heists in California and the Pacific Northwest. One of the cars lost $3.6 million to five heavily armed white men. Another lost $500,000. Other members were suspected of the machine-gun murder of Denver talk show host Alan Berg, a politically liberal Jew. The government saw these actions as the evolution of militant fascism.

Richard Kemp doesn't quite fit the mold of violent revolutionary or red-eyed racist. A tall man at six feet five, and well-mannered, with large, limpid blue eyes, his discourses on the evils of our system are subdued, with no signs of repressed violence.

"The way it is now," he says, "you can't even go to the bathroom without Big Brother telling you how to do it. I had a Forest Service contract in the state of Washington where the National Forest Service gave us a thick booklet of rules. One entire chapter was devoted to how to properly relieve oneself.

"Too much government is bad, and it's my hope that one day it will become top-heavy and topple itself. People think that being a racialist I advocate fascism. I don't."

Nowadays, the betrayal by his friends seems to cut deeper than anything else.

"I'm embarrassed to say I was ever a part of this thing," he says softly. "The informers were among our most violent agitators. I feel sorry for Bob Mathews. He had high ideals and thought he was doing right. I had a good job, a car, a truck, and a nice home. Now everything I own in the world I can put in a paper sack, and this," he says, looking around his small cell, ". . . I didn't need any of this."

Mathews, thirty-two, along with Kemp, Gary Yarbrough, and several other members of The Order, went underground in 1984 and became fugitives. The FBI was on their trail. Mathews wounded an FBI agent while shooting his way out of a stakeout in Portland, Oregon, on November 24, 1984. Yarbrough was injured in the shootout. He was captured and later convicted of racketeering.

Mathews was finally run to ground on December 8, 1984, when agents surrounded him in a small two-story house on Whidbey Island, Washington, near Seattle. After a blazing shootout in which agents in helicopters burned the house down around him, Mathews's body was found in the smoking ashes. Clutched in each hand was a burned AR-15 rifle. A Bruder Schweigen silver-and-gold medallion was melted into the charred bones of his chest.

Kemp was captured in Kalispell, Montana, in January 1985. He was indicted in Seattle, along with twenty-two other members of the Bruder Schweigen and The Order under the RICO statutes (Racketeer-Influenced and Corrupt Organizations). To convict under the RICO statutes, the government must tie the accused to specific criminal acts committed as part of an organized conspiracy. Kemp was tied to one of the armored-car stickups.

Ten of Kemp's twenty-two codefendants rolled over and became government witnesses. Some of those ten received full immunity for their testimony. Bill Soderquist took the stand for the government and gave evidence against Kemp.

When Kemp arrived here at Lompoc, I expected to see a goosestepping Aryan with half his ear bitten off—a man ranting about termite Jews and ready for war with nonwhites. I expected him to embrace a philosophy of hatred, mixed with Nietzschean mightmakes-right slogans. Having enough enemies of my own, I made up my mind to steer clear of this fellow.

He wound up, of course, in Cell B-4 on the first tier of H Unit. I live in B-5, next door. He lived there a number of weeks before I realized he hadn't said a word except maybe a "good morning" on his way to work at the prison industries business office or to the exercise yard, where he keeps himself in top physical condition.

Kemp's cell, like the others here, is small, with bars across the front. We mount our lockers on the front bars for some added privacy. The basic furnishings are a sheet-metal bunk and a fold-out table, with a toilet, sink, and bookshelf at the rear. There is nothing quite like cold iron and cement to help one understand the creeping pace of interminable days and lonely nights.

Kemp is so tall that he sits on his bed while writing at his table affixed to the opposite wall. He is working on a screenplay. His bookshelf holds three volumes of Dante's *Divine Comedy*. *Will*, by G. Gordon Liddy, reposes next to the Bible. Education and self-help books complete the collection, along with a Viking Portable Kipling that I loaned him.

The cell walls are bare except for a pinup of a young, beautiful Nordic woman. His pictures of friends and family are displayed on the inner door of his locker. Patient with my probing curiosity about "racialism" and politics, he stops writing and unfolds back on his bunk.

"Jews? No, I don't hate Jews," he replies, "or any other race of people. I just don't think my children should be forced to study their culture or theirs to study mine. I don't get technical about a person's ethnic origin. If I feel a strong bond and we fight for the same cause, that's enough for me.

"The white man in America is losing touch with his ancestors. We're more concerned with our jobs and a six-pack and sports on weekends. The melting-pot theory is a sick philosophy. All races stand to lose by mixing and becoming a mass of consumers seeking pleasures and money.

"But," he continued, "I do believe the Jews control the news media. Josef Goebbels's propaganda ministry has been improved upon by Jews and turned against the white man. Look at the Palestinian issue— we only see one side of it on the news. No politician who is anti-Israel could ever be elected president of this country.

"I don't know when I've felt more shame for the white man than when I saw a picture of George Bush in the newspaper wearing a yarmulke and kissing the Wailing Wall."

Kemp relates well with blacks, Chicanos, and other racial groups in the prison.

Somehow, I can't get racialism and racism separated in my mind. He explains to me that a racist is a bigot and a racialist is one who furthers the cause of his own kind.

I ask him about religion. "My race is my religion," he declares. "How I carry myself is my form of worship. Nature is my god, and nature's laws are the laws of my god."

After all our conversations, the Nazi connection lingers in my mind. Swastikas seem to appear everywhere these individuals gather. I wonder if there is something in our country analogous to the growth of fascism in Hitler's Germany.

"I think some of our people are so wrapped up in the fate of Nazi Germany because it was the last, true white government on Earth," he says. "Americans fought a fratricidal war to wipe Germany out. Today, Germany is even more decadent than the United States.

"Those fascists, unlike the white men in our country, didn't send hard-earned money to feed Ethiopians while whites starved at home. Our nonfascist children pump poison into their veins, and our women flush babies down toilets. Our whites watch news of foreign countries and say it's bad over there, while the white race is dying all around them. The white man has lost this country and is now too weak to take it back. We tried; you see how far we got."

I don't really see how far they got, but it's plain to see how much time they got. I can't help but wonder how many other young students sitting in boring political science classes are being gently tugged toward a maelstrom of political chaos.

It isn't that long a journey from Hartnell College in Salinas to a maximum-security cell at the U.S. prison at Lompoc. About 150 miles as the crow flies.

---

As was his practice, Dannie had confirmed his quotations with Kemp before submitting the article. Interestingly, Kemp and his friends were so delighted with the piece that they were betting I wouldn't run it all. In fact, I later learned that when I met Kemp briefly in the Lompoc visiting room during my first visit with Dannie, he was afraid to tell me how much he liked the upcoming piece for fear I might change it.

"Looks like 'Another Myth Shattered,'" wrote Dannie.

More high praise came from Dannie's unit manager, who called the convict into his office to tell him how much he liked this article.

Dannie's next essay originated in a letter to me in which he described his errant typist's latest siege of inebriation and then commented:

It's really a strange feeling sometimes to wake up in Isolation and wonder what you did to get in there. Mostly you hope it is only a drunk charge. I used to do it now and then but got so ashamed of the ignorance involved that I quit drinking. I'm sure glad I don't have to deal with all that anymore.

And he proceeded to reminisce about Death Row Charlie. It was a powerful letter, and I suggested he expand it into a story.

## WHEN MURDER IS A DRUNKEN MISHAP

*LOMPOC, CALIF. (JULY 19, 1987)*—We called him "Death Row Charlie." There were several men named Charlie on the yard at Folsom State Prison in 1975. Someone would say, "Where's Charlie?" We would ask, "Which Charlie?" They would reply, "You know, uh, Death Row Charlie."

He was usually playing marbles at the marble ring in back of One Building. The nickname was added to his given name in 1972 when the California supreme court outlawed the death penalty. Charlie was among several of the condemned men who were transferred to Folsom.

I met him one day when I overheard him telling a funny story about a harrowing escape he once made from a chain gang at the Davidson County workhouse in Nashville, Tennessee. In 1967 I had served six months on the same chain gang. I felt we had a lot in common. He was a fun-loving man with a cheery disposition, and we became good friends.

One day during a quiet moment on a shady bench alongside One Building, he told me about his crime. As he told me the story, I

remember looking at the cracks in the huge granite block wall opposite us—wishing I could see further into the cracks, or further away.
As I listened, I wanted to look anywhere but into his eyes.

He said it began with a day of drinking in bars in Sacramento. He
had a job, a car, a nice home, and a wife and kids. He was having a
few drinks on his day off.

After hitting several bars and consuming prodigious amounts of
alcohol, he began to brood about his past. Thinking of days and
nights in jails and prisons and the indignities he had suffered in
them; the hate and rage he felt toward those who had treated him
like an animal. He wasn't sure how his drunken rage segued into
the idea of an armed robbery, but it did.

He obtained a handgun and drove his car to a loan company in
Sacramento. By the time he parked out front, he was so dead drunk
that he had a difficult time leaving his car and entering the place he
meant to rob.

He took a woman employee to a back room, telling her he had to
tie her up. As he drunkenly attempted to bind her, she began pleading in a soft and terrified voice.

"Please don't hurt me. I don't care about the money, but please
don't hurt me." He shot her. He meant to kill her, but he was so
drunk he didn't hit a vital spot.

She told him that was enough, that he didn't have to hurt her any
more. She told him about her family, begged him for her life. He
killed her with the next shot.

As he finished the story, I turned to look at him. Tears ran down
his cheeks, dripping from his chin.

"It was pitiful, Red," he said to me in a broken voice. I have never
seen a more crushed and heartbroken man than he was at that
moment.

I wished I hadn't asked him, and more, I wished he hadn't told
me. I now understood the importance of why convicts never ask
one another about their past or their crimes. I had violated the
unwritten rule, and somehow I was violated in return.

Charlie looked different to me after that, and my view of the
world was also changed. Some enigmatic force upset the balance of
my existence and left my mind tattooed with an indelible image.

I am also chilled by memories of waking with a hangover to
hear my girlfriend shout: "Well, buddy, that's the last party I will
attend with you!" And I would ask, "What happened? What did

I do?" I feel very grateful that it was only a party I had killed.

The theme recurs with astonishing regularity in prisons. In 1983, I met a man in L Unit here at Lompoc. I'll call him William. At the time, I was developing an interest in becoming a writer. William was a beginning writer also. We talked writing. A couple years passed before some facts about his case began to emerge.

He is a middle-aged man, very quiet and courteous. With the demeanor of an accountant or business executive, he seems out of place in a prison setting. The first few years I knew him, I assumed he was an embezzler or white-collar criminal.

In 1965, William was convicted of murder in Washington, D.C. A woman had been strangled, and there is no doubt William committed the crime. The court saw fit to recommend life in prison instead of a death sentence.

William escaped from prison in 1972 and made his way to the Bay Area. He took a pseudonym and went to work for a local computer corporation. He married and worked there until the FBI tracked him down a few years ago. Everyone who knew him, including his wife and employers, was shocked and incredulous at his exposure as an escaped killer.

By February 1987, I was aware of these facts about his past. On a gloomy, cold, overcast day that one can only appreciate in an iron-and-cement cellblock, William and I stood talking, huddled near a sputtering steam radiator along the cellhouse wall. The conversation turned to his arrest and conviction for murder.

"Red," he said to me, "it was a drunken mishap." I stopped him right there. I did not care to hear the sordid details. We stood there awhile, listening to the clang and sputter of the radiator. A fitting harmony to the awkward, screaming silence that bound us there together. I hoped it wouldn't follow me as I walked away. William's first parole hearing will be in 1998.

Then there is a man I'll call Shelley, who made the journey to Death Row and back, but not back to freedom. He languishes in prison today, doomed more by his own principles than by the crime he allegedly committed.

Shelley's story starts in the mid-'60s when a man—let's call him Sam—was paroled from San Quentin. A prison heavyweight boxing champion, Sam was one of the meanest bullies who ever prowled the big yard. After his release, he joined a woman, "Jean," who had been a "momma" for an outlaw biker gang in the San Joaquin Valley.

Those were the years of the Seconal craze. Most street people called them "reds" or "red devils." Sam and Jean ate them like popcorn and washed them down with whiskey.

One morning in the fall of 1967, Sam had a quarrel with Jean and chased her down the street with a butcher knife. They reconciled somewhat and attended a party that night. Shelley and several other men and women were at the party. Everyone was taking Seconal and drinking whiskey.

Sam, with Jean's encouragement, started beating up on people at the party. The following morning, his bullet-riddled body was discovered in a fig orchard in the valley. Jean's body was found in the Sierra foothills with a .45 slug in the head.

Several people who had been at the party were arrested for murder, including Shelley. A member of an outlaw biker gang turned state's evidence on a plea bargain. He testified that he and Shelley had killed Sam and Jean. In effect, what he said on the stand was: "I confess, your honor—he done it." Shelley testified that he hadn't killed or helped to kill anyone.

The biker was sentenced to a life term with a seven-year parole eligibility and has long since been rewarded with a parole for his adroit if odious maneuvering. Shelley, the recipient of the biker's "confession," was sentenced to die in the gas chamber at San Quentin State Prison.

In 1972, with the abolition of the death penalty, Shelley escaped the cyanide gas. His sentence was commuted to life in prison, and he was moved to Folsom. He remains in prison to this day.

I've never met a nicer person than Shelley. When he first arrived on Death Row, I wrote him a note and asked him what it was like up there. He wrote back and said there wasn't much to do but the food was good and the servings were very generous.

After he came from Death Row to Folsom, we played checkers every day. His favorite expression during those games was "Come on, Red, am I going to have to call a guard to make you move?"

He still maintains his innocence, which the parole board views as a "lack of remorse" for the crime. It is nearly impossible for a man to gain a parole from an indeterminate life sentence unless he is willing to grovel, lie, and demean himself. Shelley won't ever do that.

These three never died by the hand of society, although they came close. There are worse men than them who won't die in the gas chamber and better men who will.

I've often heard proponents of the gun lobby say, "Guns don't kill people; people kill people."

We shouldn't forget alcohol, drugs, and cyanide. They also get their share.

---

Dannie continued to case the joint for other stories of interest to his readers. In portraying what he knew was an alien world to most of them, he often relied on analogies to the world they inhabited, most notably in his next piece.

---

# THE WORLD IN MINIATURE

Lompoc, Calif. (Aug. 16, 1987)—An old convict at San Quentin in 1964 said to me with outflung arms that embraced the entire upper yard, "Son, a prison yard is a microcosm of society at large. What you see here is a miniature replica of the entire world."

As I followed his gaze to that windblown, rain-battered patch of asphalt, pigeons, and gulls, I struggled to make some sense of his statement.

It was hard to see the analogies to the free world. Convicts in raincoats played dominoes while rain ran off their hats. A beady-eyed gun-rail guard stood above them with a .30-30 rifle in his hand, watching every play.

After seeing many years and prison yards go by, I've found his words held a lot of truth.

We have our own economy in prisons. Cigarettes were 20 cents a pack in 1964, with Camels the preferred currency. Camels were to Philip Morris what the dollar now is to pesos. Sandwiches were a "pack" back then. A pack would get a shirt or a pair of pants pressed, or "Bonarooed," as we call it. A quart of prison wine, or "pruno," cost five packs, and interest on loans was 50 percent. Most of those prices are still the same, though cigarettes will cost you 85 cents a pack these days.

The only real price increase has been on hard drugs, and that's entirely understandable. The heroin business is a much more dirty and dangerous occupation today than it was twenty years ago. The demand has gradually surpassed the supply.

We have our rapos (rapists), serial killers, con men, factory workers, pimps, whores, religious groups, wine shops, grocery stores, lenders, laundries, artists, musicians, intellectuals, and people of all political persuasions. You name it, we've got it. We've got the whole world in our can.

We also have our rumors. Probably better ones than the free world's. Rumors in our little society travel far and fast, often lifting convicts on majestic waves of hope, only to batter them mercilessly at the shoals of despair.

Our last warden here at Lompoc has finally retired, and thank God, say most of the cons. After his arrival in 1981, it seemed to us he began transferring out convicts who live in this part of the United States and bringing in cons from places like Alaska, Maine, New York, and Vermont. Convicts who call our potato soup "chowdah," and now it's the "toid tieh," instead of the third tier.

Someone—and there's not a shred of evidence to back this up—started a rumor that the reason the warden brought all these frontiersmen and Ivy Leaguers here is because he supposedly owns the only two motels in Lompoc. The convicts' families have to stay at the motels while visiting the black sheep of the family. Even a rumor as farfetched as that plays pretty well in here if we have a particularly unpopular warden.

We even have a prison ecology movement, and that same warden had the prison ecologists passing on some awfully scary facts. Soon after he arrived here, he built a little cinder-block shack right inside the double gates of the north sally port where trucks enter the prison. He had an X-ray machine installed in the shack, and now all the food entering this prison, including our milk and vegetables, is X-rayed before it reaches our table. The warden said it was done for "security reasons."

The building of the shack and the X-raying of food are facts, but the ecological rumor mongers say the X-raying has nothing to do with "security purposes." They say it's all some kind of test to study the long-term effects of irradiated food on human beings. Many of us who have eaten the X-rayed food for a few years are indeed acting a bit strange, but it's very hard in here to discern normal strangeness from radioactive weirdness.

The technological revolution has had as much impact in prisons as it has on the free world, though the issues in here may seem Neanderthal to readers in the world of VCRs and compact discs.

For years now, convicts at the 'Poc, as we call this place, have been able to buy "ghetto blasters." With 120 men in each cellblock, from all different cultures, the noise level rivals Vandenberg airfield right next door. Many times, a giant missile has been launched at Vandenberg and we didn't know it until we read about it in the newspaper.

Our dearly departed warden put out a memo that all big radios will be sent home or disposed of by 1988. Henceforth, the only radios allowed will be of the Walkman type, with headphones. So all the convicts who have spent big money on big radios must now dispose of them and spend big money on small radios.

As in the free world, we can either dine in the dining room or "eat out," and if our à la carte runs pretty much to baloney, cheese, and hamburger, it is sometimes attractive as a lesser evil.

In the years since 1981, we have had some terrible food managers here at the 'Poc. There was some respite during the Carter presidency when we got all the peanut butter we wanted. We even had peanut butter soup a couple times.

Recently, we got a new food manager who's putting out *nouvelle cuisine* in the land of wilted lettuce and half-cooked pork steaks.

He has served more fresh vegetables and fruit since his arrival than I've seen in the past seven years. Farewell, pork and beans; hello, *haute cuisine*. The baloney peddlers are suffering a severe decline in their cash flow.

And so it goes. As it is out there, it is pretty much the same in here. Some might cavil that there is straight sex and travel out there and not much of either in here; I'd have to admit they're absolutely correct.

But then, we have free rent and groceries in here, and there's not much of either out there.

---

Soon after that essay appeared in the paper, Dannie got involved in another spinoff from his *Chronicle* writing that gave him great satisfaction. Two teachers independently asked him if he would be interested in corresponding with their students about criminal justice issues. Dannie, who has always loved children, readily consented and soon found himself in deep correspondence—individual and collective—with dozens of students at two schools in Northern California.

The two classes were, in Dannie's words, "not only miles apart, they are worlds apart." One was a government class of college-bound students at Menlo-Atherton High School in a high-income suburb of San Francisco. The other was at a "community school" for troubled and delinquent children—many of whom had spent time in "juvie"—in Willits, a rural town several hours north of San Francisco.

With the Menlo-Atherton students, Dannie discussed issues of penal philosophy across what, for him, was a cultural divide. He asked me in a letter: "How in the hell am I supposed to inform an upper middle class student body that police forces were created to protect the moneyed class (read status quo) from the poor folks? Let me have an answer on that soon!"

And with the Willits class he had to answer questions of more desperately immediate concern from students whose families were poor, often mired in drugs, and sometimes also imprisoned.

Dannie gave them all advice and intellectual perspective and nuggets of street-smart criminology. He taught his students how the criminal justice system is "held hostage to the prevailing political mood" as the pendulum swings between liberal and conservative philosophies. "When it filters down to us," he wrote one student, "we've got the guard on day shift wanting to punish us and the guard on night shift wanting to educate and rehabilitate us."

Despite his teaching load, he continued sending me his prison stories. The next one was a further bit of prison folklore.

# IT GOES AROUND AND COMES AROUND

LOMPOC, CALIF. (SEPT. 6, 1987)—Every prison is built with a track around the perimeter of the exercise yard so that convicts can walk around and around in their spare time. It works off some of our energy and frustration the way a wheel does in a cage of pet mice.

Usually there are benches near the track, and as you sit on one you can watch convicts go around and come back around.

There is a universal cliché that goes: "What goes around comes around." It's a common saying among convicts, too—its significance enhanced by the movement of cons on the track. To us, it's more than a cliché.

There was an old convict in the Carson City, Nevada, prison in the early 1950s called "The Deacon." The Deacon had occasion to verbalize what those words mean to convicts, and his speech is talked about today in many prison yards.

He had been a deacon in a Mormon church in Utah. He was a tall, taciturn man with a wild bush of a beard. The cons respected his religion because he wasn't pushy about it, and they respected him because he recognized their codes and carried himself like a man.

In those days in Nevada, a life sentence amounted in practice to nine years. The Deacon had pursued one of his wives to Reno after she fled there seeking a divorce. In the midst of a violent argument, he killed her, and he received a life sentence.

The prison at Carson City was a small, self-sufficient operation back then. All the meats and most of the vegetables used at the prison were the yield of a good-sized farm worked by convicts outside the walls.

The warden ran this little kingdom, and his word was law. What with gambling tables in the prison yard, ample food and supply budgets, and well-to-do criminals, there was money to be made. A governor of the state of Nevada once remarked that he wished he had the warden's job instead of the governor's.

Just outside the main prison was a corral that was used to break wild mustangs to the saddle. Men inside the prison would sometimes watch and laugh as inexperienced convict cowboys learned how mean a wild stallion can be.

The story of The Deacon's speech begins with the arrival of a man named Clifford Helms at the prison in the early '50s. He was serving a life sentence for murder. Helms had worked for Bugsy Siegel's gang in Las Vegas and killed a man over a gambling debt.

He thought he was a big shot because of his mob connections, but he wasn't well-liked. His bragging—and the fact that he had killed a square businessman over a debt—didn't sit well with the other convicts.

Soon after his arrival, the appropriate payoffs were apparently made, and he was sent to the ranch outside the prison to work at breaking wild horses. The only time he entered the main prison after that was to buy his canteen supplies. He was even assigned a little shack where he bunked alone.

Helms hadn't been there long when three convicts inside the walls decided to escape. They grabbed the trash truck one morning when it entered the prison and took the guard-driver hostage at knifepoint.

When the tower guard at the back gate refused to open up for them, they crashed through the gate in the truck. The guard opened fire and killed the hostage by mistake.

Just outside the prison, the truck died, and the three escapers hit the desert on foot. Two of them were recaptured right away, and a huge posse was formed to search for the missing fugitive. Clifford Helms was issued a rifle and a horse and joined the hunt.

They searched the surrounding desert all that day and way into the night. It began to look as if the man had eluded them.

When the other members of the posse gave up on finding him near the prison, Helms doggedly kept searching. Late that night, his determination paid off. He found the convict hiding under a pile of brush and marched him at gunpoint back to the prison.

He was an instant hero in the eyes of his keepers and just as instantly a pariah in the hearts of the convicts.

Men stood near the fence yelling foul epithets as he went about breaking mustangs. No longer could he come to the main prison yard for any reason. A guard had to buy and deliver his canteen goods.

The hatred for Helms lay heavier than the desert heat on the prison. It was the sort of palpable mass feeling that all convicts experience in times of exaggerated racial hatred or accumulated frustration induced by the torture of confinement. This time it was felt by all toward one man. Many in that prison would have killed him and gladly done nine years for the deed.

Things came to a head at lunch one day. A man thinking about Helms and muttering to himself slammed his fist into his beef stew and splattered everyone seated nearby. When he refused to apologize, an argument ensued and progressed into the yard, where people began to arm themselves with clubs, knives, and pipes. All the convicts by then were fully determined to vent their frustration on one another.

About this time, the old Deacon stepped right into the middle of the fray and made his speech.

"Hold it!" he told them. "A lot of us here are friends, and we are getting ready to kill each other over a no-account stool pigeon." He stood there glaring as if he meant business, and the collective anger began to soften as he continued.

He told them that when he first came to jail he was a scared and confused man who had never done a day in jail or planned on doing one. After he was booked, the jailers shoved him into a cell with about fifteen of the ugliest cutthroats he had ever seen, then slammed the iron door behind him. He said three or four of those men were right in the crowd around him that day. The tension eased a bit as the cons began to look around with him.

"I was scared stiff," he told them, "when this evil-looking, tat-tooed fella walked up to me and asked if I needed anything—some tobacco, a toothbrush, soap, or whatever. Then he helped me find myself a bunk and some decent blankets. I took some of the things he offered, and when I tried to pay him back, I think you all know what he said to me.

"He told me, 'What goes around, comes around,' and the only way I could pay him back was to help another convict sometime when I saw one broke or in need of a friend. He told me that, being a deacon, I could understand it when he said that this was the convict's Golden Rule. I've never forgotten that, and I'm telling you all not to forget it. Clifford Helms will get his without us hurting each other."

His speech broke the mood enough that everyone put up their weapons, but the rage was still at a high level. Not for long, though. The next day an event occurred that made The Deacon look like a veritable prophet.

After the lunch break, most of the men were in the yard watching as Clifford Helms tried to calm a maddened wild mustang stallion. As he jerked the halter rope, the stallion reared and kicked him in the head. Clifford went down, and the horse stomped him to death with as much determination as if he were stomping a rattlesnake. When the dust cleared, the hate and rage had evaporated.

The Deacon's little sermon lives on. His story is told today on prison yards from the East to the West Coast. It never fails to remind us that what we send around will surely come back around. Even if a wild horse has to bring it.

---

The story of Clifford Helms's comeuppance meant a great deal to its author. It's the kind of prison homily that played well within the walls, but the story also gave Dannie a chance to tell the public something he was always eager to convey. "I was able to say that as thuggy as we are," he wrote me the day after the piece was published, "we have some values and feelings also. Many [readers] won't notice, but some will."

Although Dannie's writing never lost its engaging, folkloric tone, over time his essays exhibited more sense of audience, more social consciousness. Increasingly, he seemed to work deliberately to educate the public about the prison experience—the role, for example, of the guards and of the bureaucracy. His next essay, although occasioned by events in his prison, strives for broader understanding of convict psychology and of one all-important feature of prison life: the yard.

---

# A PLACE TO SHAKE THE GLOOM
# OF THE CAGE

*Lompoc, Calif. (Oct. 18, 1987)*—Once you get in here behind the double iron doors and the double rows of razor wire, there's a kind of calm. It's a precarious calm, like the eye of a hurricane, but we cons come to rely on it.

It's the calm of "the yard" and everything it represents. Mess with our yard and reap the whirlwind—and I'm beginning to feel a wind coming up.

A little background:

Many criminals, drug addicts, and alcoholics outside of prison can't deal with their lives or their habits. Their waking hours become a foggy maze of pain and lawless destruction, blended with intermittent moments of peace and gratification. They are forever tortured by the knowledge that the release they seek will only bind them more securely in the cage they build for themselves.

One day they are shoved into a real cage, and the iron doors slam shut behind them. The most common look in their eyes at the moment the last door clanks firmly shut is a strange mixture of resignation and relief.

Suddenly they are able to handle their habits and to get a grip on their lives. The choice isn't theirs anymore.

Jail restores order and certainty in a person's life. Meals are served according to a rigid schedule, laundry exchanged at definite times; sick call, mail call, and visits are all at fixed hours on designated days.

We can't see out the windows of the jail, but we see the future stretched before us in a rigid, orderly fashion. From lives of chaos, uncertainty, and danger, we are thrust into order, security, and boredom.

Jail is a prep school for prison. We learn some of the values and etiquette of convicts, and above all we learn to do our suffering as quietly as possible. Our neighbor has his own cross to bear.

We learn never to awaken a sleeping convict, because in this world of noise and agony, sleep is precious. We learn that it's a cardinal sin to interfere in an argument between another convict and a jailer. It isn't done. Taking the jailer's side can cost a man his life.

By the time we reach prison we are becoming clear on the subtle lessons of the cage, and we are accustomed to breakfast at six and supper at five. McDonald's is only a dim memory.

In prison we are confronted with another certainty, a job. Everyone in prison works unless physically or mentally unable to do so. The employment ranges from factories to janitorial, kitchen, laundry, and maintenance crews. There are also vocational and educational programs. Everything is scheduled.

Federal prisons are more relaxed these days than state prisons. The prisoners are of a more cosmopolitan type, and there is very little racial tension. A convict can also get a shot of dope or a drink of booze now and then. Not enough for a habit, but enough to take the edge off a bit.

These few amenities, however, do have their price. The federal Bureau of Prisons accepts convicts from state prisons and mental hospitals who are too unstable, violent, or sensational for local jails and prisons. The more violent of these are kept medicated on strong psychotropic drugs. They walk among us like zombies in slow motion. Others carry on lengthy conversations with imaginary companions or affect poses resembling the Statue of Liberty—they can remain motionless for hours on end.

We endeavor to ignore these unfortunate souls as we go about the business of serving our sentences.

A mental patient here not long ago walked into a cellblock office where a guard was sitting and began cutting the officer in the head with a single-edge razor blade. They never exchanged a word. It took a multitude of stitches to close the wound.

As a result of that type of incident, we are all treated like mental patients instead of convicts. Most regular officers aren't certain whether we are here because of insanity or criminality. In a cellblock with only one guard and 120 convicts, they can't afford any chances. This attitude breeds distrust and bad communication between staff and convicts.

Now that our existence is orderly, we are easily upset by tentative or uncertain measures. Yet much of this we take in stride, as just another part of our judgment and sentence.

In the prison setting, we begin to understand that the most important thing we have is our set routine. Something we do every day. Our routine is the motor that drives us over the hump of time. We fine-tune it and get it down to a science.

We are confined to one cellblock and not allowed in any other. From our cellblock we can go to the yard, the mess hall, or our job. Movements are allowed hourly during a ten-minute period. Many of us spend our free time in the yard, which is a precious place indeed.

In the yard, we have handball courts, tennis courts, weights, basketball, volleyball, a running track, green grass, and miles and miles of blue sky and fresh air. It's the place where we play, shaking off the dust, disease, and gloom of the cage.

A man with an afternoon job may come to spend his mornings on the yard, afternoons at work, and his evenings studying in his cell. This routine is as certain to him as the years he must do.

When we meet a new convict, he doesn't inquire as to the health of the family; he asks: "What kind of routine have you got?"

But there are changes these days in our routine. The Bureau of Prisons' punishment of choice now seems to be closing the yard. More and more reasons are found to close it. In the federal prison in Marion, Illinois, convicts are confined to their cells twenty-two hours a day.

What is happening at Marion is the end result of the tactics being used here. A man who has to do ten or twelve years locked in his cell for twenty-two hours a day is definitely a man I do not want for a next-door neighbor.

It used to be that the only reason for closing our yard was severely inclement weather or heavy fog. Then one day, as some convicts from the prison camp next door worked between the double fences, spreading lime to kill the grass and enhance the view, someone inside yelled an insult at them. Now our yard is closed when a crew works between fences.

A few years ago, five convicts stole the prison trash truck and crashed through the fences. One was killed by gunfire, and the other four were captured immediately. Since that incident, our yard is closed when any truck or other motor vehicle enters the prison. Many trucks come here to bring groceries and other supplies. Before the breakout, the yard had remained open when trucks came to call because there is the protection of a fence between the yard and the trucks.

Seldom does a week pass now when our yard isn't closed a few days for one reason or another. Guards, when asked why, will say, "Truck," "Men working," "Lack of staff," or just that it's closed and that's that.

Back in the cellblock, some of us remove our running shoes and go back to bed, sleeping all day and tossing and turning all night. Others sit in the stuffy cellblock and watch the rays of sunshine filtering through the iron security screens on the windows.

Taking away the yard spoils our routine and unbalances our body clocks. Tempers begin to go bad; we snap at each other like too many rats crammed into a cardboard box; hating becomes second nature.

Some of us believe that there are conservatives on the staff who are bent on "getting tough on criminals." They seem to be responding to a mood prevalent on the outside—both in the courts and among the general populace. These staff workers, we believe, would like to start "getting tough" by locking us in our cells twenty-four hours a day. This belief, whether right or wrong, fuels our cloistered hatred.

No matter how we approach the issue intellectually, it doesn't dampen the rage we acquire from being packed in gloomy cages while there is blue sky and sunshine just beyond the wall. We have to share this place down to our germs. If one gets the flu, we all get it.

When our routines are disrupted, chaos is once again among us. The future seems fragmented, uncertain. A strange type of resolve takes hold among the convicts: Should our keepers choose to deal in pain, chaos, and destruction, we will try to give them a good game. After all, we invented it.

---

Dannie's story on the yard also originated in letters to me. He had talked for some time of the prisoners' growing frustration with yard closure policies, and a month before this article appeared he wrote me a vivid letter describing a volatile episode on a morning when the yard was closed. I converted part of that letter, word for word, into a story that ran as a sidebar to "A Place to Shake the Gloom of the Cage."

---

# A MORNING IN THE CAGE

*LOMPOC, CALIF. (OCT. 18, 1987)*—It's Sunday morning and I'm all dressed up with nowhere to go. . . .

I had put on my running outfit when I woke up. There is a ten-minute "movement" at eight o'clock and another at nine on weekends. That's when we're allowed to move to or from the yard.

At the eight-o'clock movement, I went for the yard but found it closed. Sign up on the "control" booth said "Fog Line"—which means it's too foggy for the gun towers to see well enough. I went back to my cell and waited until nine.

At the nine-o'clock movement, I went back, and the sign was still up there, but we could all look out the windows and see the sun shining; there was no fog in sight. We can see all the way to the fields beyond the fences.

All the cons who work on weekdays and can't get outside then were there, some of them with tennis racquets. There were four cops standing by the locked gate hard-eyeing everyone.

Someone yelled, "You assholes! What the fuck is goin' on here!"

The cops started saying, "Clear the hall! Move it on!" People yelling, "Open the fucking yard, you assholes!"

The yard was closed all day last Monday (reason unknown), half the day Tuesday, half the day Wednesday, and, so far, half the day today. That's close to the weekly average.

In another disquieting development that no one has explained to us, workmen have recently started taking all the windows out of the hallway and putting solid sheet metal over them. I guess they don't want us to see outside, either.

---

The Lompoc prisoners' troubles with yard closure policy continued after publication of Dannie's articles, and when next he broached the subject in print, it led to the crackdown that was still reverberating in court briefs five years later.

As word of Dannie's newspaper writing spread in the prison, the convicts doing time with him frequently approached him with information and story ideas. Some of those ideas ultimately saw print. Others, by far the greater proportion, had to be rejected. In many cases, the convicts' story ideas didn't check out when Dannie asked for documentation; in others, the idea-monger turned out to be seeking self-serving publicity or revenge for some personal grievance. Dannie says that one man who was "stone nuts" tried to persuade him to write a story based on his unhinged delusions.

Several prisoners wanted him to write about how they'd been "screwed by the parole board" but then refused to share with the writer details of their crimes and sentences. "Why do you need to know that?" one asked petulantly. And the author replied, "Every story has a beginning, middle, and end. You want me to tell just the middle and end. My editor won't let me do that."

Dannie set high value on his credibility, and he lectured more than a few convicts on his obligations to his readership. Meanwhile, he continued to sift through the suggestions brought to him by friends and acquaintances. It was one such personal contact that led to his next story.

Many convicts with long experience in courts and prisons have a fine-tuned sense of justice; they can spot a moral outrage or a legal injustice across a crowded catwalk. Often, prisoners seem to sense better than judges who does and does not belong among them.

When one of Dannie's friends met newly arrived prisoner Kevin

Sherbondy through his job in the prison dental office, he was stunned by the story the young man told him in a casual chat, and he urged Dannie to talk to him. Dannie and Sherbondy were housed in different housing units, but the dental aide introduced them the next time they were all on the yard together. The two did a couple of laps on the track, with Dannie questioning Sherbondy as they ran. The story Dannie first heard that day catapulted the author from the feature section of the paper to the news pages. It also changed Sherbondy's future.

## THE 23-YEAR-OLD 'CAREER CRIMINAL'

*LOMPOC, CALIF. (NOV. 29, 1987)*—On Monday, November 17, 1986, a revised federal career criminal statute passed into law. That same morning, a twenty-three-year-old man from San Clemente, California, was arrested for possession of a firearm. After a one-day trial in U.S. district court in Los Angeles, Kevin Sherbondy became the first person in the United States to be sentenced under the statute. He received fifteen years in a federal prison.

The career criminal law provides that any person found in possession of a firearm who has a record of three violent crimes and/or serious drug offenses shall be sentenced to prison for no less than fifteen years and up to natural life. A sentence under this section is nonparolable.

U.S. district court Judge Harry Hupp seemed to agonize over Sherbondy's sentence but concluded that he had no choice.

"If I was given discretion," he said at the time, "it would not be a fifteen-year sentence; because of your youth and intelligence, I'd think a shorter sentence would be in order."

Kendra McNally, the U.S. prosecutor, disagreed with Hupp. Citing Sherbondy's past record, she called the sentence "entirely appropriate." "The law is designed to take career criminals off the streets," she said. "He qualified."

This past September 16, Kevin Sherbondy arrived at Lompoc to begin serving his sentence. Here at the penitentiary, when we think of career criminals, we picture a big-time dope dealer or a violent thug involved in organized crime—at the least someone with a long history of criminality. So it stunned many of the convicts to see a twenty-three-year-old "career criminal."

At six feet three and 220 pounds, Sherbondy is a strapping young man. He's a bodybuilder and has the looks of a star in a surfing movie. But his eyes don't play the part; these days, they hold the dull sheen of hurt and bewilderment.

His intelligence is obvious, but his words are slow and labored when he is asked about his sentence.

"I don't really know," he says, studying the ground between us. "It's a denial of everything I believed in. I'm not a career criminal, you know. I've never hurt anyone or stolen a dollar in my life. I can't really define what I feel, but I suppose pain would be a good word."

Kevin never knew his father and was eight years old when his mother died. His maternal grandparents, Arthur and Ethel Sherbondy, adopted him and his eleven-year-old brother, Danny. The children were raised in a secure, upper-middle-class environment.

Arthur Sherbondy, before his retirement in 1978, was a district vice president at Bank of America. Ethel still works part-time as a dental hygienist. Kevin was raised in their home near San Clemente, overlooking the Pacific. The Spanish-style house is located one mile from Richard Nixon's former Western White House at Cotton Point. Arthur and Ethel were both advocates of law-and-order politics.

Kevin's first brush with the law came when he was twelve. He was arrested, handcuffed, and read his rights for skateboarding in a drainage canal.

"That was my first inkling of how repressive our government can be," he said, gazing balefully toward the corner gun tower. "But I'm just beginning to understand how thoroughly Big Brother can crush someone."

Kevin steered clear of trouble for the next six years. He says now that he was so square he couldn't even lie to Ethel Sherbondy in order to cut school and go surfing when the waves were high. He would plead and show her the waves. On rare occasions, she would relent.

The worst argument he had at home was when he wanted to skip a grade in high school and begin college early. Barely into his teens, Kevin had developed a burning desire to study drama and become an actor. It's a desire he nurtures to this day.

The beginning of the end was a purchase he made at a yard sale in 1979 when he was sixteen years old. A neighbor who was moving sold Kevin a beach bike, some stereo components, and a Sturm Ruger .44 long-barrel revolver—an unwieldy twenty-to-thirty-year-old gun with Western "frontier" styling. The gun came complete with a tie-down holster and a cartridge belt—hardly the kind of easily hidden weapon commonly used in criminal endeavors. The seller told Kevin it was old and inoperable and cautioned him never to attempt to fire it.

Kevin's yard-sale gun was no secret in the family. He kept it hanging on his bedpost. "It was sort of a macho thing—an old relic in a pretty leather holster," said Ethel Sherbondy, who never gave the gun much thought until it cost her grandson fifteen years of his life.

In the early 1980s, the cocaine epidemic bloomed in Kevin's neighborhood. Suddenly, everyone was using coke. His first arrest was for possessing a half ounce of cocaine. On March 12, 1982, he was bailed out, and on April 11 of the same year he was rearrested and charged with robbery as well. An acquaintance had charged that Kevin threatened him with a BB gun in an argument over money. Kevin pleaded guilty to that charge and the cocaine rap and received a nine-month sentence in the county jail.

On October 26 of the same year, before he was to do his time in jail, Kevin pleaded guilty to a burglary in which no money or property was taken. This case arose from yet another neighborhood cocaine argument. He was sentenced to prison for that crime and served thirty-five months at San Quentin and Chino.

On February 9, 1986, Sherbondy visited a friend to beseech him not to testify against another friend in a coke case. The man reported the contact, and Sherbondy was jailed again, this time for intimidating a witness. He received three years' probation on that charge.

"I know all those convictions look bad," he says, "but those first three convictions leading to my going to prison all happened within a nine-month period of time. All of them involved the same people more or less, and no one was ever hurt. The worst I've been accused of is threatening someone. Right there you have my entire career in crime."

Upon his release on probation in July 1986, Sherbondy decided enough was enough. After a heart-to-heart talk with Ethel and Arthur, he enrolled full-time at Saddleback College in Mission Viejo, a few miles from San Clemente, carrying a full load of business management courses and one drama class—all the while holding down two jobs.

One of his employers later wrote to Judge Hupp that Sherbondy, on his release from prison, "seemed to have a new determination and zest for life. Everyone noticed it. His temper had disappeared and he was there for anyone who needed him, [going] out of his way on many occasions to help my family, our friends, and even people he did not know."

He also stopped using cocaine, and he quit hanging out with friends who led wilder lives. That resolve proved to be his undoing.

He had taken up residence with his girlfriend in a condominium owned by Arthur Sherbondy on the San Clemente golf course. His girl still liked to party, but Sherbondy, as a full-time college student with two jobs, had no time for nights on the town.

Their discordant relationship fell apart in early November 1986, and Sherbondy asked her to move. She moved out and on November 12 contacted Otis Weichum of the Orange County sheriff's department and told him that Sherbondy was on probation and had a gun in his bedroom. The old-style pistol was hanging on his bedpost in its tie-down Western holster.

Weichum then contacted Sherbondy's probation officer, John Fadule, who for some mysterious reason said he wouldn't be available for a search until Monday, November 17. The 17th was also the day the new career criminal law was to take effect. Weichum then contacted a federal Alcohol, Tobacco, and Firearms agent named Jimmy Searls.

That call, according to Searls's affidavit in the court file, was made on November 13, and Weichum told Searls that he had a man who might qualify for the new career criminal law. Searls agreed to participate in the search on the 17th.

Monday morning, as Sherbondy was driving to his grandparents' house, he was pulled over by law officers. His house was then searched by Fadule, Orange County sheriff's deputies, and ATF agents. The gun was found on the bedpost, as reported by Sherbondy's ex-girlfriend.

Agent Searls said in a report for the grand jury that he tested the gun and it "operated as designed." Sherbondy says—and his grandmother confirms—that an Agent Pruitt of the ATF testified at his trial that in testing, the gun froze and was inoperable. In any case, in order to convict under the statute, the gun need not be operable.

Arthur and Ethel, along with Sherbondy's friends and employer, have been devastated by his judgment and sentence.

"We all thought I finally had it made," Sherbondy says. "I'd had that old gun so long it was like an old tennis shoe. I never dreamed I could get fifteen years in prison for owning it."

The employer who wrote the judge on Sherbondy's behalf offered to house as well as employ the young man, adding, "Surely he's paid for his past."

Sherbondy's grandparents are anxious to appeal his "career criminal" conviction but have been stymied in their efforts to do so. The attorney for the original case, according to his grandmother, charged $15,000, of which the couple still owe $10,000. They are living on retirement income and unable to finance a full-fledged private appeal.

"We don't know what to do now," said Ethel Sherbondy. "A public defender has been assigned to the case, but we've left messages at his answering service and he never calls us back." She says they have written to the public defender asking to be called collect but, again, have received no response. They do not know where to turn next in their efforts to free their grandson from the fifteen-year sentence.

Now in Lompoc serving his sentence, Sherbondy is still haunted by questions. "Two things really puzzle me," he says. "One is why the [federal] government got involved in a state probation case and why they waited a week until the law took effect to come and arrest me. If I'm such a dangerous criminal, why wait? I think they were looking for a good, white, middle-class example, and like the woman said, I qualified."

Whatever happened, fate rubbed it in some. Just before sentencing, Sherbondy received a certificate from Saddleback College saying that he had made the Dean's Honor List for the fall semester. A few days later, he received fifteen years as a career criminal.

Now the taxpayers will have to feed and care for him until November 2001. But society won't have to fear him anymore. It would indeed be frightening to know there was a twenty-three-year-old career criminal lurking out there somewhere with an old inoperable gun hanging on his bedpost.

And the letters came. Hundreds of them, some with checks attached, went to me and the newspaper; to Dannie and to Sherbondy; and to everyone our resourceful readers thought could assist: Judge Hupp, President Reagan, California Governor George Deukmejian, members of Congress, the prison, attorneys, and other news media (a *60 Minutes* producer said readers had sent them "no less than five" clippings of the story in the first two weeks after it ran). Pervading the letters was a single impulse: to help in any way possible.

One correspondent assured Sherbondy, "If the story as depicted in the *Chronicle* is accurate, somewhere, somebody important is going to get angry and help you." That somebody important turned out to be Connie Lurie, a prominent, wealthy, and indefatigable San Franciscan who has long been active in charitable affairs but was best known to the general public because at the time her husband owned the San Francisco Giants.

Lurie was very moved by Dannie's article and wrote to Sherbondy, telling him, "There must be some way to get this nightmare to end." She then set about seeking advice from her well-connected acquaintances. Lurie joined forces with another tireless supporter, software executive Ed LeClair, and state appeals court Justice William Newsom, who said, "I've been a judge for almost fifteen years and this is the worst single injustice I've encountered." Together, they founded the Sherbondy Action Association.

The group went to work on Sherbondy's behalf with custom-designed stationery, determination, and a list of recruits that included *Chronicle* readers who had written Sherbondy as well as Lurie's own circle of socialites, lawyers, businessmen, politicians, and even a former San Francisco police chief. Among the politicians were two top officials of the San Francisco Republican Party.

It was a group with clout, and they weren't afraid to wield it. Under some of the most prestigious letterheads in town, they wrote "Dear Ed" letters to Attorney General Edwin Meese; they asked President Reagan for executive clemency; they asked members of Congress for investigations.

They did get promises of investigations in Congress; Congressman Pete Stark said he "was told by the [House] Subcommittee [on Crime] that, on the face of it, the career criminal law was not intended to be used as it was on Kevin Sherbondy." But the rest of official Washington proved unhelpful and unsympathetic; assistants sent back letters justifying Sherbondy's sentence. Inexplicably, letters to President Reagan were "referred for response" to the new warden of Lompoc, R. H. Rison, as Dannie revealed in a follow-up story for the news section. In his replies, the warden misrepresented Sherbondy's record and then defended his conviction. It was an odd role for a prison warden, a custodial official whose judicial functions are normally limited to post-conviction behavior.

Encountering a bureaucratic wall as impenetrable as the prison's own walls, the Action Association changed its tactics, raising thousands of dollars and hiring highly respected San Francisco attorney Dennis Riordan to join in Sherbondy's appeal. (No one expected much from Sherbondy's previously assigned attorney, who had done nothing to reassure Sherbondy when he wrote him, "I have never found it worthwhile to have personal conference with appellants, since they invariably want to rehash the events of the trial concerning [evidence which does not appear] in the record and cannot be brought up on appeal. Therefore, if you have something which you think is appealable you had better write it out and send it to me, otherwise I don't think a personal conference would be in order.")

Meanwhile, the U.S. attorney in Los Angeles wrote the *Chronicle* to protest that Dannie's report on Sherbondy was "misleading and inaccurate." He argued that "the persistent violence and dissimulation in Mr. Sherbondy's criminal record demonstrate that he is precisely the type of dangerous, veteran criminal that the Armed Career Criminal statute was designed to remove from the community for a substantial period of time."

Dannie, who had based his story on a thick file of court papers and police documents as well as interviews and clippings, was incensed by the U.S. attorney's attack on his hard-won credibility. He apologized for any embarrassment the letter caused me and sent me a point-by-point rebuttal. Sherbondy, too, sent me a detailed response. To clarify the dispute from a neutral perspective, the *Chronicle* assigned an investigative reporter to do a follow-up story.

When the dust had settled, the only clear error in Dannie's story was that he had referred to a "public defender" when, in fact, the man was a court-appointed defense attorney. The U.S. attorney had charged Dannie with misrepresenting the date that the new career criminal law went into effect, but apparently his office had itself misread the law.

Most of the rest of the U.S. attorney's charges involved specifics of Sherbondy's criminal record. As with any crime, the tangled details and motivations of Sherbondy's misdeeds are subject to widely divergent interpretations. Dannie and Sherbondy clearly put a far more benign interpretation on Sherbondy's actions than did the U.S. attorney's office. In addition, the government had found it necessary to ignore judicial actions in reaching some of its conclusions on Sherbondy's crimes. And in the process of evaluating the government's claims, the *Chronicle* also uncovered new evidence in Sherbondy's favor.

Finally, the fact remained that a law designed for "armed, habitual drug traffickers and violent criminals" had been applied to a young man on the shakiest of technicalities. As the *Chronicle* news-section story stated, "At his trial, no evidence was introduced that Sherbondy had ever used the gun to commit a crime or had ever fired the weapon."

As Riordan told the *Los Angeles Times,* Sherbondy is "no saint, and there's no reason you should like him. But I doubt he's the type of criminal Congress intended when it established the statute. . . . I hate all the posturing involved. They're trying to justify this as the equivalent of landing Al Capone."

A year after Dannie's story on Kevin Sherbondy ran in "Sunday Punch," the Ninth Circuit court of appeals upheld Sherbondy's gun-possession conviction but threw out his sentence. The court, as it so often does, chose to rule on narrow grounds, glossing over the most troubling issues raised by Sherbondy's conviction and sentencing. It found that one of Sherbondy's prior convictions—urging a friend not to testify against another friend in a cocaine case—did not qualify as a "violent felony," and it therefore overturned his sentence.

Riordan told the *Chronicle* that the appeals court decision would not have occurred without Dannie's article. In fact, the reversal of Sherbondy's sentence is compelling testimony to the importance to our judicial system of the kind of inside-the-joint writing for which Dannie himself was subsequently punished.

Sherbondy was finally freed from prison on March 29, 1989, twelve and a half years short of his full fifteen-year sentence. Late that year, Connie Lurie accepted, on behalf of the Sherbondy Action Association, the Citizen Involvement Award of the California Attorneys for Criminal Justice.

■

Dannie followed the big splash of the Sherbondy article with a story that generated less controversy outside the prison but aroused some dissent within it.

## THE PRISONERS ON THE OTHER SIDE OF THE BARS

*LOMPOC, CALIF. (JAN. 31, 1988)*—He stopped me in the hallway one day, and I thought he wanted to shake me down. But he just wanted to talk, which is unusual for a prison guard. He told me he'd just transferred here from a Southern prison where he knew a friend of mine.

After I inquired about my buddy, our conversation lagged, so I asked him how it felt to be working in a prison.

"It's scary," he replied, "real scary."

I remarked that he didn't look all that scared.

"Out here in the hallway it's not so bad," he said, "but when I work one of those cellblocks with a hundred and twenty convicts— and ten or twelve of them yelling at me at the same time—I'm terrified. Even though I look outwardly calm, inside I'm trembling."

I managed to depart without telling him he'd get used to it. We both knew he wouldn't.

Some convicts hate all prison guards. They perceive them as the physical manifestation of their own misery and misfortune. The uniform becomes the man, and they no longer see an individual behind it.

Many guards react in kind. The hatred is returned with the full force of authority. These two factions become the real movers and shakers in the prison world. They aren't a majority in either camp, but the strength of their hatred makes its presence known to all.

Most guards in the federal system come to the job from the military. But even among men used to taking and giving orders, many find it hard to adjust. Amid all the hatred, insanity, and violence, large numbers of them quit before long. The ones with families who need the job find themselves trapped in a cage of their own.

The pay for a beginning prison guard in the federal prison system is pitifully small. The entry-level salary for guards at the lowest experience and educational level is $15,118 a year, according to a Bureau of Prisons spokesman. (By contrast, salaries for guards at California state prisons begin at $28,032, a figure higher than the top scale for rank-and-file federal guards.)

Many of the guards here work a lot of overtime shifts in an attempt to make ends meet. Often I see a guard who worked my unit on the day shift working another unit on the evening shift. Some of them seem to spend almost as much time in this prison as I do.

Things happen in prison that a person would never encounter on any other job. The day before Christmas Eve here at Lompoc, a convict was murdered in a cell sometime during the day. He wasn't discovered by the unit officer until the 4:00 P.M. standing count. He had been killed and stuffed into his bed.

That evening, as the officer worked overtime to make his report, he looked pale and haggard. A few days later, while working another unit, that officer was severely beaten and injured. He left here with a bandage across his nose. His holidays weren't filled with yuletide cheer. I sometimes wonder what years of that kind of stress will do to a man.

Each unit, or cellblock, has a little cubicle of an office with a phone. From there, the officer dispenses toilet paper, envelopes, mail, request forms, aspirin, and other supplies. He also must write reports, venture out on shakedowns and at mealtimes and hourly movements, running back to the office when the phone rings.

I found an officer there during a rare quiet moment. He was working his second shift of the day. I said something about him working a lot of overtime.

"Hey," he shouted, "I don't like it here any fucking better than you do. I don't have much choice!" He told me that he had three kids and that he'd read in the paper recently that it takes $100,000 to raise and educate a child through three years of college.

"At that rate," he mused, "I don't think I can get mine through high school."

I couldn't get him to discuss the madness. He went shifty-eyed on me as soon as I mentioned it. But it's here.

Every few weeks, newly hired officers tour the prison with a senior officer as a guide. We gawk at them while they gawk at us and our surroundings. I asked an officer one day why I never saw a large number of those recruits again after the tour.

"They quit right there, before they even work a day," he said. "They think you guys are locked in your cells all the time. When they see all these convicts out prowling the hallway and walking the yard, they say: 'No way!' And they quit right there."

One officer, who always seems to be smiling and has an upbeat view of life, summed up the prison guard experience this way:

"The way I see it, man, is that we got our own kind of society here. The director and his assistant—that would be the cream of the crop, you know, like Nob Hill. The regional directors and wardens is the upper middle class. The captain, now, he's plain middle class. All the lieutenants are lower middle class."

Then he smiled at me and said: "Guess who that leaves for the prisons and the low-rent districts?"

It was the easiest trivia question I've ever been asked.

---

Lompoc's guards loved Dannie's story. Several came up to the convict to express their appreciation. Others ran off copies and passed them around. One copy was posted on the bulletin board in the officers' lounge.

From the beginning, the guards and counselors in direct daily contact with prisoners had shown interest in Dannie's writing, asking for copies, encouraging him to continue and discussing individual stories with him. But, as Dannie's article makes clear, there is a class system among prison employees. "No lieutenant ever asked me for one of my stories or made favorable comments," he says.

Predictably, the other convicts' reactions to this story were ambivalent. Most liked it, but there was an undercurrent of grumbling. When word reached Dannie that there was some muttering on the yard about his sympathetic story, he sought out the complainants and told them he could not dismantle free-world stereotypes of convicts by pandering to the convicts' own stereotypes. He said he had to play it straight, and he said he expected them to bring future complaints directly to him.

Dannie encountered similar suspicion on one other occasion, when he wrote about prison drug use. A prisoner said that was tantamount to informing, to which Dannie replied, "Everyone knows there are drugs here, man."

In both cases, the objections were successfully defused, and Dannie regained the respect of the few complainants through open discussion. On neither occasion were any threats made against Dannie.

The potential hostility of fellow convicts was among the reasons later cited by federal prison officials as a hypothetical danger of prison journalism.

∎

The convicts one meets in Dannie's prose are individuals, not types. None was more distinctive than the subject of his next profile.

## THE GUY WAS ROBBING 'EM BLIND

*LOMPOC, CALIF. (MARCH 6, 1988)*—I first saw the blind man in the prison cafeteria. He was using a white-tipped cane to negotiate the chow line with the assistance of another convict.

It isn't often one encounters a totally blind man in a maximum-security federal prison. After lunch, I walked up beside him and, as a joke, asked: "How did you rob a bank without being able to see?" I had already guessed he was an embezzler or computer scammer.

"I took a cab over there," he replied, grinning and gazing about four inches north of my right eyebrow. I collected him the following day and guided him to the yard. I had to hear this.

His name is Robert Toye. He's a forty-two-year-old native of San Diego and suffers from a hereditary degenerative eye disease called retinitis pigmentosa. Since being declared legally blind in 1974, he has robbed more than seventeen banks.

"I robbed eight banks in New York in 1974 and 1975," he says. "I wasn't completely blind at that time. There was about a two-inch tunnel of vision in one eye, so I could distinguish objects pretty well."

Apprehended by the FBI in the spring of '75, Toye went to prison and was scheduled for parole in 1983. By then he was just about totally blind.

The tunnel now is the size of a BB, he says. "If I hold a book right up against my eye, I can read it one letter at a time. But I have to put my finger on it before I go to the next letter or I'll get the lines confused."

Retinitis pigmentosa, or RP, is a name given to a group of diseases affecting the retina. Located in the back of the eye, the retina acts like the film in a camera. It is a delicate layer of cells that picks up the image and transmits it to the brain—where "seeing" actually occurs. In RP, the retina begins to degenerate. One of the earliest symptoms is a difficulty seeing at night. Many people know the disease as "night blindness." There is no known cure or effective treatment.

Toye was released by mistake from the Metropolitan Correctional Center in New York in February 1983. He had been scheduled for transfer to a halfway house, but the move had been denied because the halfway house would not accept a blind man. A jailer, unaware of the denial, released him.

Toye walked two blocks down the street from the correctional center to a Citibank branch and robbed it of $9,500.

His modus operandi in all his bank robberies was to wear a large, heavy coat. He also carried a zipper bag and kept a pellet gun up his coat sleeve. After entering the bank, he would stand in line until he reached the teller, hand the bank employee the bag, and flash the gun in his sleeve. More often than not, the other bank customers weren't aware that a robbery was taking place.

The day of his mistaken release in New York, he'd been issued a heavy coat and a carry bag, but he lacked a gun. On his way to the bank he fished a Coke bottle from a trash can and put it up his sleeve. He robbed the bank by pretending the bottle was a gun.

Using some of the money from that first caper to fly to Las Vegas, he rented an apartment in a nice residential area. He shied away from all centers and services for the blind, knowing that the FBI would be watching for him there.

In Las Vegas he made three important purchases: a pellet gun, a nice leather carry bag, and a telescope that enabled him to read a phone book by holding one end of the scope against his eyeball and the other against the phone book. Once again, he was in business.

In the following three months, using his Las Vegas apartment as a base, he journeyed to New York nine times and robbed nine banks. Every one of them was a branch of Citibank.

He would go to the phone company in Las Vegas, affix his telescope to a New York phone book, and write down the address of a Citibank branch.

After flying from Las Vegas to New York, he would ride the shuttle bus into Manhattan and take a cab to the bank. Immediately after each robbery, he would reverse the process and return to Las Vegas.

"The reason I always robbed New York banks," he said, "was because there's always big crowds in New York. I need those crowds to get away from the scene. The reason I always rob Citibanks is they don't have bank guards in Citibank. Simple as that."

Not simple to me. I wanted details.

"After leaving the cab," he replied, "I would stand in front of the bank until a customer entered. By staring at the ground, I could just make out the back of someone's shoe. I would follow the shoe sole and line up behind them in line. When my turn came, I'd hand the teller the bag, flash the gun, and tell them I wanted all the money.

"After retrieving the bag, I'd walk to the wall of the bank, feel my way to the door, and leave. Out on the sidewalk, I'd take my fold-up cane out of my pocket and blend with the crowd. After walking half a block or so, I'd stand on the curb and wave my arms for a cab."

I told him he had more faith in New York cabs than I have, but he said he never had a problem. He was always careful to check the weather forecast on the day he robbed a bank, because in foul weather, cabs are hard to come by in New York.

Toye did have some harrowing experiences in a few of the banks he robbed. There was, for example, the incident in May 1983 when he was in the process of robbing a teller in an uptown Manhattan Citibank branch.

"Everything was going smooth," he said. "I'd just showed the teller the gun, and she was filling the bag when this lady ran up and elbowed me out of the way. She threw a bill on the counter and told the teller she wanted change for the phone right now. I elbowed her back and told her to wait her turn. She became so indignant and pushy I finally yelled, 'Dammit, lady, I'm robbing this bank!' Then she began elbowing me again, trying to get her bill back so I wouldn't take it with the bank's money. In the middle of our shoving match, the teller pushed the bag in my chest and said, 'Get out of here!' "

Another time, he'd just made his exit and was tapping along in the crowd with his cane when the police arrived. One of them shoved him against the wall, and he thought he was being arrested. But they were just beating a path to the bank.

By far the most embarrassing episode was the time he robbed a bank and the teller put a red dye bomb in his bag. The bomb was designed to explode at the door of the bank. He heard it explode as he left and quickly zipped his bag shut, but dye bombs also emit a terribly foul odor. When he hailed a cab, the driver began complaining.

"Jaysus, mister! What's that smell? Have you got a dead jackrabbit in that fucking bag?"

Toye pacified him with a large tip. He says he washed the money in a Las Vegas laundromat and salvaged most of it.

Toye was arrested on May 24, 1983, when he deviated from his normal methods. Early that day, when he retrieved his luggage at the New York airport, he found the lock on his suitcase was broken and the case itself badly damaged.

So, after robbing a Citibank branch at 46th Street and Third Avenue, he took a cab to Eighth Avenue—to buy new luggage—instead of returning immediately to the airport. A cab driver on Eighth Avenue recognized him from a wanted poster and called the robbery task force.

The first he knew of it, he was spread-eagled on the street with a dozen guns pointed at him.

Toye doesn't use drugs or gamble, and he won't say what became of the money from his stickups. He learned to read braille in a prison class in Talladega, Alabama, but events on the night of June 14, 1987, made it impossible for Toye to serve out his sentence at that institution.

The Talladega prison doesn't have gun towers, but it does have double hurricane fences with rolled razor wire on top and in between. The prison perimeter is patrolled by two white vans containing guards armed with shotguns and pistols.

On the night in question, Toye hid in the yard with the help of other convicts. At eight o'clock, when the yard was clear, he climbed the first fence, using his white cane to hold down the razor wire. He jumped down, made his way over the second fence, and headed for the pine trees 150 yards from the prison. The motorized guards spotted him, and in his haste, Toye ran smack into the first tree he reached. Stunned and demoralized, he surrendered. He was transferred here to Lompoc for that escape attempt.

Lompoc penitentiary wasn't designed to accommodate a blind man, so Toye spends most of his time listening to television. He's been in prison this stretch since 1983 and is looking forward to a parole in July 1995. He expects that even his BB-size tunnel of vision will be gone by then.

"When I say the future looks dim," he laughs, "I mean it literally."

---

Among the responses to that profile was a telegram to Toye, phoned in to the warden's office: "I recently came upon Dannie Martin's article on you . . . and am very interested in talking with you about the possibility of doing a similar piece for *People* magazine. . . ."

A "similar piece" did finally run in *People*—without giving credit, though, to the man who first brought Robert Toye to the attention of the reading public and that magazine's local bureau.

Dannie's myth-deflating reassessment of prison operations took him next to the very heart of the prison power structure.

# INSIDE REPORT FROM A PRISON OF PAPER

*LOMPOC, CALIF. (MAY 29, 1988)*—Out in the free world, people have only two notions of how prisons are run. Some believe prisons are staffed by sadistic guards, and others believe social-worker types are in control. Both kinds can be found working in prisons, but neither has any say at all about how a prison is operated.

Bureaucrats run prisons. Sadists and social workers come and go, but the paper-shuffling bureaucrats endure forever. They rule a world of numbers and written regulations in which convicts obey the law of "the pass."

We go nowhere without a pass, and nothing gets done that isn't initiated by paperwork and concluded with paperwork.

When you approach a prison official with a problem, his standard reply is: "Send me a cop-out, and I'll get back to you."

A cop-out is a form obtained from the unit office. It's entitled "Inmate Request to Staff Member." Across the top, the convict fills in the name and title of the recipient and the date. Under that line is a space labeled "SUBJECT: State completely but briefly the problem on which you desire assistance. (Give details.)"

After you've completed this space, there's another category: "ACTION REQUESTED: (State exactly how you believe your request may be handled; that is, exactly what you think should be done, and how.)" The convict then signs his name, number, work assignment, and housing unit. Small print at the bottom of the form warns that failure to "specifically state your problem may result in no action being taken."

If you fail to get a reply and complain to an official, his response will normally be: "Send me a cop-out about it, and I'll get back to you."

Illiterate convicts find this process daunting at best and nerve-racking at worst.

In this world of locked doors and gates, it's the pass that really counts. Walking down an empty hallway between sanctioned movement periods, a convict will be stopped by guards who want to know why he is out there. But if he's carrying a pass in his hand, he won't be bothered at all.

Bad things happen to those of us who fall between the cracks of the paper trail, but human nature and regulations being what they are, it happens often. When it does, it's like being trapped in an infuriating maze of paper.

Recently I visited the dentist here at Lompoc for a partial root canal on an abscessed tooth. When he finished, he told me to pick up some penicillin at the pharmacy window in the hallway at lunchtime. But when I got there, the pharmacist informed me that the dentist had neglected to send him my chart.

I asked the pharmacist to call the dentist, but he declined. When he said no, I felt the paper crack yawning beneath my feet.

The pharmacist told me to have my unit officer call the dentist, but the unit officer refused to call and told me to go see the dentist at the 2:30 movement period. I was stopped by a guard at the hospital door. He demanded a pass. After some argument, he agreed to call my unit officer and instruct him to issue a pass.

After a phone call and more argument, I was back at the unit, where the unit officer abruptly wrote me a pass, which I left with the guard at the hospital door.

When I returned from seeing the dentist, the guard couldn't find a pass with my name on it. After a long search, we realized that the unit officer had written "Miller" on my pass instead of "Martin." The number wasn't mine, either.

One day late, I got my penicillin.

The same day I was chasing after my penicillin, a friend of mine, Joe, also suffered a "pass deficiency." His prison job boss went home early and told him to return to his cellblock. When he got there, the unit officer wouldn't let him back in during working hours without a pass. As Joe walked back down the hallway, he was stopped and told to leave the corridor and get a pass. When he attempted to enter the lieutenant's office to explain, he couldn't get in without a pass.

"I became so frustrated that I almost knocked on the door of Isolation and told them to let me in there," he said.

The isolation unit is one of the few places you can get into without a pass, especially if you are in a hurry. Luckily, a lieutenant happened out into the hallway and escorted him back to the cellblock.

In the land of serious paper shufflers, things like interview forms and passes are at the bottom of the paper chain. They feed on the lowest forms of life; convicts are the plankton and complex algae of this ecosystem.

In 1986 a man arrived here and set up shop in an empty office off the main corridor. A sign was placed above his door that read "Research Coordinator."

Equipped with the latest in computer technology and a printer, he sat behind a desk for nine months, working over voluminous files and printouts. As convicts walked by and eyed him suspiciously through the office window, he glared back and went on about his work. No one had any idea what or whom he was researching.

When the silent stranger finally packed up his gear and broke camp, he left behind the issue of his nine-month labor.

It was a ten-page booklet of charts and graphs concerning our weekly unit inspection scores from the period of January 1, 1986, to September 30, 1986. Its title was: "Year-to-date unit sanitation scores. Dan McCarthy, Research Analyst USP Lompoc."

There are ten 120-man cellblocks here at Lompoc, plus the one isolation unit. We have weekly safety and sanitation inspections at each cellblock. The highest-scoring units are placed at the head of the eating rotation the following week. The scoring runs from 80 to 100 points, and the inspectors are usually one administrative official, one representative of the safety office, and one staff member. This weekly inspection has been a practice at this prison for many years, but I doubt it had ever been quantified as thoroughly as it was by Dan McCarthy, Research Analyst.

McCarthy's booklet contains a page of background information on his study. To refrain from stretching my own paperwork intolerably, I quote only the final paragraph, which says: "As in any analysis based on a scoring scheme, the scoring system itself is of critical importance. The results of an analysis can only reflect the accuracy of the scoring instruments and the consistency of the scoring personnel. The aim of this presentation is to present the produced scores without regard to the scoring system."

In all candor, I am not a smart enough convict to know exactly what that statement means. But as a fledgling writer, I have learned to recognize a self-destructing paragraph when I see one.

One of our more intellectual convicts did form a suitable analogy concerning this body of work. After going through the book, he turned it upside down and went through it again. He then turned it sideways and thumbed it one more time, then laid it back down and stared off into space for a moment before pronouncing: "If the government was a dead log, man, this guy would be a toadstool peeking out from under it."

No one has any idea how many of these booklets were printed. The big question is: Who could possibly care? Actually, as convicts we are in pretty good hands. Bureaucrats neither hate us nor love us. They practice the ancient art of creative avoidance, hoping that if they shuffle us around on paper long enough, either our problems or we will simply go away. Whichever goes first.

They are firm believers in the old adage that time heals everything, and who can argue that premise? But here at the bottom of the heap, two things never change.

If your paperwork isn't in order, you can't even get into a prison, and once in, you will never get out without a pass in your hand . . . and you'd better make sure that the one you try to leave with has your correct name and number on it.

The idea for that story was Dannie's—he'd been living it for years—but he was indebted to another convict for the pamphlet with the "self-destructing paragraph." Unauthorized copies of documents such as that one float around the cellblocks at all prisons, but at Lompoc most of them seemed to end up in Dannie's hands. Not only did he give *Chronicle* readers access to the prison world, he was also a conduit to the outside world for the prisoners.

And that role made him dangerous to the prison—how dangerous we could not have guessed before publication of his next essay.

# II

## THE GULAG MENTALITY
## JUNE – JULY 1988

Peter: I'm in Isolation. They won't give me *anything*. Not even a pencil or paper. I borrowed this stub from the man next door. . . .

I am sending this letter by way of [attorney] Mike [Schwab] as I *know* if it was addressed to you it would never arrive there. . . .

The problem I'll have here is that I'm allowed to write letters but they won't give me stamps, envelopes, paper, etc. I believe I can get some somehow, but it's shaky. I think I'm about to be put on the "merry-go-round." The feds do this when they are mad at a convict. . . .

Okay, so I'll write an article about all this and send it to Mike to send you. I'm saving the good stuff for that.

I hope you won't feel bad about all this. I'm okay really. I doubt their sanctions will hold up. We will see. . . .

Can you send your home phone number? I don't have my address book. Maybe they will have to allow me a call sometime. Also if a subscription to the paper was sent here right from there they'd have to give it to me. So if a subscription can be worked out, I'll have Mike send the money.

I'm worried now that they will just trash all my books in

my cell. I have some beautiful books, including your Schopenhauer, works of Shakespeare, etc. *That* would really fuckin
hurt.

—*Letter from "the hole," Lompoc*

■

The chain of events that led to that dramatic letter began in the visiting room at Lompoc three months earlier, on a Saturday afternoon in
March 1988.

It was my third trip to the penitentiary. I was still not comfortable
there—I never could be—but I *was* comfortable with Dannie and the
other prisoners I chatted with that day. By then, Dannie's work was
widely admired not only among the other convicts but among their
visitors. Their support was palpable. Various prisoners and guests
stopped by our small table in the visiting room to say hello and to pass
along story ideas. Others smiled our way from afar. They all seemed
to know who I was: "The Editor."

For months before our visit, Dannie had been writing me ominously
about the rising level of tension he sensed within the prison. "Convicts
are like a bunch of caged-up dogs in a way," he had written in one
letter, "and when they get irritated, they begin to bite each other." He
blamed a clampdown by the prison administration, including petty
harassment of visiting teachers and the yard restrictions that he had
begun writing about for publication months earlier. In another letter,
he told me, "This joint is getting so repressive now and violent that I
don't know where it will end up. There's a lot of fistfights breaking out
everywhere. . . . I'm glad I've only got three years or so left to do."

During that March 1988 visit, Dannie mentioned other apparently
minor policies instituted by Warden R. H. Rison (who had taken over
the previous summer) and how they added to the air of repression.
They were the sort of accumulating irritants, he said, that sometimes
lead to major disturbances.

The tension Dannie was feeling resembled inmates' experiences at
Rison's previous post, as warden of the Federal Correctional Institution
at Terminal Island in Long Beach, California. I was later to see reports
from that era in the *Long Beach Press-Telegram*. "There is the perception
among a number of inmates that Rison has made changes simply to
irritate them," a reporter had written in 1984, and he quoted an inmate
as saying, "It's an accumulation of straws. I'm wondering how many
more straws until it breaks the camel's back."

When a riot occurs in a prison, the convicts' first demand is generally to meet with the press or a public figure to pass along their grievances. Why, Dannie asked me during our visit, did you have to wait until *after* a riot occurred? Why couldn't you try to cool the tensions by talking about those grievances *before* they reached the boiling point?

I told him I saw no reason why you couldn't, and the article that resulted from that discussion ran three months later in the *Chronicle*. Our joint venture was never the same again.

## THE GULAG MENTALITY

*Lompoc, Calif. (June 19, 1988)*—As the saying goes, it's the little things that make a house a home. To those of us who face the mind-killing boredom of long prison sentences, small changes take on large significance in this, our home-away-from-home.

Among the small things that matter most to us here are our routines and perks and possessions. They help to personalize this cold world.

And it is these important little things that are most in jeopardy when we convicts get a new "landlord."

A change of wardens often brings trauma for a prison population. New wardens have different ways of doing things.

A few years ago—in what convicts now call the good old days—there were said to be two kinds of warden: those who lean toward punishment and those who believe in rehabilitation.

These days, it seems there is only one kind. But the different ways they choose to do their punishing make a great difference to us, the punished.

The warden here at Lompoc from 1982 until 1987 was Robert Christensen. We who lived here during his tenure called him "Defoliating Bob."

He earned that nickname upon his arrival by chainsawing a row of stately and beautiful old eucalyptus trees in our "backyard," trees that for fifty years or more had served as a windbreak about 150 yards from the prison perimeter. Our cellblock view apartments had lost another amenity.

Not long after cutting down the trees, the warden poisoned all the squirrels that convicts enjoyed feeding near the prison fences, then mounted a genocidal war against the cats and raccoons that had roamed the prison grounds.

He also managed to curtail most of the small liberties enjoyed by the convict population. Before his arrival, we had been permitted to wear our own clothes. Now we were to wear strictly tucked-in and buttoned-up government issue. And our recreational opportunities and food went from bad to worse.

He did away with little niceties like Christmas packages from home and unrestricted telephone access. As he made these changes, he was busy installing electronic grille gates in the hallway so that the prison could be sectioned off in case of emergency. Sheet-metal plates went up over windows with an outside view.

To a group of captive spectators, it looked as if he was battening down the hatches and preparing for a storm. But we knew that wardens don't last forever, and we hoped things would calm down when he left.

Defoliating Bob retired last year. One of the first official acts of our new warden, R. H. Rison, was to close down our recreation yard until noon every weekday. Those of us who work on night jobs and run and exercise in the mornings now sit in gloomy cellblocks watching the sun shine through the window bars.

Closing the yard is a hard policy to understand. "He's tryin' to start a riot," one agitated convict exclaimed at the dinner table, waving his plastic spoon at those near him. "We might just as well give him one and get it over with."

Someone at the table inquired as to why a warden would want to start a riot in his own prison.

"If a riot jumps off," the man replied, "all the guards get overtime, and the warden gets more money to spend on security. Plus the fact that a locked-down joint is easier to run. Look at Marion"—the federal prison in Illinois. "It's been locked down seven years now. This yard's been open forty years. Why else would he close it now?"

No one has been able to formulate a credible answer, but if we are skeptical of the new warden's motives, we are also leery of riot rumors. They're too often the figment of a captive imagination.

No sooner did the warden close the yard than we lost our chairs, and that hurt.

For as long as most of us can remember, we've had our own

chairs in the TV rooms as well as in our cells. There's little enough in here for a man to call his own, and over the years these chairs have been modified and customized to an amazing degree—legs bent to suit the occupant, armrests glued on, pads knitted for comfort. And the final personal touch is always the printing of a name on the back.

Gazing down a row of chairs in a TV room, you would see on the back of each the prison nickname of its owner: 415 (the San Francisco area code), Shorty Blue, Big Red, Monster Mack, Mukilteo Slim. Names that run from somber identification of the occupants to bizarre sobriquets. But whatever the name on the back or the condition of the chair, those chairs were ours.

A couple months ago, the guards came one day with no warning and confiscated all our chairs. Each of us was issued a gray-metal folding chair, along with a memorandum from the new warden stating that anyone writing on or otherwise defacing these chairs would be subject to disciplinary action.

It was startling to see the rage some convicts felt when they returned from work in a prison factory to find their chairs gone and replaced by a stark folding metal chair.

"I've been here nine years," one older convict said. "Always tried to get along and do my own time, but if someone wants to burn this place down, I'll be glad to help. I wonder how he would feel if I went in his house and took his recliner?"

That sentiment was echoed by many here. The sanctity of our home was being violated. And adding up other clues, there was a widespread belief here that the prison authorities had set out to demolish the last vestiges of privacy in the prison.

A woman psychiatrist was hired here recently to handle the entire prison caseload. No one resented the fact that she was a woman or even the fact that she has a difficult time communicating in English. But what all her patients do resent—and she has many of them—is the fact that the warden won't allow her and a male patient to be alone in a closed room together.

When she conducts a session with a patient, the door to her office must be left open so that a guard or staff member nearby can hear every word. It doesn't help that her desk is in one corner of the room whereas the patient's chair is against the opposite wall. Sometimes two or three people can hear the conversation out in the hallway.

One of her more needy patients had this to say: "Man, I don't even go and see her anymore. One session like that is enough. I can feel someone breathing on my neck while I talk to her, and I get the feeling if I say the wrong thing he's gonna step in and say: 'Hold it right there. Let's just put the SOB in Isolation and forget all this crap!' "

It may be none of our business as convicts how the warden runs his prison. But we are seeing an awful lot of violence here lately— and that can become our business very fast.

There have been two murders and more than six serious assaults here at Lompoc since Christmas. The fistfights are becoming too numerous to count.

We can understand the forfeiture of our privacy and small liberties in the name of security or retribution. But we become uneasy when the more driven and frantic psychopaths among us can't get effective treatment.

Somewhere between the closing of our yard and the inexorable tightening-down on small privileges, the prison is evolving from a boring but mellow place to a caldron of fear, hatred, and violence.

We wait and watch for the next move. Many of us older convicts feel that if the lid stays on until our next "landlord" arrives, it will be a small miracle.

. . . And that's the news from my house.

---

Three days after "Gulag" appeared, on the afternoon of Wednesday, June 22, I received a rushed call from convict Kevin Sherbondy, the young man whose unjust sentence Dannie had exposed the previous fall. "Dannie's been taken to the hole for inciting a riot," he told me in a clipped and breathless voice. "It's because of his article Sunday." He knew no further details.

With that phone call, the prison story Dannie Martin was telling merged with the story he was living. And with Dannie in "the hole"— also called "solitary" or "isolation" by the prisoners but known to prison officials as "administrative detention" or the "special housing unit"— my role changed, too. I became a participant in this new story as well as the editor of the convict's commentaries.

Dannie was a time-hardened con, and he knew well the risk he was taking in writing critically about his warden. Before publication of "Gulag," he mentioned the danger in phone conversations with me and other friends. But he also felt a duty to Lompoc's prisoners to "get their concerns out to the public." A number of convicts had been asking him if he would do a story on "the way they are cracking down on us." Two or three, he said, had "really bugged me to do something."

The author later testified in court that if a riot was truly imminent at the prison, "I figured if the public knew about it they might try to do something to keep that from happening. . . . And if they do let it happen, then at least I'd feel better about it, knowing they knew about it." But a riot was the last thing he wanted, because if there's violence in a prison, "that's a threat to me personally."

In editing the manuscript for "The Gulag Mentality" together, Dannie and I had worked to assure that no one could interpret his piece as advocacy of rioting. We buttressed the "featurish" nature of his story by emphasizing the "prison-as-home" theme. We played down the talk of a potential riot, too. Dannie's original manuscript included the remark "we are also leery of riot rumors," but in the editing process he underlined the point by adding, "They're too often the figment of a captive imagination."

The only advocate of rioting mentioned in the article was an obviously uncredible character at the dinner table who was described as "one agitated convict . . . waving his plastic spoon at those near him." Clearly, this man was not the Lenin of Lompoc. (Warden Rison, however, later put a sinister interpretation on that dinner-table scene. "I considered the message, based on my correctional experience, to transmit the possibility of being considered as a weapon, did not consider it a spoon," he said in a deposition. ". . . You don't wave utensils in the middle of the dining room. That is out-of-the-ordinary behavior.")

When a free-lance artist hired by the *Chronicle* to illustrate the article came up with a drawing of figures with matchstick heads, I vetoed it because it gave too much weight to the threat of a riot. The substitute drawing showed a convict holding aloft a personalized chair, with rows of folding metal chairs in the background. Dannie, of course, had no say in the selection of illustration or any other aspects of headline or graphic display—those were entirely *Chronicle* editorial decisions. Yet later testimony by prison officials cited that drawing and "the way some . . . things were exhibited" in the article as among the concerns that led to the convict's special confinement.

Although Dannie was pleased to give prisoner grievances a public airing, he did not want to get typecast as a convict "sniveler." Indeed, even before "Gulag" was published, he had another submission on my desk—written in a lighter tone and accompanied by the comment "I felt like having some fun. Tired of doing that old bureaucrat and evil-warden stuff."

After publication of the "Gulag" article, the reaction from other inhabitants of "Dannie's house" was positive. Fifteen or twenty convicts came up to him to praise his essay and thank him. Not a single prisoner expressed anger or criticism.

In fact, "The Gulag Mentality" caused no perceptible stir among the convicts. One prisoner later testified in court that the essay "settled things down a little bit. . . . After it was written, it was like, 'Maybe this will help. Let's sit back and wait.' "

Another convict wrote the *Chronicle:* "It [the article] was nothing to get excited about. We got a few chuckles, muttered 'right on' a couple of times."

"It was pretty well forgotten about by the next day or the day after that," a third convict later testified.

But someone evidently had not forgotten it. Kevin Sherbondy made that alarmingly clear in his brief phone call three days after publication of "The Gulag Mentality."

As the prison's apparent retaliation developed into a court case and a First Amendment "cause," I was dropped into the same world of Silly Putty rules that Dannie had inhabited for years. I came to see it as a place where men who got there because they had trouble with rules are bound in by so many regulations that even their keepers don't know them all. (Several of the prison officials responsible for the ultimate charge against Dannie testified that they were not at first aware of the existence of the rule he was said to have violated.) It is also a world where the guarantees of the Constitution sometimes seem no more than a distant rumble and where even federal judges fear to tread.

And, incredibly, I learned that the free-world rights of outsiders—newspapers, for example—are limited by the same set of undefined, prison-issue regulations that govern convicts.

Trying to find justice in that distorted environment has been one of the most exasperating experiences of my life, but such a broad assessment was the last thing on my mind when I got Sherbondy's phone call. I was stunned and outraged. I felt personally offended because Dannie was apparently being punished for a newspaper article that I had published.

I needed first to get the facts. So while Dannie sat incommunicado in solitary, scrounging for a pencil stub with which to record his experiences, I notified the *Chronicle's* city desk and asked that a reporter investigate the action taken against him.

The reporter assigned to the story learned that Dannie had indeed been sent to "the hole," although prison officials called it "protective custody." Prison spokesman Paul Hofer said the action was taken "for his own safety" when prison authorities received word that Dannie's life might be in danger from fellow inmates upset with the article. The special detention, the prison's spokesman said, could last for up to two weeks while authorities investigated.

Hofer told the *Chronicle* that the several convicts who had indicated they were angry enough at Dannie to want to hurt him were upset for two reasons: because Dannie supposedly represented himself as their spokesman and because his article mentioned the possibility of riots. By the time prison officials were compelled to defend their actions in court a year and a half later, all that remained of those several angry convicts bent on personal injury was one prisoner who, it was said, had passed Associate Warden Thomas Curd in a crowded hallway and "in passing said that . . . not all of us agree with that article that's in the paper, something to that effect, and just kept on walking."

Another conjecture popular among top prison officials—and a reason later cited for sending Dannie to the hole for his own safety—was that the unnamed spoon-waving prisoner who had suggested a riot in a chat with his dinner-table buddies would attack the writer to prevent him from revealing the spoon-waver's identity to prison investigators.

Many prison officials choked on just one word in Dannie's article: "riot." The prison's chief of security, Captain William Brew, says that he "started to [read Dannie's article], but I just couldn't hardly believe what I saw. The word that jumped out at me was 'riot.' "

Warden Rison also revealed that a key factor in his conclusion that something dangerous was afoot in the institution was his slowly dawning recognition over the two days after the article was published that he "had been avoided" by the inmates, especially during his daily lunchtime availability on the chow line. He said that when he first saw Dannie's article two days after it was published, he "started to put pieces together."

When prison officials spoke with the *Chronicle* and other media in those first few days, they emphasized the issue of Dannie's safety, but they simultaneously expressed their anger at the content of his article, with Warden Rison calling it "half-truthful in places and nonfactual in others." He rebuked the *Chronicle* for publishing the piece and added that he was preparing a letter to the editor denouncing the paper's action.

███

The *Chronicle*'s reporter was not able to contact Dannie or any other prisoners, but he did print my reaction, which included the charge that if Dannie was being punished because of the content of his *Chronicle* article, then it was "a serious violation of the First Amendment. As to alleged threats by other convicts, I can only be dubious. If he is being held in solitary only for his own protection, then there is no reason why he cannot be allowed to communicate with this newspaper and the public about the veracity of his article and the circumstances of his solitary confinement."

The First Amendment is a blunt, powerful instrument. It sits in the bottom of every journalist's toolbox, but in twenty-four years as an editor, I had never before had occasion to reach for it. It is no easy matter to know when to make use of that preeminent principle. No dispute comes prelabeled "First Amendment." Except in rare, contrived "test cases," we generally find such fundamental constitutional issues hidden in a welter of mundane circumstances. I was uncomfortable even citing such a lofty principle in answer to a reporter's question—it's a bit like chatting with a colleague in iambic pentameter.

The next day before work, while out on my morning run, I chanced across some neighbors, Jeff Leon and his wife, Debbie—both lawyers. I stopped for some streetcorner advice on the First Amendment, which I had so casually brandished the day before. Our conversation was brief, but later, after he had read the article on Dannie in the morning paper, Jeff Leon phoned to tell me, "I think you have a hell of a case there, and if you're interested, I bet my firm would let me represent Dannie pro bono."

I told Leon that I hoped the dispute could be resolved informally after the issues were aired in the press, but we agreed that he would make inquiries at his firm in case he was needed in a hurry. Our informal conversations that morning were the beginning of what was to become a major legal challenge to the regulations that silence many federal convicts.

■

When Dannie was finally able to communicate with the outside world, he revealed that the detention order he had been handed on his second day in the hole informed him that "Inmate Martin is under investigation for possible attempts at encouraging a group demonstration"—a charge that had not been announced to inquiring reporters. The detention order added as an afterthought that "he is also under investigation that there may be a threat to his safety if left in open population."

The "possible" group demonstration charge remained baffling, because there never was such a demonstration and the prison spokesman told the *Chronicle*'s reporter on June 22 that "there is no indication that there is any riot in the offing" at Lompoc.

Dannie later told me that among prisoners, to be locked in protective custody is "a real shame on your name"—a signal that the convict is a snitch, a child molester, a homosexual, or someone who won't pay his debts. Those are the people who generally need protecting in a prison. Dannie said that prison officials know this and sometimes apply the "protective custody" label to besmirch a convict's reputation among his buddies.

Usually, before placing a convict in protective custody, prison officials offer him the opportunity to sign a waiver denying he is in any danger on the mainline. Dannie asked to sign such a waiver when he was brought to Isolation, but his appeal was ignored until his ultimate release from special confinement.

Dannie was later quoted in the *Los Angeles Times* as saying, "In a place like this there are a lot of things that can threaten your safety more than writing a newspaper article."

The Bureau of Prisons' ploy of putting an outspoken convict in the hole "for his own safety" did not originate or end with Dannie. In one now-celebrated case just four months later—four days before the 1988 presidential election—the BOP placed Brett Kimberlin in solitary confinement and out of reach of the media hours after it was revealed that he was prepared to announce he had repeatedly sold marijuana to vice presidential candidate Dan Quayle years earlier. That action came from the top—BOP Director J. Michael Quinlan—and followed complaints from high-level officials of the Bush-Quayle campaign. The reason given for putting Kimberlin in solitary was that his life was in danger. No such threat was ever verified, and the prison later determined that he was not in any danger.

It all sounded so familiar.

■

The *Chronicle* published its report on Dannie's plight on Thursday, June 23. Other news media immediately picked up on the story, calling me for comment.

As a journalist I felt awkward about being interviewee rather than interviewer, and I was not accustomed to speaking for the newspaper. Soon after the first of a flurry of interview requests, I informed a *Chronicle* executive who was passing my desk that I was being asked to comment on the paper's behalf. "Say good things," he advised me, and continued on his way.

For the next four years, with no further briefing, I was by default the paper's "Dannie Martin spokesman." Calls came from local newsletters and national wire services, from trade journals such as *Editor and Publisher* and national newspapers such as the *Christian Science Monitor, Washington Post,* and *Boston Globe.* The interest ranged as far afield as the *London Financial Times* and *Asahi Shimbun.* And that was just the print media.

In short, I no longer had the luxury of hiding behind a blue pencil.

The reporters who phoned me for comment also called the prison for details on the popular writer's status. In those interviews, Warden Rison repeatedly blamed the controversy on the *Chronicle* for not including his comments in the "Gulag" article.

"As long as I'm not going to be given a chance by the *Chronicle* to respond and the newspaper publishes whatever [Dannie] writes unedited, as fact, I don't plan on leaving this fellow in this institution," Rison was quoted in an *Associated Press* dispatch. ("I don't recall saying that," the warden later testified at our trial.)

The same day, the *Lompoc Record* quoted Rison as saying, "I can't have someone producing editorial copy that I have no control over." ("I don't recall a statement to that effect," the warden later testified in a deposition.)

Rison also angrily denounced Dannie to the media, telling radio station KUHL in nearby Santa Maria, for example, "This prison isn't big enough for him and me." And, in fact, we later learned that on the same day, in what he called a routine memo, the warden recommended to his boss, BOP Regional Director Jerry Williford, that, based partly on the overcrowded conditions at Lompoc, "we feel a transfer to the State of Washington is appropriate. Mr. Martin has been a model inmate the last two years. . . ."

On Thursday afternoon, spokesman Hofer said that the prison's investigation had "turned up little evidence that there is any significant threat" to Dannie. Although he said Dannie's article "was way out of line," he added that "the institutional tenor right now is very calm. There's very little indication of any major conflict."

Or, as the warden told the *Los Angeles Times,* "The inmates could care less about Dannie Martin." (The warden later could not recall either conversing with the *Times* or making that statement.)

So, in midafternoon on Thursday, June 23—half a day after the *Chronicle*'s story on the detention hit the streets—Dannie was released back to the general prison population. One of his first actions was to mail me his account of his trip to solitary.

Here's the published version of Dannie's own story of his two days in the hole, written before he knew of his impending release back to the mainline. When he wrote it, he told me, "I thought I was gone."

## A REPORT FROM 'SOLITARY'

*LOMPOC, CALIF. (JULY 3, 1988)*—I have written a number of pieces for "Sunday Punch" concerning prisons, their administrators and inhabitants. It's time, I suppose, to write one about isolation status in prisons. I won't need extensive notes for this one as I woke up in Isolation this morning.

The Sunday, June 19, issue of "Sunday Punch" carried a story of mine entitled "The Gulag Mentality." It referred to our new warden, R. H. Rison, and some changes he and the previous warden had made here at Lompoc.

On Tuesday, June 21, I was arrested as I went about my job emptying ashtrays in the main corridor. It was a tough job that took about fifteen minutes each evening, but someone had to do it—and I'll certainly miss it.

Two guards walked over, looked balefully at me for a moment, and said: "Let's go, man." I went, and as I walked between them down the hall, I thought we were going to the lieutenant's office, which is a pit stop for the average miscreant. But when we passed his office, I realized that I'm not average. I was on my way to the hole. Do not pass go.

I asked each guard in turn, "What seems to be the difficulty here, officer?" Each kept looking straight ahead. No response. Their visages were grim, their jaws determined.

The guard in charge peered through a little window in "I Unit," opened the door, and motioned me in. "I" cellblock is Isolation, and as one enters, there is a little cubbyhole where you are relieved of all possessions. An "I Unit" guard waited on the far side of a barred door to receive me. He handed my escorts a rolled towel containing one pair of green boxer shorts, a green T-shirt, and a green pair of woolen socks.

I didn't have to be told to strip, and I was soon naked. The guard in charge told me to turn around, bend over, and spread my cheeks. I always have to be told to do that.

I don't know what they hoped to discover. Perhaps they thought I had a newspaper article stashed away there.

When I had put on my boxer shorts and T-shirt, the "I Unit" guard handed a pair of handcuffs through the bars, and my escorts handcuffed me behind my back. In "I Unit," prisoners are handcuffed every time they move anywhere.

Once I was cuffed, they opened the barred door and motioned me up a flight of stairs. I felt some relief that I wasn't going to the basement. Basement cells have big iron doors instead of bars, and it's dark and you can't talk to your neighbor. I've been there a few times and don't really enjoy it.

After passing two more locked gates, the "I Unit" guard escorted me down the second tier to cell A-13. These doors are barred, with a slot for a food tray, and they open electronically. We waited as the guard at the front opened the door.

As I walked past the first twelve cells, I noticed that they all contained double bunks, and there were two men to a cell.

My door slid open. I entered, and the door slid shut. A familiar old clanking sound of finality. I backed up to the bars while the guard removed my handcuffs and handed me two sheets and a pillowcase. I noticed that the double bunk contained only two mattresses and no blankets. I told the guard I had just got over a bad flu and I needed a blanket.

"I'm out of blankets," he replied and walked off. By this time, I began to realize that I wouldn't get much from the staff. They all acted as if they were afraid to even talk to me.

It gets extremely cold in here at night. I spent the night under my two sheets feeling like a supermarket chicken in a meat-display counter. But I did have some company. I got a cellmate about an hour after I arrived. The first thing he told the guard was: "Hey, I need a blanket."

The guard looked at him, then over at me, and replied, "I'm out of blankets," and walked off. I told my new cellmate that he was just unfortunate to get me as a cellmate because the guard couldn't very well give him a blanket after telling me there weren't any.

I asked him what he was locked up for. Prison protocol demands that you don't ask a man about his original crime, but it is proper to ask what he's in Isolation for. It's hard to sleep in a cell with a man you know nothing about, as he could be a homicidal maniac.

He told me he was called to the lieutenant's office and told he was observed near the cell of a man who had been cut up badly with a razor blade in "K Unit." He was then escorted over here. He's twenty-one years old and a state prisoner from Alaska. He said he came to prison when he was fifteen years old and is serving ninety-nine years for murder. Other than that, he seems to be a pleasant, mannerly young man. We get along fine.

The following morning, a guard brought me a piece of paper signed by Lieutenant C. Gramont that says: "Inmate Martin is under investigation for possible attempts at encouraging a group demonstration." And "He is also under investigation that [sic] there may be a threat to his safety if left in open population." So I guess I'm here for my own good, but somehow I can't follow this line of logic.

This "investigation" is evidently independent of me. No one has asked my feeling on the matter, and the form made clear that I was under investigation for "a violation of Bureau [of Prisons] regulations."

A medical-staff type walked by my cell in a white smock. I told him I had an appointment today with the dentist. I'd had half of a root canal done and was to have it finished today. He told me to write down my name and number. I told him I didn't have a pencil. He had a notebook in his hand and a ballpoint pen in his smock pocket.

"I don't have one either," he said and walked away.

A convict brought me and my cellmate a blanket, writing paper, and a pencil stub, with which this article is written. So things are looking up. He said today (Thursday) it was on the news that I've been locked up. Every little bit helps.

Directly in front of my cell is a cage made from wire like that which you see on a hurricane fence. Daily, one or two convicts are allowed in there to walk back and forth like caged timber wolves. It's called recreation, but I'll probably pass when my turn comes. I'm an old, tired wolf who enjoys his bed and leisure time.

I'm sure I'll be transferred to another prison but don't know where or when. Or I could be put on the "merry-go-round."

In federal prisons, when a prisoner is en route, he's not allowed phone calls or mail privileges—the reasoning being that he could attempt an escape. So what is sometimes done is that they put a fellow like me on a bus and drop him off at Isolation for a few weeks at every prison they stop at. I've seen convicts get caught up in that for nearly two years, never able to contact anyone. It's known as the merry-go-round. Old convicts call it "bus therapy."

If things get really bad, I could be pumped full of psychotropic drugs like Prolixin or Haldol and locked up in 10 Building at the Springfield, Missouri, prison, which is the final stop for troublesome federal prisoners. But that's another story. While the warden's options aren't unlimited, they are awesome in a way.

I hope this doesn't sound like sniveling, because it isn't. I knew the stakes of the game when I sat down, and I'll be in it until I'm cashed out.

There is massive prison construction going on in our country now. I feel that if the taxpayers have to pay for all this, they are entitled to an accurate view of how the prisons are staffed and oper- ated. They are also entitled to know the thoughts, feelings, and viewpoints of the men in those prisons. I plan to keep telling it like it is. If I get on the merry-go-round, I'll find a way to talk about that.

I received eight letters last night from people who read me and appreciate my articles. My thanks and gratitude to them and all the others who have written. Please stay tuned.

Warden Rison later said, "I wasn't totally comfortable with [my] decision" to release Dannie from administrative detention, although "the safety issue was really not a major concern" anymore. He attributed his reluctant decision at least partially to "pressure from the news media."

Perhaps his sensitivity to press reaction was an attempt not to relive his experience as warden at Terminal Island, where he had tussled with the local newspaper over a similar issue. One element of Rison's frosty dispute with the *Long Beach Press-Telegram* involved the isolation of a "whistleblower" prisoner whose letter to the editor had been published in that paper.

In any case, the warden was betting, he later testified, "that Dannie Martin and the editors and people had their laugh and they got their good story and they beat the warden up a little bit and that things would probably turn to normal in a day or so."

At the time, he summed up for a *Chronicle* reporter by saying, "We're going to have an open-door policy with the news media. I would just like an opportunity to respond when the administration's view is an issue." He said something similar in a conversation with a freedom-of-information official from the Northern California Society of Professional Journalists, adding that he would be willing to talk with me in order to iron things out.

With Dannie reportedly out of the hole, I gladly called the warden's office and had a lengthy, open, and reassuring talk with him. He told me that Dannie was indeed back on the mainline and at the time of our phone conversation was at dinner. He assured me that Dannie would be allowed to call me after dinner, outside normal phone hours, even if it was on the warden's personal phone.

Rison reiterated what he had told other journalists in his hectic day of media inquiries: that he was a great believer in the First Amendment and that he had no beef with Dannie. His problem, he said, was with the *Chronicle* for not soliciting the institution's responses to the convict's essays.

I explained that Dannie did not write news stories but first-person commentaries from a prisoner's perspective and that his stories ran in a features-and-commentary section, clearly labeled as the work of a prisoner. Rison said, "I still think I have the right to reply."

Over a period of two years and twenty articles, the prison had never before requested an opportunity to respond to Dannie's pieces, but most important, I told the warden, the prison had indicated on two occasions that what Dannie was doing was illegal. I asked how I could have sought his reaction to articles written "illegally" by one of his convicts.

Rison assured me that what Dannie was doing was not illegal and that he was free to continue. I replied that the prison had even sent me a "program statement" setting forth the regulation that Dannie was apparently violating. "Would you like the number on it [the program statement]?" I asked, turning to my file cabinet to retrieve the document.

"That won't be necessary," the warden replied. "If there is such a program statement, it will be ignored by this administration." (His point was that I had been informed of the rule by his predecessor's administration.)

"In that case," I said, "since you don't believe his writing for the *Chronicle* is illegal, I would be happy to give you an opportunity to respond in advance to anything Dannie writes when I think you might have a contrary view."

I placed two conditions on my offer. First, Rison had to guarantee me that no action would be taken against Dannie for exercise of his First Amendment rights. Second, there must be no attempt at prior restraint of upcoming articles. Both conditions were based on the fact that in soliciting his comments, I would be giving the warden information from the articles in advance of publication. He had Dannie in his control, and I feared his reaction to any upcoming article with which he disagreed.

I also asked that he personally reply to my requests for comment and not shunt the calls to press officers. One reason for that request was that it appeared we had established good rapport in our conversation and I felt we could implement our arrangement best if there were no go-betweens. The warden agreed readily. His satisfaction with our understanding was confirmed when he said he no longer saw a need to send the *Chronicle* the angry letter he'd been preparing.

At another point in our lengthy conversation, the warden indicated that prison officials had preliminary evidence that Dannie was perhaps being paid for his writing and that there was a rule against that but that he didn't feel it was applicable in these circumstances.

Now, years later, I have such a strong recollection of the wording of our conversation that I can even visualize myself turning to the left, toward the file cabinet, when I asked him if he wanted the number of the program statement mailed to me by the prison. But Warden Rison has subsequently denied under oath much of this conversation as I have just related it. Although he acknowledges that he had an agreement with me to get his response to Dannie's articles, he repudiates much of the substance of our conversation.

Specifically, Warden Rison denies telling me he had no objections to Dannie writing for the *Chronicle*. He also denies telling me he would ignore Dannie's apparent violation of prison writing rules in the future, although it was that very concession that formed the basis for the agreement he concedes we reached. It has never been clear why I would want to print his reactions to a story that I was not allowed to publish. What would the warden be reacting *to*?

My conversation with Rison ended as cordially as it had begun, except for the warden's edgy quip that he hoped I had got as little of my work done that day as he had his work, because of the blitz of media calls.

The next day, June 24, prison spokesman Hofer reiterated in an interview with a magazine reporter what the warden had told me: "From now on, Dannie is free to write anything he wants."

■

**D**annie was jubilant about his release back to the mainline, he was drained by the experience, and he was awed by his support on the outside. "Oh, man, it's been a long week," he said in one phone call. "Thank you for everything, buddy."

I suppose Dannie and I had become crime partners. The crime was "committing journalism," in Dannie's felicitous words. That phrase originated in one of his early newspaper interviews: "I committed bank robbery and they put me in prison, and that was right. Then I committed journalism and they put me in the hole. And that was wrong."

Dannie told me in one call that more than a hundred convicts had come up to him soon after his release to offer support. They praised his "Gulag" article and disputed the reasons given for his solitary confinement, assuring him that there was no threat to his safety from the inmates. They told him of petitions that had been circulated in his behalf. Many convicts presented him with letters they had prepared to send to me. "I think the whole joint was writing you over that," he said.

I, in turn, told him about the flood of letters and phone calls from his worried readers on the outside, as well as the overwhelming attention from the news media. Dannie was heartened both because he knew that such attention was his greatest protection and because it was another indication of the impact of his previous writing.

Dannie and I reviewed by phone the developments during the time he had been incommunicado. I told him of my agreement with the warden, and I described my plan to get Rison's consent to a written text of our understanding, including one clarification—his assurance that the prohibition against retaliation included retaliatory transfer. I wanted that written version published in a *Chronicle* news article in the hope that having it "on the record" would further ensure Dannie's protection.

In the same calls, Dannie and I edited his upcoming article on his stay in Isolation, and like everything we discussed over the phone in the week after his release, that editing, too, became a bone of contention with the prison. Distorted reports of those phone calls were later used against us in court.

Jeff Leon had by then secured permission from his firm to represent Dannie if he needed counsel, and the attorney had Dannie's grateful acceptance. Leon, a brilliant young bulldog of a lawyer, was suggesting that Dannie go to court immediately to request a formal injunction against prison retaliation. He, even more than Dannie, was worried about a retaliatory transfer—"bus therapy"—but I and the *Chronicle* attorneys with whom I had been consulting were inclined to trust Rison's word and not litigate needlessly. Dannie concurred.

For three days, June 28–30, in the first test of my compromise agreement with Rison, I tried repeatedly to reach the warden to get his comments on Dannie's "Solitary" manuscript. Each time, I was connected with prison spokesman Hofer, who informed me that the warden was at a conference in Georgia but that Hofer had forwarded the request for him to call me.

On at least two occasions, Hofer relayed word from the warden. One of those times, in answer to my desire for a written version of our agreement, he passed along Rison's mangled version of our understanding. The other time, Hofer relayed a formal statement expressing the warden's "serious concerns about the *Chronicle*'s current stance in having paid an inmate journalist." Alarmed by the tone of that communiqué, I redoubled my efforts to speak with Rison in person, as we had agreed.

∎

On June 30, soon after one of my unsuccessful attempts to contact Rison, I received a call from the prison. It was Kevin Sherbondy again, and there was desperation in his voice. "More bad news for you," he said. At 12:45 that afternoon, he told me, Dannie had been searched and handcuffed by a lieutenant and three officers in the middle of a handball game and hustled off the yard.

In a second call, a short while later, Sherbondy told me, "They took him right . . . out the front gate . . . so he's not here anymore."

I called Hofer yet again, this time to find out what was happening to Dannie. He seemed as surprised as I had been by the news and promised to call me back in minutes. When he did, he said he had just been handed a press release by Acting Warden Thomas Curd confirming Dannie's transfer. For security reasons, he refused to divulge Dannie's destination.

The action was obviously irrevocable. Hofer and I spent a few minutes going over loose ends, including several questions I had planned to ask the warden. I wondered, for instance, what the origin was of the "encouraging a group demonstration" charge, which was never formally invoked. Was it, I asked, based on any overt action in the prison, such as getting up on a soapbox in the dining room? He said no, it was based entirely on the contents of Dannie's "Gulag Mentality" article, especially the use of the word "riot."

The press release issued by the prison at the time of the transfer said:

> It has come to our attention that inmate Dannie Martin . . . has become a compensated byline journalist for the *San Francisco Chronicle* which is in direct violation of current Bureau of Prisons Policy as published in Title 28 Code of Federal Regulations Section 540.20(b). Evidence has surfaced that inmate Martin will continue to publish as a compensated byline journalist in violation of Policy. . . . In order to minimize disruption to the safe and orderly operation of the institution and pending the outcome of a full investigation into policy violation by inmate Martin, he has been transferred to another Federal facility.

The prison's new chief of security, Captain William Brew, later testified that he recommended the transfer to protect Dannie "from retaliation by a volatile inmate population" and "to prevent a full-scale disturbance."

Although the press release made clear that violation of 540.20(b) was Dannie's infraction, he was formally charged with "conducting a business." Transfer is not one of the stipulated sanctions for such low-level offenses. Inexplicably, Dannie was being transferred to a *lower-security* institution although he was declared a security threat and charged on his way out the door with violation of prison regulations.

By the time Dannie was accused of violating 540.20(b), I was quite familiar with the rule. It was the regulation that had accompanied return of Dannie's first check from the *Chronicle* in 1986, and it was the regulation whose number I was about to give to Warden Rison when he informed me that it would not be enforced by his administration. In fact, the rule had never been enforced in the decade it had been on the books. Specifically, 540.20(b) states: "The inmate may not receive compensation or anything of value for correspondence with the news media. The inmate may not act as [a] reporter or publish under a byline."

---

I was devastated by Dannie's transfer. It was clearly the end of quiet accommodation and the beginning of a bitter legal dispute. And because of my agreement with the warden, I felt personally betrayed by him. Strangely, he later claimed to feel betrayed by *me*. As he said in court papers:

> I . . . thought that the editor and I had an agreement that I should at least have an opportunity to respond to any negative criticisms made by Mr. Martin in future articles. However, I was apparently mislead [sic] by the editor. . . . as far as I was concerned, I had worked out a relationship with the *Chronicle* to provide me some type of equal time in future articles that were critical of my administration.

He amplified that statement in a sworn deposition, saying that, in violation of our agreement, I had made no attempt to contact him before publishing "A Report from 'Solitary,' " and "there was no message for me to get hold of Mr. Sussman to return a call."

But when he was asked by a *Chronicle* attorney, "Do you feel that Peter Sussman lied to you?" Rison replied, "I don't feel Peter Sussman was being totally untruthful, no."

■

Dannie was hustled out of Lompoc penitentiary so swiftly that he was not even able to retrieve his watch from a post near the handball court. After a brief grilling about his writing, he was led in chains out the prison's front gate, bypassing the normal receiving and departure office. It's a procedure that Dannie says he has seen only during bad riots. One prison official conceded that it was "something of a rush job."

"I was outraged," Dannie later told an interviewer. ". . . They wanted to put chains and shackles on my voice. I'm not going to let anyone do that."

Dannie was driven to the Metropolitan Correctional Center in San Diego by two officers who not only wouldn't explain why he was being transferred, but wouldn't even acknowledge his presence throughout the hours-long drive. That trip brought a flood of feelings to Dannie, some of which he described in his next "Sunday Punch" essay, published after a subsequent transfer to Phoenix.

## MY EYES WERE LEFT FREE

*PHOENIX, ARIZ. (AUG. 7, 1988)*—After being starved for eight years on a diet of concrete and wire, my visual senses have recently been stuffed with some of the finest images freedom has to offer. It was a brief respite.

Now I'm back in prison, with a view of the desert. It's pretty much the same area where Snoopy's brother Spike is living. I've seen the cacti with their limbs raised in supplication to the rain gods, but no Spike.

Old convicts tell the young that the best way to do a long sentence is to free the mind of debris left over from the free world. The idea is to acclimatize oneself to the world within the fence or wall and to erase all that lies beyond.

Of course, it can't all be forgotten, but as time goes by, more and more becomes dim and foggy.

The stress of long, boring days and nights diminishes accordingly. It's not a bad system, and in recent years I've found myself teaching it to young convicts. I tell them that all they need is a good prison routine.

My own adjustment to the wire-and-concrete jungle was disrupted suddenly when the gates at Lompoc penitentiary rolled open and I was deposited in the rear seat of a station wagon. My hands and feet were shackled, but my eyes were left free to do as they pleased.

Having been away from cars so long, at first it seemed we were traveling at a dangerous speed. But a glance at the speedometer showed we were going fifty-five miles an hour.

Then I saw the ocean for the first time in eight years. Big, foamy waves washed up on a sandy shore. A group of youngsters with surfboards was taking full advantage of a warm, sunny day.

As we drove along, the wildflowers and thick, verdant growth of Santa Barbara hit me with an almost physical force. A magnificent mirage.

Even the gridlock on the freeway that began fifty miles before we reached Los Angeles seemed new and exciting. People who pulled up alongside us would roll their eyes in our direction.

Their expressions were amusing as they took in the two stern prison guards in the front seat and their khaki-clad ward behind a protective plastic shield. A few inquisitive children had the temerity to wave at me, but my hands were hooked to a dog chain around my waist and I couldn't wave back.

When we passed Los Angeles and headed toward San Diego, through Richard Nixon country, there was the ocean again. I watched with awe as the foaming waves rolled in under the burning, glinting sun.

It was night when we reached the Metropolitan Correctional Center in San Diego. I was unceremoniously placed in a two-man cell on the ninth floor, but I was the sole occupant. A narrow window about a foot wide ran from the ceiling to the floor of my cell. I was so tired that I didn't gaze out until the next morning.

Because there are two levels to each floor of the center in San Diego, the ninth floor is actually the same height as the eighteenth floor in a regular office building, so looking out my window I discovered a million-dollar view.

Directly beneath me was the red tile roof of the U.S. Courthouse, with the stars and stripes fluttering in the breeze. I've looked at many U.S. courtrooms from the inside, but this was my first overview.

Beyond the courthouse were the twin towers of the Americana Hotel. High-tech architecture that looked like burnished chrome reflected shards of morning sunshine. Beyond the hotel and marina lay the bridge to Coronado Island. The distant cars looked like bugs on an ivy stem above the silver water.

Beneath the bridge, sailboats and blue-gray military ships plied the waters under fluffy clouds. It all looked more like a convict's daydream than a real view.

As I watched the sailboats running before the warm breeze, I thought about an old song, "Red Sails in the Sunset." Refrains of the song kept running through my mind as I waited for evening. I wanted to see those billowing sails glowing red in the evening sun, but when the sun fell like an orange into the blue water, the sails remained white.

I stayed in that cell for a week and spent most of my time looking out the window, dreaming of faraway exotic places. When I wasn't looking out the window, I was lying on my bunk like a mountain gorilla, picking things out of my hair and rolling my eyes toward the locked cell door.

Now I'm in the desert near Phoenix. I was driven here in a van. Looking out its windows, I found myself thinking of the living things that abound in the desert, even though they aren't in evidence. But what I saw was as limitless and still as a postcard mailed from antiquity.

This is a new prison, and now and then we still discover a rattlesnake in the yard. Last night a friend brought a box over to my cell and introduced his pet, which turned out to be a big, hairy tarantula.

I noticed some birds flying around a high-security floodlight late one evening. I asked someone what kind of birds flew at night and he replied: "Bats."

My view now is stark desert with a barren hill next door. A lone green cactus sits on the hill, with seven limbs raised toward the burning sky. I'm still looking for Spike, but then I don't get much opportunity to go sightseeing in the neighborhood.

Dannie called late at night from San Diego to inform me of his location. I had already begun consultations on a possible lawsuit in his behalf, and he backed my efforts.

He informed me that he had been moved without even being allowed to gather his possessions, a highly unusual procedure. As a result, he did not have toothpaste or stamps or the money to purchase them in the commissary. I promised to lend him $50, and the next day my wife sent a postal money order for that amount.

The gesture went awry in the aura of official suspicion that seemed to surround everything Dannie and I did together. My wife's postal order was returned to me by the San Diego warden with a letter: "As you are aware, it is contrary to Bureau of Prisons regulations for an inmate to receive compensation for being a reporter or by-line journalist. In accordance with those regulations . . . we are returning herewith your Postal Money Order in the amount of $50.00, Dannie Martin payee."

Of course, when the *Chronicle* pays writers, it does so with its own checks, not with postal money orders purchased by the wives of its editors, but the Bureau of Prisons once again took action based on its suspicions, without requesting explanations.

That pattern of suspicion and conjecture turned out to be a big reason why Dannie had been transferred out of Lompoc. The disciplinary infraction he received on his way out of the prison, Associate Warden Curd later testified, was "because of conversations that he had with Peter Sussman at the *San Francisco Chronicle*." Curd's only source of conversations between Dannie and me at the time was our monitored talks on the phone.

While Warden R. H. Rison was out of town and Dannie was back on the mainline at Lompoc, the prison had been run by Curd. It was later revealed that he and security chief Brew had reviewed tapes of monitored phone conversations between me and Dannie and played them for Rison by long-distance phone. So while I was trying to reach the warden for his comments on Dannie's upcoming story, Rison was trying to read my mind and Dannie's by eavesdropping on our conversations. The warden even listened to me telling Dannie what I would like to discuss with the warden when (if, as it turned out) he returned my call.

Curd and Brew were security hard-liners. Both had disagreed with

Rison's decision to release Dannie from Isolation. Brew has testified that "the first thing" on his mind after reading Dannie's "Gulag" article was "thinking we were going to go get Dannie Martin and bring him in and try to squeeze some truth out of him or the inmate who made this flagrant comment" in the "Gulag" article.

In just about every conversation Dannie and I had on those tapes, Curd and Brew heard numerous causes for alarm. Brew found our conversations "explosive, flamboyant, and flagrant to the point of inciting at least a disturbance, if not fully intimating a riot by the inmate population." (If so, it would be Lompoc's first one-person riot, because only one convict was a party to those supposedly inflammatory phone conversations.)

The two officials relayed to Rison their alarm about what they thought Dannie and I were discussing. The warden then conferred with his superiors and recommended transfer.

Like anyone listening in on a conversation between two friends, Curd, Brew, and Rison misinterpreted much of what they heard. And they heard what they wanted to hear in the obscure references that sprinkled our chats.

For example, Dannie had referred in his "Solitary" manuscript to a racial imbalance in the special housing unit. In our telephone editing session, we agreed to drop the reference. The transcript of that taped conversation shows Dannie commenting that he was "uneasy" about his numbers because of later admissions to the unit; I replied, "No, I took out the whole black-white issue. . . . It adds another issue, and I don't want to add a lot of new ones at this point."

Here's how prison officials interpreted that brief exchange:

Captain Brew: ". . . with my knowledge Martin and Sussman were preparing an article concerning racial and protective custody issues of inmates housed in the SHU [special housing unit, informally called Isolation] based on the taped evidence."

And Warden Rison: "There was reference to 'Let's talk about the racial imbalance,' as he perceived it, 'while I was in administrative detention. Let's talk about protective custody cases.' "

Even if what these men heard bore the slightest resemblance to what we said, and it did not, they were acting out of a suspicion more dangerous than the problem they were trying to avoid. If there was a racial imbalance in the special housing unit, that fact would already be common knowledge within the inmate population because of the constant movement back and forth to the detention units.

The use and misuse of our casual banter by third parties was deeply disturbing. Ironically, the mere act of eavesdropping suggests a furtive guilt on the part of those being overheard. As prison officials and, later, lawyers and judges pawed over our private conversations, I felt a kind of guilt akin to what a rape victim must experience.

In the final analysis, Dannie was apparently transferred less to punish him for his past writings and more to control what the *Chronicle* published from the prison in the future. As Curd put it:

> Martin was not transferred because of the "Gulag" article. He was transferred because of the upcoming articles that we were unsure of what was going to be said, and it was evident that we were going to continually be disrupted as long as he was in the institution. And my personal feeling was that if we moved him out of the institution, that the *Chronicle* may not even print the stories about the conditions of confinement in solitary, as he stated it, because Martin would not be in those conditions.

Similarly, Brew was concerned, according to the prison's paralegal, that "we didn't know what is going to be in the [next] article. We don't know anything about it. We don't know what is going to be said."

Neither official called me to request the opportunity to respond that I had already granted the warden, and neither apparently considered another option: to keep the presumably subversive edition of "Sunday Punch" out of the prison so other prisoners couldn't read it.

When Rison recommended that Dannie be transferred based on reports from Curd and Brew, his suggested destination was to another maximum-security penitentiary—Leavenworth or Lewisburg, "I get them mixed up." However, regional director Williford, who is formally responsible for transfers, decided on the lower-security Federal Correctional Institution at Phoenix, via San Diego.

▪

Our legal case began to take shape within minutes of the call alerting me to Dannie's hurried move from Lompoc. I unleashed Jeff Leon, who had been on standby expecting just such a transfer, and he began preparing papers requesting a temporary restraining order to protect Dannie's First Amendment rights.

I was soon called by the Southern California branch of the American Civil Liberties Union. It had received calls a week earlier from Lompoc prisoners upset about Dannie's banishment to solitary, and unbeknownst to us, an ACLU attorney had warned prison officials that any further action to deny Dannie his constitutional rights could lead to a lawsuit. With Dannie's transfer, they were prepared to go to court. I put them in touch with Jeff Leon, and the ACLU's John Hagar signed on as Dannie's co-counsel.

I had earlier been in touch with the *Chronicle*'s attorneys at the suggestion of the paper's executive editor, and I alerted them to Dannie's transfer and the pending lawsuit on his behalf. Within days, the *Chronicle* was on board as a co-plaintiff. It was a fitting recognition that the paper's rights were at risk as well as Dannie's.

At the time, the issues appeared so clear-cut that I doubt anyone in the *Chronicle*'s hierarchy thought that the paper was committing itself to a costly, years-long free-press campaign. And the *Chronicle*'s top executives would surely not have *chosen* to ally themselves with a convicted bank robber—it's not the sort of image a major corporation promotes these days. But the First Amendment is a newspaper's birthright, analogous perhaps to a physician's Hippocratic oath, and I watched with pride as the *Chronicle* backed me and a convicted bank robber.

■

The passionately dedicated Leon became point man in the suit. He worked night and day through the long Fourth of July weekend of 1988, emerging from his office on the first working day with a brief arguing that Dannie's and the *Chronicle*'s First Amendment rights had been violated by the prison's retaliatory actions.

The lawsuit, filed on July 6, named the BOP director, the warden, and a number of other prison officials as defendants. The Bureau of Prisons itself was later added to the list. The suit requested various forms of relief, including an immediate court order to prohibit further transfers of Dannie pending resolution of the legal case; allow Dannie to continue writing for publication without punishment; and prohibit enforcement of 540.20(b). The suit also sought personal guarantees for Dannie such as protection from parole-board retaliation and return of his writing supplies, manuscripts, and notes. And it asked for unspecified damages and attorneys' fees.

Hours after the suit was filed, a government attorney confirmed the suspicion expressed in the suit that Dannie was scheduled for further transfer within hours or days. The attorney said the transfer from San

Diego to his "permanent" but undisclosed destination was scheduled for 9:00 A.M. the following day, so federal Judge Charles Legge set an emergency 7:00 A.M. court hearing.

At the hearing, Leon and *Chronicle* attorney Lisa Zinkan said that transfer is ordinarily in the discretion of the Bureau of Prisons, but not when it is in retaliation for expression protected under the Constitution. They argued that moving Dannie farther from San Francisco would diminish the value of his writings to his Northern California readership.

Justice Department attorney George Stoll replied, "He's not Bret Harte or somebody who is uniquely describing the California experience. He's a federal prisoner and he's moved around from time to time."

But, said Judge Legge, "this isn't your ordinary transfer. It looks like you're bouncing the guy around. It really does." To which the government attorney added, "At least one bounce."

In the end, Legge ruled that "it seems obvious that there's been retaliation . . . for the exercise of First Amendment rights," and he issued a temporary restraining order granting much of what we had requested but refusing to block Dannie's transfer out of California. "I don't think it's my function to tell the Bureau of Prisons where to put prisoners," he said.

Legge left the status of 540.20(b) ambiguous in his order. He refused to declare it unconstitutional immediately, but he also said that "there's no restraint on the *Chronicle* to publish whatever it gets."

Legge, finding "no threat to safety or order within the institution" because of Dannie's writing, subsequently followed up with a preliminary injunction against the defendants. He said there was substantial evidence that the actions taken against Dannie had been based on the content of his articles. Citing a Supreme Court ruling, the judge said that "prison walls do not form barriers separating inmates from the protection of the Constitution, and that certainly includes protections under the First Amendment."

Legge's ruling also suspended enforcement of 540.20(b) until after a trial of the issues, but when he later issued the written version of that ruling, Legge limited the suspension of regulations to Dannie only, excluding other prison writers from protection. In the interim, at least one other prisoner—Christopher Boyce, the "Falcon" of the book and film *The Falcon and the Snowman,* who was serving his federal sentence in a Minnesota state prison—had begun writing under a byline for the

*Minneapolis Star Tribune* because of the protection afforded by Legge's oral ruling.

■

Shortly after the initial court hearing, the *Chronicle* received a lengthy manuscript from BOP western regional director Williford, one of the defendants in our lawsuit. He requested that we publish his views, and we did so in mid-July. The response ran in "Sunday Punch" in a format and length nearly identical to "The Gulag Mentality."

In a mirror image of Dannie's views, Williford denounced the media's "sensationalized" and "stereotypical images about prisons," by which he meant "oppressed inmate . . . victimized by a brutal, unfeeling, pot-bellied and cigar-smoking warden" and "stunted 'guards' " in "an old, dark, and ominous walled fortress shrouded in myths and secrecy and inacessible to the outside world."

He argued that prisons have "dramatically changed" and that modern prison officials are much more accessible to the media. And he chastised the *Chronicle* for not balancing Dannie's views with those of the prison administration.

Williford was scathing in his denunciation of me and Dannie, although he did characterize Dannie's writing as "an intriguing and unique inmate's view." He said that I "embraced" Dannie's version of life at Lompoc because it "is entertaining, possesses pizzazz, and sells papers." Of my First Amendment views he wrote:

> Mr. Sussman . . . was recently quoted in the *Chronicle* as saying Dannie Martin's "transfer jeopardizes the public's access to inside information about a public institution paid for by taxpayer's money." He goes on to say, "If the only way to find out about that institution is through the warden, then we don't have the public accountability that taxpayers have a right to." How idealistic, how commendable, and what a bunch of "baloney."

I received a number of interesting responses to Williford's article. The first was from Dannie, writing from his new home in Phoenix. "Very good thinking on your part" to run it, he told me. "I believe you'd have been an excellent bank robber." I took it as a compliment.

Several former prisoners wrote to challenge Williford's views on conditions inside the modern prison.

■

Through all of the legal arguments and personal recriminations, Dannie and I were sustained by the vocal and articulate support of our readership. Of the hundreds of letters and phone calls we received during the crackdown, no more than two were negative. Many were from political conservatives who were unable to see the threat in the articles they had been enjoying for two years in the *Chronicle*. Several letters began almost identically: "I'm no bleeding-heart liberal, but . . ."

Two particularly moving letters—one to me and one to Dannie—were written by a woman of seventy who was fighting cancer. "Your writing," she told Dannie, "has a special meaning to me—what right have I to be depressed when you, Dannie Martin, can turn out such marvelous writing under such hideous circumstances. . . . Dannie, I would give my good right arm and my front seat in hell if I could live long enough to greet you in person."

Her letter to me concluded, "Keep up the good work! The First Amendment is worth fighting for."

The frail but spunky writer of those two letters didn't quite make it to Dannie's release, but she got to meet him through a glass barrier during the trial of our lawsuit. In spite of her deteriorating physical condition, she attended every court session and called frequently to receive legal updates and to offer assistance and encouragement. She was every editor's dream reader—informed, concerned, and always responsive. It is to the memory of that woman, Mrs. Gay Eddy, that we have dedicated this book.

Also writing eloquently on behalf of our readers was Nancy Hoffman, a correspondent who came to play a personal role in the lawsuit. Hoffman suggested in her letter that the Bureau of Prisons' treatment of Dannie suggested that the bureau had "something interesting to hide," and she asked:

Aren't you even a bit curious to know what dirty little secrets they are so anxious to protect? I am! If Dannie Martin is denied the opportunity to write about what he sees and experiences on the inside of the prison system, his rights have been violated and so have mine. . . . Dannie Martin . . . when you are denied your constitutional right to freedom of speech, I am simultaneously denied my right to hear what you have to say.

At our invitation, Hoffman joined our lawsuit as a co-plaintiff to represent the interests of *Chronicle* readers, but Judge Legge ruled that she had no legal standing.

Meanwhile, Dannie—shielded for a time by the preliminary injunction, and with an audience now educated to the risks he was subjecting himself to—continued to exercise his constitutional right to freedom of speech from his new home in the Arizona desert.

# III

---

# EXILE IN
# THE DESERT
# AUGUST 1988 –
# NOVEMBER 1989

Dear Peter: . . . I can't get much help on my current project from these convicts here. It's not that they wouldn't like to help. The gulf between us and the law-abiding public is even more daunting to them than it is to me. I can't help but think the people who build and operate prisons like it that way.

No one has any confidence in the idea that we can explain things to people who have never wanted to discuss anything with us. We're probably like slaves in a cane field listening to someone say we should explain to the master that this ain't right. . . .

—*Letter from Phoenix*

■

$\mathbf{D}$annie had an uneasy transition to his new prison. It wasn't the prison itself; he liked it. The Federal Correctional Institution at Phoenix had none of Lompoc's pervasive tension, the food was good, the yard was open from 8:00 A.M. to 9:00 P.M., and air conditioning protected convicts from the heat of the surrounding desert. Also, Dannie knew some of the convicts from other prisons.

The physical plant is newer than Lompoc's. Unlike that World War II–era fortress, the Federal Correctional Institution at Phoenix looks like the low-budget campus of a community college. The prison had about a thousand inmates at the time, more than double the rated capacity, but the single-story cinder-block structures are spread out, with less of the maddening, high-voltage feeling of Lompoc's echoing, three-tier cellblocks.

But the Phoenix prison was isolated, far from Dannie's family and readership. Moreover, he had not yet acquired a feel for the pulse of the place. He had described the process once for me in a letter:

> There's a term known as "a corner." Older convicts know the term well, but the new breed has no concept of it. . . . A corner is defined by who a man hangs out with. That's his corner. Lots of times even a loner is hooked to a certain corner, so within that you've got "strong corners," "weak corners," etc. Once you know all the corners and where they are and what their guidelines are, then you get an easy feel for the pulse of a prison.

Dannie made it a practice to work the corners—all racial groups and cliques—to get the feel of the joint. It had always helped the convict survive, and, he later testified in court, it's "sort of the same system that I use for acquiring knowledge to write about things. Some of it will work in a story, and some of it won't."

Dannie was even more uncertain of his position than most newly transferred prisoners because of the circumstances under which he had left Lompoc. The guards at Phoenix all knew of his history there, if for no other reason than the posting on the Phoenix officers' lounge bulletin board of both Jerry Williford's "Sunday Punch" rebuttal and Dannie's own sympathetic story on guards.

When he arrived, Dannie couldn't yet identify informers, and he wasn't sure how tight an official rein was being kept on him. In fact, there were early indications that he was being watched closely. Otherwise routine decisions on things such as phone calls and mail inspection sometimes had to be kicked upstairs to the warden's office for a ruling. Dannie said lower-level officials seemed afraid to decide such questions on their own.

At times, these niggling daily pressures became so galling that Dannie yearned momentarily for the harsh clarity of a serious penitentiary like Marion or Leavenworth. There, at least, you know where you stand.

Both Dannie and I also felt a loss because of the journalistic task that remained undone at Lompoc. We had started a story that we could not finish. We continued to receive letters from convicts and former staff members at Lompoc talking of petty crackdowns, irregularities, and erratic personal behavior by prison officials. But we had no credible or effective way of following up. In addition, any critical stories about the Lompoc administration would have appeared to be warden-bashing; the *Chronicle,* after all, was a party to a suit against the top officials there.

So in that sense, the Lompoc administration had accomplished its aim in moving Dannie. The spotlight was off.

◾

Jeff Leon and I went to Phoenix to begin working with Dannie on the lawsuit within weeks of his arrival there. It was the convict's first chance to meet his lead attorney in person. From then on, running like a subplot through Dannie's time at Phoenix and mine at the *Chronicle* was the laborious year-and-a-half-long process of preparing for trial— reconstructing our experiences at Lompoc, assembling evidence, contacting sources and potential witnesses, and raising funds for Leon's expensive, largely pro bono representation of Dannie. (The *Chronicle,* of course, paid its own way.)

The media, too, kept tracking the case. After the hectic weeks of tit-for-tat accusations while Dannie was at Lompoc and San Diego, they began to flesh out the story. TV producers requested interviews in Phoenix and San Francisco. Arizona papers interviewed their new resident, and national publications such as *Time* magazine also covered the story.

Such attention fueled the interest of prisoners across the country. As late as two years after *Time's* story appeared, convict letter writers were referring movingly to that article in mail to me. And Dannie received other indications of his importance to prisoners elsewhere. One Phoenix convict told him that at a rural California jail where the man had done time, photocopies of Dannie's "Sunday Punch" articles were stashed behind a telephone, where convicts could find and read them.

Not all the recognition came from the media and fellow prisoners. The San Francisco board of supervisors, the city's governing legislative body, passed a resolution citing Dannie's "unique and eloquent portraits of prison life [that] have won him a large and devoted following in San Francisco." Arguing that "the residents of this City have the right to continue to read his views," the unanimous resolution urged the Bureau of Prisons "to recognize and guarantee the First Amendment rights of all Federal prisoners, including Dannie Martin, to prepare and write articles for publication in the news media."

It is hard to overestimate the effect that such a governmental gesture has on a man in a prison cell.

Among the unfinished business facing Dannie was his disciplinary write-up, or "shot," for violating the compensated byline journalist rule. He finally got a hearing on that charge in Phoenix in late July. He reported that the hearing officer reviewed the BOP's case and concluded that there is "such a thing as due process. I don't see any evidence to support this shot." The hearing was adjourned indefinitely.

■

**D**espite his many distractions and readjustments, Dannie began to focus again on his writing. "I don't plan to go out of my way to criticize anyone," he told me in a letter, "but I also don't plan to be intimidated by what has happened."

When he got his bearings at Phoenix, he returned to print with a story he had been working on before his transfer.

## PEN PALS IN THE PEN

*PHOENIX, ARIZ. (SEPT. 18, 1988)*—Many women at some time or another think of writing a convict. Most of them don't. Others do, then wish they hadn't. And there are those who marry convicts and live happily ever after.

A distraught Arizona woman wrote me recently about a predicament she got herself into by writing to a strange convict.

His picture was published in a Southwestern newspaper because of a good deed he'd done for the community. She liked his looks and thought he was nice because of his good works. She wrote him a letter, and a warm correspondence ensued.

He wouldn't reveal his original crime to her, but that seemed okay. She didn't want to pry.

Early in the correspondence, he wanted to share some fantasies. Hers were nothing unusual or bizarre, so she shared a few. That's where all the trouble began.

He began sending her ten-page accounts of violent rape in which she was the victim and he was the perpetrator. It didn't take a big intellect to realize that these graphic "fantasies" were based on actual events. She informed him that their correspondence was terminated.

He then began writing her threatening letters, describing in gruesome detail what he would do to her when he got out. She called his caseworker, who confirmed that he was in prison for a violent sex offense.

The caseworker told her that the man had been a model prisoner in the sex offender program and was due to be paroled soon. That's all the information the caseworker would give out.

Police agencies the woman turned to for help implied that it was her own fault for writing to a convict in the first place.

Another woman from the Bay Area wrote to me more than a year ago with a hair-raising tale of how she had been defrauded by a convict. She's a lovely, kind woman—the sort who cries over stray cats.

Some time ago, she began writing to a convict. A mutual correspondence ensued, lasting almost a year. They talked often on the phone, and the woman also visited him in the prison. Eventually, he got a substantial amount of money from her by telling her that his release on parole depended on his posting bond that he did not have. That story, it turned out, was a total fabrication.

He wound up leaving her destitute. She found out later that he had done the same thing to several others, including one woman who died on welfare after giving her money to the convict.

I gave those two women all the belated help and advice I could. But the sad fact is that had they known a few things about checking out convicts, they might have been able to avoid those situations.

Those are extreme cases, but the practice of women writing to convicts is far from unusual. It's a subspecies of "pen pal" that deserves more attention than it has gotten. Nor is this all a horror story—there are some roses among the thorns.

Last November, I wrote a story in "Sunday Punch" about twenty-three-year-old Kevin Sherbondy, who was convicted under a harsh new career-criminal law. He is a photogenic young man, and his photograph accompanied the article. Sherbondy received many letters from women in California and neighboring states, and the only problem they encountered by writing Kevin was that there wasn't enough of him to go around.

Convicts can make good spouses for those who treasure their own freedom. A woman said to me once: "I enjoy having a convict for a husband. It enables me to have a husband and still do as I please." There are other women—the social-worker types—who write to convicts with the goal of changing them into something other than what they are. Those relationships usually end with a lot of heartache and disappointment.

Then there are the sexually frustrated women—some of them fascinated by the idea of handcuffs and chains—who write to convicts mainly for excitement. They usually initiate the correspondence by explaining that "all the men out here are either married or gay." Their letters get quite steamy at times.

Some of the women who habitually write to convicts have been, or perhaps expect to be, abused by men. Communicating with a convict may seem a safe way to act out their unconscious expectations. Their image of convicts may be misleading, but many of them "shop around" until they find one who fits their expectations.

Older women, perhaps widowed and lonely, sometimes write convicts while thinking of their own sons. Other elderly women, who have experienced a full life in society, become curious in their golden years about prison life. Those writers are a treasure to a convict. I have an elderly pen pal I wouldn't trade for a trainload of teenyboppers.

Then there are just plain nice women who happen to like outlaws. It's a phenomenon I'm at a loss to explain, but there are plenty of them.

The story is no simpler behind the bars. There are all types of men in prison—good men as well as very bad men. They run the gamut from extreme sickos to honorable lawbreakers. The trick for a female correspondent is to find out which is which.

If a woman knows how to "qualify" convicts, her chances of finding a good one are better than they are in a singles bar—and she can find out more about a convict than she can about a stranger she meets outside. But there are a few things every woman should know about writing convicts.

The letter writer can look at a convict's entire past record, whereas she can learn from a stranger in a singles bar only what he chooses to tell her. And she has the advantage of seeing the bad side of a man first—a process that is usually reversed in the free world.

The first two questions a woman writing a convict should ask are how much time he is doing and what he was convicted of. His answers can easily be verified by calling his caseworker.

Under the Freedom of Information Act—Title 5, Section 552—a caseworker can give out certain information about a prisoner without his consent. This includes the type of crime, length of sentence, and other pertinent information.

But that isn't all that can be discovered. If the prisoner is willing to sign a release-of-information form, the caseworker is free to divulge his entire past history. I would advise a woman to be very leery of a prisoner who won't reveal his past to her.

In any case, it's wise never to send money to someone you don't know thoroughly. A prison caseworker will know something about a convict's financial needs on the outside.

Nowadays, there are many people in prisons who are totally insane. Some of them are fugitives from mental hospitals doing time for crimes of pure madness. It's difficult to identify one of these monsters by talking with him. They often present to the world a naive and likable persona.

Even convicts have a hard time identifying them, and they are right here among us. The caseworker won't tell us anything about another convict under any circumstances. I spent time in Folsom Prison with a quiet, well-mannered man who killed three of his cell partners before the authorities decided to give him a single cell.

The diminutive word "con" has unfortunate consequences for all of us. The word is derived from "confidence man" as well as "convict." As a result, society tends to view all convicts as essentially fraudulent people.

We do attempt to con prison guards, parole officials, and judges. It's an age-old law of the dungeon that lies open doors and gates much more easily than truth. But in personal relationships, many of us are scrupulously honest. Our word is what we live by, and we keep it good.

I could hear a chorus of groans and fiddle bows on taut strings as I wrote that. But the truth is that it's the rare convict who has the finesse to con society. It's more typical of a convict to draw a gun and hand a victim a sack to put the money in.

There are a lot of lonely men in here, good men. For them, there is nothing quite like a letter from a woman. It puts a note of hope into a litany of despair and renders the boredom less formidable. It brings thoughts of perfume and silk to the concrete jungle. It often enables a man to smile in the dour face of adversity.

There's one other bit of advice I can offer about choosing whom to write. Shy away from those convicts who keep protesting their innocence and choose one who says he is guilty as hell. He'd be the fellow more likely to be telling the truth.

---

In that story, Dannie turned the most gruesome of incidents into an informative public service. The "distraught Arizona woman" whose letter first got him thinking about writing the article had told us a story so horrifying that we could not print most of the details. We decided, too, to disguise some elements of her experience in order to protect her.

In his next article, Dannie again relied on memory rather than fresh experiences. It was an indication, perhaps, that he still was not entirely comfortable in his new surroundings.

## THE MEMO OUTLAWS

PHOENIX, ARIZ. (OCT. 23, 1988)—The most cunning, feared, admired, and hated prison inhabitant is the memo phantom. There is one or more in every prison, but it's seldom that anyone knows who they are. Secrecy to them is as sacred as their desire for chaos.

Prisons are run by memorandum. An operations memorandum from the warden or associate warden sets forth a rule or new procedure, for staff and convicts alike. Custodial memos, by captains and lieutenants, announce new head-count hours, leisure activities, and the like. Program memos, by the chaplain or some academic nabob, deal with educational and religious activities.

Convicts send "cop-outs"—a sort of reverse memorandum—to officials to request some type of assistance.

These instruments of communication give the memo phantom generous latitude in his quest for disharmony within a prison population.

What happens is that a new memorandum will appear on all cellblock bulletin boards at the same time. The memo phantom's work is always cleverly written and signed and appears to have the signature of the warden or other appropriate official. Frequently, the content of a bogus memo will drive someone up a nearby wall.

One of the more famous stunts took place at the Oregon State Prison in the late 1950s. The warden at the time was a strict disciplinarian who ruled convicts and staff alike with an iron fist.

There are four cellblocks at the prison, all branching out from a common control area, or "rotunda," as it's called by convicts. The cellblocks are designated A, C, D, and E blocks. Evening lockup in those days was 3:45 P.M. Convicts were not to leave their cells after that, except for dinner.

One day, a memorandum signed by the warden appeared on the bulletin boards of all four cellblocks. It stated that considerable strain had been put on the inmate population by the housing of relatives, friends, and crime partners in separate cellblocks.

It went on to say that in order to reduce visiting in the workplace, a new inter-cellblock visiting procedure would become effective immediately.

Cellblocks A and D would be opened from 7:00 to 9:30 P.M. on Mondays so that convicts could visit back and forth. C and E would be open on Tuesdays at the same time. The visiting was to continue on weeknights on a rotating basis.

The final paragraph noted that this new procedure was experimental and subject to a future custodial appraisal. The guards didn't relish the extra work, but they dutifully complied with the memorandum.

The new procedure was a huge success with convicts until one evening when the warden decided to take a walk through his prison. He was dressed in a nice suit, complete with necktie and hat.

He entered the rotunda and saw two cellblock doors standing

open while convicts ambled back and forth with cups of coffee in their hands. When he observed the guards standing around watching them, he went crazier than a wood rat on ether.

People who were there at the time report that his face swelled up as if his tie were choking him to death. He ran to the nearest guard and yelled: "What the hell is going on here?"

Before the guard could reply, he ran to another guard and yelled: "I said, what in the hell is going on?"

Before the second one could reply, he ran to still another guard, pulled off his own hat, and began jumping up and down on it, all the while yelling: "What in the hell is going on?"

The memorandum was rescinded immediately, and rumor has it that some guards lost their jobs over that one. Apparently, the warden was the only one who didn't know about the new visiting procedures.

The "foot letter" was perpetrated on the same warden not long after the visiting scam.

A new convict came to the prison, and he had a terrible foot odor. No amount of bathing or powder would help his condition. It was chronic, and he was sensitive about it. No one ribbed him much, though, because he was about as dangerous as a coral snake.

Someone forged a letter on the warden's stationery and slipped it into the guards' mail sack so that it was delivered to the convict with smelly feet in the regular evening mail.

The letter informed him that the warden had received numerous complaints about his feet. It went on to say that his feet should not be the responsibility of this prison administration. But if he wouldn't assume responsibility for his own feet, then staff would be forced to "take appropriate measures."

The convict angrily confronted the warden about his letter the next day. For quite some time after that, the only ones bothered by his feet were his neighbors in Isolation.

Another time, a friend of mine was called to the prison psychiatrist's office, where the psychiatrist informed him that he did indeed have a problem.

"What do you mean?" my friend asked him.

"Well, there are rules against kissing another man in the visiting room," the psychiatrist replied.

After a heated discussion, the truth began to emerge. Someone had sent the shrink a cop-out requesting counseling and signed my friend's name and number on it.

The request stated that he had a personal problem in that one of his gay friends was planning a visit soon. The friend would be expecting a kiss upon his arrival, and that would surely harm my friend's mean, macho image in the prison. The cop-out asked the shrink's assistance in resolving this dilemma.

He finally convinced the doctor that they had been victimized by a memo phantom. But my friend told me later that the shrink acted as if he still thought he had sent the request, then lost the nerve to discuss it.

Reading this, someone might think convicts and guards are awfully gullible to fall for these bogus edicts. But when you realize that prisons are run by memorandum and bulletin board, it becomes more understandable. Another reason the phony memos work so well is that some legitimate memos are more bizarre than those penned by memo phantoms.

Early this year, Warden R. H. Rison put out a memorandum at Lompoc penitentiary stating that our recreation yard would be closed during the morning hours. The memo went on to say that this was necessary so the yard crew could "refurbish" the yard.

Older convicts laughed when they read that one. It had the distinct odor of the memo phantom. In the first place, the yard had been open forty years or more. We knew that the so-called yard crew consisted of a few hard-core ne'er-do-wells who wouldn't make their own beds, much less "refurbish" anything.

The last laugh was on us, of course. Rison was dead serious about closing the yard. That memo set the stage for one of the cruelest stunts I've ever witnessed.

The right to receive Christmas packages from home had been discontinued by the previous warden at Lompoc. But an outside Christian group was allowed to give packages to convicts who didn't have enough money to buy the generic Christmas packages available in the prison canteen.

Last Christmas, some 250 convict paupers were approved to receive free Christmas packages. At the last moment, Warden Rison put out another memo disallowing all but about sixteen convicts.

The rumor was that our packages had been given to the Cubans who had been transferred there recently, after the prison riot in

Atlanta. The rumor was verified by some of the guards, who weren't too happy about the situation.

Everyone was surprised in June of this year when a memo concerning the packages appeared on all unit bulletin boards.

The memo explained that during a recent audit of the warehouse, some 250 undistributed Christmas packages had been discovered. The men who hadn't received their packages were instructed to bring a cop-out complete with their name and number on Monday evening. They were to form a line at the group activities center near the lieutenant's office.

The next Monday, guards were startled to find a line of unruly convicts waving cop-outs in the main hallway. They wanted their Christmas packages. What they got was an unforgettable lesson in the art of bogus memos.

In the middle '60s at the conservation center at Susanville, California, a memo appeared on the bulletin board that almost caused a riot.

It expounded on the unfairness of some convicts being paid $15 a month while those who didn't work received nothing. It went on to explain that henceforth (a word often used in legitimate memos) one-half of each convict worker's pay would be put into a slush fund for indigent and unemployed inmates.

As I stood there reading it, I became as angry as everyone else. The final paragraph was really infuriating. It said: "Whatever is brought upon thee, take cheerfully and be patient when thou art changed to a low estate, for gold is tried in fire and acceptable men in the furnace of adversity."

I've read many bogus memos since that one, but not one of them ended with such good advice.

---

Within weeks of the appearance of that article, things began looking up for Dannie. On November 3, he and I were presented with the Elsa Knight Thompson Award for Special Achievement by the Media Alliance, a San Francisco organization of media professionals. Dannie followed every detail from afar, receiving photographs of the ceremony and several reports by letter. I sent him a photocopy of the certificate—the most he dared have in his possession in that unpredictable environment—and sent the original to his father in Texas, to hang in his barber shop.

Red Hog was big with pride. The award "will look good on my résumé," he joked in a letter. "Hog futures are looking better all the time."

That award was followed by others, including freedom of information awards from the local and national Society of Professional Journalists, the Scripps Howard Foundation, the California Society of Newspaper Editors and California Freedom of Information Committee, the Prison Law Office, the Playboy Foundation, PEN American Center and Newman's Own, Inc., and others.

"I've always had some contempt for the society we live in," Dannie wrote me, "and lately I've been ashamed of that. These awards help me to feel that I'm making small amends."

Powerful organizations such as The Newspaper Guild also backed our legal position. The guild's resolution, passed unanimously at its international convention, began, "Dannie M. Martin is a bank robber and convict. He also is a writer. Being the former should not separate him from the protections the U.S. Constitution offers to the latter."

Such recognition played a major role in bringing us the media attention that was Dannie's greatest guarantee of protection. Without the continuous attention of people of principle on the outside, Dannie would not have been able to continue acting on principle on the inside.

By the time of his next story, it was apparent that things had improved for him on the inside, too. He was starting to write about the people around him again. The writer had found "the pulse."

## DRESSING FOR SUCCESS IN A FEDERAL PRISON

*PHOENIX, ARIZ. (DEC. 18, 1988)*—Robert Stroud—the notorious Birdman of Alcatraz—killed a prison guard over the denial of a visit with his mother. His was an isolated incident, but it's an example of how emotional an issue a visit can be for convicts and their loved ones.

It's a hard blow to a family when a member is convicted of a crime and sent to prison. Time becomes another form of confinement for those who wait and hope.

A prison visiting room is the hard way of keeping families and friends together. But for convicts, it's the only place there is. Even the most enduring emotions need the regeneration of sight, sound, and touch now and then.

The institution here in Phoenix is a level 4 prison—a place ostensibly for less dangerous offenders. High-security prisons, such as Lompoc and Marion, Illinois, are designated levels 5 and 6. Yet the visiting regulations here are as stringent as those of high-security prisons.

When we enter the visiting room here, we are stripped, thoroughly searched, and forced to don a pair of baggy, wrinkled coveralls with a zipper all the way up the back. We also must wear a pair of canvas sneakers that have been worn again and again by other men.

The coveralls are designed to prevent convicts from secreting drugs in a body cavity. But the problems this procedure alone have caused one convict, wheelchair-bound Richard Jackson, are enormous (see accompanying story below).

In addition to Bureau of Prisons policy on visitors, attitudes of individual wardens and associate wardens are reflected in memorandums. On September 6 of this year, a memorandum was placed on all cellblock bulletin boards at this prison signed by Joseph Van Kemper, associate warden in charge of programs. Among other things the memo stated:

1. No female visitor will be allowed to visit if, in the staff's opinion, her dress is inappropriate and/or provocative.
2. No tube tops or tank tops will be allowed.
3. No shorts of any kind are allowed.
4. No skirts or dresses that are more than two inches above the knee are allowed.

It went on to say that effective October 1, visitors would be turned away if not in compliance with the dress code.

It's difficult for the convicts and their guests to discern what may be "inappropriate" in the staff's opinion. But a newly arrived convict's wife ran afoul of these rules on her first visit.

She drove here to visit from Salt Lake City and was turned away because she was wearing a tube top. The guard informed her that it was "too tight." She returned to the parking area and retrieved a shirt to wear over the top.

A roving security guard who patrols the prison fence was parked nearby. The convict's wife approached the guard to ask if the shirt would be acceptable. As she drew near the truck, the guard jumped out and leveled a shotgun at her, yelling: "Get away from the truck, lady!"

She, of course, was petrified.

The way visits are handled here at Phoenix seems to run contrary to a public policy statement put out by the Bureau of Prisons on July 22, 1986. It is entitled "Program Statement 5267.4" and subtitled "Purpose and scope 540.40." It reads:

> The Bureau of Prisons encourages visiting by family, friends and community groups to maintain the morale of the inmate and to develop closer relationships between inmate and family members or others in the community. The warden shall develop procedures consistent with this rule to permit inmate visiting. He may restrict visiting when necessary for the security and good order of the institution.

The policy looks good on paper, but it doesn't work that way in practice. Visiting applications are routinely denied if the prisoner didn't know the applicant prior to incarceration.

For a citizen of the underworld, the only visitors he could get approved are his old underworld friends. But there's a catch to that also. All applicants with a serious criminal record are automatically denied.

Immediate family members are generally approved routinely, although even spouses have been denied visiting privileges if they have arrest records. Many close relations who would have been welcomed in the past are now having terrible experiences with visits.

Jerry Armijo's home and family are in Denver. He's been in prison for six years, and during that time he has never had a visit. His family wasn't able to travel to the prisons he was in at Sandstone, Minnesota, and Ray Brook, New York. In June of this year, he was transferred to Phoenix.

He told his counselor that he would soon be getting a visit from his sister and brother-in-law, who live in Denver. The counselor replied that it would be "no problem."

When they arrived here at the prison on a Saturday, they were told bluntly that they wouldn't be allowed to visit. His counselor had neglected to give his visiting list to the visiting room officer.

A phone call to his unit would have verified that it was his family, but no one would do that. The family members drove back to Denver without a visit. When Armijo found out about the incident and confronted the warden, he says the warden had this to say: "If you continue this attitude, it could lead you to Isolation and a trip back to New York."

Many of us believe that nowadays our keepers will do everything possible to discourage visiting. Visitors, far from being welcomed as guests, are treated as potential criminals. This is a turnabout from a few years ago, when visitors felt welcome at prisons.

It's becoming apparent to us that the concept of rehabilitation is a thing of the past in modern-day prisons. The focus has shifted heavily toward warehousing, punishment, and retribution. Convicts believe that long-established visiting protocols have become the first casualty of this new mentality.

Others believe that the drug wars have fostered the official animus toward visitors, and it is true that most of the drugs that enter a prison come in by way of the visiting room.

No matter what brought about the change, some of the incidents are downright heartbreaking to convicts and their families.

Isaac Conchola has a twenty-seven-year-old son, Jon, who is mentally retarded. The boy lives in Los Angeles with Isaac's wife. He has the mind of a happy-go-lucky eleven-year-old.

The boy loves the Dodgers, and Isaac used to take him regularly to Dodger Stadium to watch the team play. Jon remembers the trips well and longs for Isaac to return home so they can go again.

Four months ago, Isaac informed his counselor that Jon and his wife would be here to visit in November. He was told it would be "no problem."

When his wife showed up with Jon for the visit, she was told that Jon would have to leave the premises because he wasn't on Isaac's visiting list. She had to take Jon to Phoenix by cab and put him on a plane back to Los Angeles.

I've known Isaac for twenty-five years, in and out of some of the toughest prisons in the country, but the day of that aborted visit is the first time I've ever seen tears in his eyes.

"It was pitiful, Red," he said. "That boy just had no way to understand why he couldn't see me."

Until a quarter century ago, convicts pretty much ran the inner community of prisons where they were confined. They allotted many jobs and had a bigger say in the everyday operations, including some input on visiting procedures. Administrators usually went along if things remained calm, secure, and reasonable.

Today, convicts have no say whatever in a prison's operation. This change, along with overcrowding and bureaucratic bungling, has caused tremendous resentment and pain among convicts and their families.

The new rules, policies, and attitudes don't enhance humanity in either us or our keepers. Especially when our loved ones begin to suffer their ill effects.

It could be argued that prisons are more efficient now, but I believe they ran better when convicts had some input. If memory serves me right, everyone was at least courteous and polite in those days.

---

Running with that story was this sidebar:

---

## 'NOT IMPORTANT ENOUGH TO GET KILLED OVER'

PHOENIX, ARIZ. (DEC. 18, 1988)—Richard Jackson, twenty-seven, is paralyzed from the waist down and confined to a wheelchair. His paralysis, he says, was caused by a beating he received from guards in a federal prison at Bastrop, Texas, in 1985. His wheelchair is now a prison within a prison.

Last Father's Day, he rolled himself to the visiting room here for a reunion with his father. The visiting room guard told him he would have to be taken from his wheelchair for a strip and rectal search before his visit.

Jackson, who wears a catheter because he can't control his bladder, refused because the guards had only a toilet seat on which to place him after removing him from the wheelchair.

He asked to be taken to a nearby infirmary and searched under proper conditions. The visiting room guard wrote an "incident report" against him for disobeying an order, told his dad to leave, and rolled Richard to Isolation in his wheelchair.

To no avail, he tried to explain that it was painful to be stripped, lifted, and moved about by untrained staff.

Jackson spent the night in Isolation, sitting in his wheelchair because there was no way for him to get from the chair to the bunk. Cells in Isolation are not equipped for the handicapped.

He was released from Isolation the next day, and the incident report eventually was torn up. But his once-cherished visiting hours with his father have evolved into total misery for both of them.

He received no further visits until late October. After much wrangling with officials from the warden on down, a procedure was worked out whereby he could be strip-searched in the hospital prior to each visit. But he then encountered a worse problem.

The guard insisted that he don a pair of zip-up visiting coveralls. Richard asked if he could cut a hole in the leg of the coveralls for his catheter and was told he could not. He had to leave himself exposed through the fly of the coveralls in order to hook up to his catheter. The officer allowed him to place a folded bath towel over his lap to cover himself.

During his visit, two children of convicts walked by and looked under the towel. They went to their fathers and told them that Richard had exposed himself to them.

When he returned from the visit that evening, he was confronted by two angry convicts, who told him in no uncertain terms that it had better not happen again. He called his father in Phoenix and told him not to come back.

"I hate the thought of not getting a visit during the years I have left," he says, "but I don't know what else to do. Visits with my father are important to me but not important enough to get killed over."

---

The new visiting rules at Phoenix were a target of opportunity, but Dannie wove into the story practices that he'd been discussing with me for years. It had always irritated him that federal prisons effectively eliminate most visits for longtime outlaws. That's because new friends are not allowed on the visiting list and old friends doubtless have records themselves. The combination of policies seems to eliminate all "friend" visits for an old-timer like Dannie.

Because many convicts had run afoul of the new visiting rules at Phoenix, there was widespread gratitude for his story. Some prisoners came up to him to relate their own experiences butting heads with guards over the new rules. One, for instance, told Dannie that his visiting wife had to go to town to change from a skirt to jeans, returning with only enough time for a twenty-minute visit.

Although Dannie never got direct word from the authorities about his article, he apparently experienced their reaction. For his many media visits, he had always been allowed to wear the pressed, open-necked khaki shirt and khaki or denim pants that prisoners wore around the yard. After "Dressing for Success" appeared, a guard informed Dannie that "word has come down" that he was now required to meet the media (and their cameras) in a brilliant orange jumpsuit with a zipper up the back.

We will probably never know for certain who ordered the change, but the effect was to humiliate the convict in his press interviews.

■

Dannie's next piece was the first of a number of moving portraits he wrote during his Phoenix years that illuminated, through cameo biographies, the operation of the penal system.

## THE STRANGE SAGA OF OKIE BOB

PHOENIX, ARIZ. (JAN. 15, 1989)—Robert D. Thomas couldn't explain to me how he wound up doing life in a federal prison for murder.

"You're the first one who ever asked me to explain it," he said. "I could explain what happened, but I'm not even sure how or why it happened."

I've always called him Okie Bob. He grew up in my neck of the woods around the San Joaquin Valley of central California. At fifty-two, he's three years older than I. In our early years, we spent time in many of the same reform schools and prisons.

He was a rowdy and tough little guy. But I remember him having a sense of fairness even when he was fighting.

In 1970, he dropped out of sight, and I never thought much about him. Many convicts straighten out their lives and don't come back to prison. When I arrived here in Phoenix six months ago, I was surprised to learn that Okie Bob has been in federal prison since 1972, doing time for murder.

He and I work together every morning raking rocks. In a lucid manner, with a date-perfect memory, he tells me what happened. But as the story unfolds, I can't escape the feeling that this is the Okie Bob I knew telling me about someone else he knew. Or someone he didn't quite know.

He was born on February 3, 1936, in Los Banos, about 120 miles southeast of San Francisco. His family were migrant farm workers, and he has four brothers and three sisters. The family was stable except for its peripatetic existence. None of his siblings or his teetotaling parents ever had trouble with the law. Although his parents were semiliterate, they were, in his words, "good, hardworking people."

Bob had a terrible time in school. Following the crops as he did, there was never time to form lasting friendships on the schoolyard. He felt alienated and finally quit attending school. The third grade was the last he completed.

"I guess I felt about school like one of those nomads that ride camels in the desert," he says.

In November 1950, at the age of fourteen, he was picked up for truancy and sent to reform school at the Preston School of Industry, near Ione, California.

The California Youth Authority sent people there up to the age of twenty-five. The bulk of the population was from San Francisco or Los Angeles. Gangs and cliques from those urban areas pretty much ran the place.

Bob says he learned early that an "Okie" with very few homeboys had to fight every day to keep from being classified as a "punk" and taken advantage of. So, although he was only five feet five and 140 pounds, he fought, and he soon earned grudging respect from his fellow convicts. But then he had to keep on fighting to keep that respect. It was a vicious circle.

He was released in March 1952. Three months later, he was returned to Preston for chronic truancy and made his way from there to Lancaster Reform School near Bakersfield. Then he was transferred to Deuel Vocational Institution at Tracy.

Deuel was a state prison that held young offenders as well as adults. Upon his release from there in May 1954, at the age of eighteen, Bob says, he had spent a year and a half in prison and two years in reform school and had never been charged with a crime.

"I never learned anything in school, but in prison I learned to use drugs and fight like a maniac," he says.

One month after his release from Deuel, Bob was sentenced to San Quentin for joyriding in a stolen car. Released in May 1956, he stayed out until October of that year, when he was charged with receiving stolen property—a bottle of wine and a carton of cigarettes. He was returned to San Quentin.

Three months after his release in September 1959, he was convicted of attempting to rob a gas station in Fresno. The station had only $35. Bob had a gun, but he says it was inoperable. He was caught in the act and sentenced to San Quentin in December 1959. Other than a brief period when he escaped in 1970, those three months in 1959 were his last stint in the free world.

Back at San Quentin, he continued fighting. As a result, he stayed in Isolation more than the average prisoner. In February 1961, the prison psychiatrist, a Dr. Schmidt, referred him to the medical facility at Vacaville for psychiatric observation.

Psychologists at Vacaville diagnosed him as having a "psychopathic personality" and prescribed group therapy. He refused the group therapy.

"Hell, I didn't think I needed it," he says. "I thought I was supposed to fight now and then in prison. That's what I learned in reform school, and I never used weapons, so I thought I was okay."

But as we stand there in the Phoenix sun, leaning on our rakes while rooting about in the rubble of his past, we both agree with clear hindsight that his refusal to attend group therapy was a terrible mistake. His refusal apparently condemned him to a netherworld of pain and madness.

Bob says the doctors at Vacaville altered his diagnosis to paranoid schizophrenia, deemed him "nonresponsive" to psychiatric treatment, and prescribed electric shock treatments until further notice.

His housing was changed to S Unit, a maximum-security psychiatric unit.

Electroshock treatments in those days were very common and indiscriminately administered. "Three times a week, five big inmate technicians came for me and dragged me to the shock room," he says. "I fought them every step of the way."

Inside the shock room, they forced him onto a table and held him down while a doctor attached metal plates to each side of his head. The doctor then pressed a button, and Bob felt a sharp, searing pain in his head and blacked out.

"I always woke up back in my cell feeling confused and disoriented," he said. "Sometimes there would be blood running out of my ears and my nose."

After twenty shock treatments, the hard way, everyone was mad at Okie Bob, including the inmate technicians who had to fight him three times a week. Another committee of doctors met, and again he was judged "nonresponsive," Bob says. He was then moved upstairs to section S-3, "the Glass House."

His cell was made of safety glass, and he was under direct observation twenty-four hours a day. No exercise periods. Showers and shock treatments were the only events he attended outside his cell. It was in the Glass House, he says, that he was introduced to Anectine.

"One day the inmate technicians came with a doctor," he recalls. "They held me down while the doctor administered an intravenous dose of Anectine. It was terrifying.

"All my muscles relaxed, and my lungs slowed until I could barely breathe. I felt my heart slow down until it almost stopped beating. All the while, the doctor was talking to me, saying things like 'I gave you this because you are violent. When you come around, you will remember to be careful and calm from now on.'

"I'd prefer ten shock treatments to one of those," he tells me.

Anectine is a derivative of curare, a deadly poison and muscle relaxant commonly used by natives in rain forests to make poison tips for their arrows.

During this period, Bob was also receiving Prolixin four times daily. Prolixin, a psychotropic drug, is like a chemical straitjacket. It is an extremely potent drug that these days is administered biweekly to violent prisoners. But in those experimental days, Bob says, multiple doses were given daily.

From 1961 until 1967, Bob was shuttled back and forth between Folsom Prison, San Quentin, and Vacaville. In all, he figures he received eighty-two shock treatments of 150 volts each. One convict technician told him that after a particularly brutal fight on the way to the shock room, an angry doctor had pressed the button fifty-six times.

"My dad died in '62, but I was totally confused during those years," he says. "From April of 1962, I don't remember anything until September of 1963. Something happened to my sense of hearing too.

"I was walking down a hallway at Vacaville when I heard a convict tell me to get a mop and mop out a shower. I became enraged and beat him severely. Later I found out he had only asked me for a cigarette. I could no longer trust my own ears."

Bob's mother visited in 1962 and was horrified by his condition. On a subsequent visit, in late 1967, she found her son on a bed in full restraints. Pulleys were attached to his neck, arms, and legs so that if he moved suddenly, his head, arms, or legs would jerk violently. He could move only in slow motion.

Bob says prison doctors escorted his mother into a room where they tried to badger her into signing papers authorizing "psychosurgery," a polite term for a prefrontal lobotomy. She says Bob informed her that he was an experimental subject in a study on leprosy and other diseases.

She refused to sign the papers and threatened to drive straight to Sacramento and expose what she viewed as the destruction of her son by prison administrators. She and a few friends began writing letters of complaint to state officials. They also complained that Bob had done close to nine years in prison for a bungled $35 robbery attempt.

Overnight, he says, he was taken off restraints, pumped full of Thorazine, and whisked to Y wing, a maximum-security unit at Soledad State Prison near Salinas. There, he says, he was kept full of Thorazine for more than eighteen months. But all his medicine was taken orally. No more shots or shock treatments.

In May 1970, his mother's letter-writing campaign apparently proved successful. Bob was removed from all medication and sent to a minimum-security camp next to the main prison at Soledad. Looking back, Bob assumes that the purpose of the transfer was to prepare him for his impending release to society.

Four days were all the preparation he received. On May 5, 1970, he scaled a fence at the perimeter of the camp and escaped.

"When that Thorazine wore off, I was crazier than a pet raccoon," he says. "I took one look around me, realized there were no gun towers, and I was gone. I stole a car in Gonzales, California, and headed for Monterey."

In Monterey, he obtained a 9mm pistol and began robbing, as he says, "everything in Monterey, Salinas, and Modesto." The string of robberies lasted ninety days, during which time he was living with a hippie commune in Big Sur and buying drugs for everyone with the money.

The FBI finally tracked him to his residence and kicked in the door. Bob happened to be across the street and saw them go in. He fled to Chicago, where he pulled another robbery and drove a stolen car from there to Detroit.

Just past the Detroit city limits, he ran into a city bus. When the driver tried to detain him, he fired a shot in the air and ran. At a nearby stoplight, he jumped into a car with two men and forced them to drive him to South Bend, Indiana. He rode in the backseat while they sat up front.

"On the way to South Bend, I heard them whispering," he says. "The driver was telling the other man to divert my attention when we reached our destination and he would kill me with a bumper jack. When we reached South Bend, I made them lay down beside the road and shot each of them in the head with a 9mm bullet."

As Bob tells me this, we're both leaning on our rakes, looking at the fence and the still, peaceful desert beyond. A pretty little bird—a cactus wren that Bob and I had provided with water last summer—runs near us and turns over a rock with his beak. He's looking for food just as frantically as I'm looking for words. A palpable silence descends on us until I ask him the only question that needs asking.

"Bob, do you think they were really talking about killing you, or was it more of those auditory hallucinations?"

"I don't know," he replies. "I've often wondered about that myself."

One of the men survived, the other one didn't. Bob was arrested in Juárez, Mexico, on August 3, 1970. He was extradited to California for robbery and escape, and kept under heavy sedation until his indictment in U.S. district court in San Francisco on a kidnap charge, with the understanding that there had been a murder involved in the kidnap. He pleaded guilty in Judge Oliver Carter's court on

November 10, 1972, and was sentenced to life in federal prison, consecutive with his state sentences.

The reports of government-appointed psychiatrists were entered into the files at his sentencing proceedings. All agreed that Bob was insane.

Dr. Bruce C. Johnston, a San Francisco psychiatrist, ended his report:

> In sum, Mr. Thomas is a severely constricted man who easily falls into the psychiatric category of schizophrenia but who further indicates a deficiency in total ego development (impulse control, rational thought, interaction with other humans) more substantial than one finds in most schizophrenics.

But Bob's attorney, an assistant public defender, told the court, "I personally feel that Mr. Thomas is perfectly competent to proceed." He then informed the court that his client wanted to plead guilty and would accept consecutive life sentences if the court saw fit to impose them. The attorney says he was acting on Bob's instructions so that the convict could serve his time in federal custody and avoid state charges that could result in a death sentence.

Bob's state of mind seemed to be expressed in a statement he was allowed to make to the court:

> Right. At the time they have me in a strip cell with two other men. There's no water in there and told me I'm going to stay in there as long as I'm there. If I could ask for a drink of water, it's ten more days. Our toilet in that cell is three inches long by an inch. I haven't had one drink of water since I have been in there. Wouldn't give us any. Said if I asked, it's ten more days. Haven't had a hearing. One of us have to sleep standing up in there while the other two sleep. No room to lay down in there.

Judge Carter had this to say in regard to Bob and his crime: "Now I guess there is the hard way to say it or the tough way to say it, that we have hotel space for people like you to retire from society. That's about as gentle a way as I can put it."

"I am aware of it," Bob responded.

The judge went on: "You are not only your own worst enemy, you are the enemy of all the other people around you. You are an enemy in two ways. It would be my prediction that sooner or later you're going to end up dead or some other people are going to end up dead or both. That would be the most complete end to this sad picture."

Okie Bob went to the federal prison at Marion, Illinois, in November 1975. In 1977, he was a suspect in the murder there of another convict. He spent three years in Isolation, and the charges were dropped.

In July 1980, he was transferred to a prison at Butner, North Carolina, and he came to Phoenix in January 1988. He has never talked to a psychiatrist or mental health worker while in federal prison. He became eligible for parole in 1985, but the parole board refuses to see him, citing "incomplete files."

Bob has educated himself and become a vegetarian and a rabid nonsmoker who has stacks of certificates for winning marathon races in prison. He seems to have full possession of his mind and recalls his past with the clarity of someone with a photographic memory. His sense of humor is good now, and he says the "voices and visions" are long gone.

I've known a lot of madmen in prison, and it isn't easy for me to really look at a man when he is insane. All I can see in his features is a confirmation of my feeling that he is mad. The true persona remains indistinguishable, because there is no common ground between me and that type of person.

Bob doesn't look like that now. To me, he seems like the Okie Bob I knew when we were kids. But all the time we've talked, I've been thinking about the death penalty. Had his crimes happened in the political climate of today—and not when the death penalty was in abeyance because of a Supreme Court ruling—Bob would have been a shoo-in for capital punishment.

I begin to wonder what it is that is put to death. Certainly not this baggage of bones and flesh, because we all have those and they can't be inherently evil.

What we must seek to kill, to destroy, is the murderous personality of a killer. But looking at this man, I think something in his personality has been killed already. Shocked and poisoned to death by electricity and potent chemicals.

What emerges now looks to be a regeneration of the old Okie Bob—not a product of any system but a being who lives on from day to day in spite of the system.

Accompanying that story in "Sunday Punch," I published excerpts from two news stories that had run in the *Chronicle* in previous weeks. Both dealt with juvenile justice, and it was easy to see from those stories that little had changed since Okie Bob's days in the same system. In one news story, a state legislator was quoted as telling a Sacramento hearing, "California has become a national embarrassment by incarcerating more juveniles per capita than any other state and holding them longer than adults convicted of the same crimes."

A juvenile court judge told the same hearing that he was "very concerned" about the effect of overcrowded, violent conditions. "I don't want a kid coming back who is in worse shape than he was when we sent him," he said.

Okie Bob liked Dannie's story, and many members of his family wrote me, seeking some tangible assistance for him. "It gave him some hope," Dannie wrote me, "and really wound him up." But Okie Bob's reaction also saddened Dannie; he knew that the article was unlikely to lead to any real change for his fellow convict.

Among those who came up to Dannie to praise the Okie Bob story were his unit manager and a number of the guards, one of whom had begun getting copies of his articles as they came out and then passing them around to other officers.

Two months later, Dannie was back with another powerful portrait of a fellow prisoner and his struggles with the system.

## HE WENT BACK TO PRISON TO DIE

*PHOENIX, ARIZ. (MARCH 12, 1989)*—Burton Parker came back to prison on Tuesday, February 21. He didn't return here because of a crime he had committed. He came back to die.

At sixty, Parker is ravaged by a terminal cancer. He was given a medical parole last November so that he could die with his wife and her family in Albuquerque.

According to Parker, it didn't take long to discover that dying in prison is much more convenient than trying to expire with any dignity in the "Free World."

"I couldn't get help anywhere at all," he says. "SSI, Medicare, welfare, the parole board—you name it, I tried it."

His treatment was costing hundreds of dollars a month. His wife, a hard-working woman, clears less than $1,200 a month—barely enough to cover rent and other living expenses.

Soon after Parker's release in November, it became obvious that his illness would drive them both to the poorhouse before he reached the grave. But for her, the debts wouldn't end at the cemetery.

By dying in freedom, Parker was building a prison of debt for the woman he loves. He wasn't willing to do that.

From November until February, they used up their meager savings and were more than $2,000 in debt.

"Medicare and welfare told me my wife made too much money for them to help me," he says.

The situation became so intolerable to him that he decided to return to prison. But doing that wasn't as easy as he thought it would be. His parole officer in Albuquerque, David Hoffman, wouldn't go along with the idea.

"He'd tried to help me every way he could," Parker says. "He even called the parole commission, trying to get them to help. But he just wasn't willing to send me back to prison."

Still, Parker was convinced that coming back was the only way left to him. His wife, he says, became hostile at the mere mention of the idea, so he didn't consult her about it again. But as the cancer ravaged him physically, the financial burden continued its own inexorable progress.

Finally, Parker took his last $10 and bought a bus ticket to Flagstaff, Arizona. When he arrived, he called the U.S. marshal's office and told them: "I'm on parole, and I've violated my parole by leaving my district. I want you to come down here and arrest me."

They came to the bus station but wouldn't arrest him because there wasn't a warrant outstanding. The marshals asked him if he would accompany them downtown, where they placed a call to his parole officer in Albuquerque.

Hoffman asked the marshals to put Parker on a bus and send him back home. When he refused to go back, they placed a call to a U.S. parole commissioner in Dallas. The commissioner issued a parole violator warrant for Parker's arrest. His next stop was the prison here at Phoenix. (He was moved on last week to the prison hospital at Springfield, Missouri.)

I visited him here several weeks ago. He seemed his old self and was lucid and direct. The only change in his outward appearance was the dark circles etched beneath his eyes by the debilitating pain of lung cancer.

He was sitting on a hospital bed watching a small television on a bedside table. A toilet, shower, washbasin, and small metal locker completed the furnishings in the room.

He turned the sound off on the TV in deference to my bad hearing and talked awhile about his past. It seemed to be a more comfortable subject than his future.

Parker was born in San Francisco on March 18, 1929, the year of the stock market crash. Growing up in those depressed times taught him the value of a dollar, he says, but he never learned to be a good citizen.

As a young teenager, he was arrested in Dallas for car theft. From that humble beginning, he went on to commit more serious crimes; he has spent thirty-six of his sixty years in various jails and prisons.

The years in prison were mainly for writing bad checks and what convicts call "businessman crime." The bank-robbery conviction in 1984 was his first venture into what we cons think of as heavy crime.

While in prison, he completed two years of college and earned an Associate of Arts degree in business administration. His jobs in prison have always been as a clerk for various department heads. He has such a reputation as an excellent clerk that when he enters a prison, administrators seek him out to ask if he will work for them.

He says he had two sons by his first wife, who is deceased. The kids are grown now, with families of their own, and he has had no contact with them in recent years. He met his current wife in 1980, after his release from the New Mexico State Prison. They've been together ever since.

"She's a good woman," he says. "She didn't want me to die in prison, but I'll be damned if I'll leave her with years of debt."

I had only a nodding acquaintance with Parker before he returned here, but I know the type of man he is well enough to ask him the foremost question on my mind.

"Why didn't you just rob a bank, Burt? I don't see what you had

to lose. If you got away, you had money, and if you didn't . . . ?"
He's looking at the silent, flickering TV screen as I speak, and taking
a last drag from a Camel. He stubs out the cigarette in an ashtray
and peers up at me out of blue eyes as clear as a child's.

"I'm tired, Red," he says, with a note of finality in his voice. "I'm
tired of all that crime."

I ask him how long he's been smoking, and he tells me "forever."
He figured the cigarettes finally did him in.

Last April, he began hacking and coughing while pain throbbed
in his chest. He made an appointment here at the infirmary for a
chest X-ray. The technician reading the X-rays found a tiny white
spot on one of Parker's lungs.

He was made to understand the ramifications of that little spot,
but prison bureaucracy works slowly, and it took seven months for
the paperwork to come through clearing him for a trip to the Bureau
of Prisons hospital at Rochester, Minnesota.

By the time he arrived there last September, he says, the spot on
his lung was as big as a baseball. The doctors there diagnosed it as
a large-cell squamus carcinoma. It was in both lungs by then and
spreading throughout his chest.

They deemed it to be terminal and inoperable. Six months was
their outside guess for his future.

At that time, he had only a year to go for a mandatory release on
his ten-year sentence. After another sixty days of paperwork and one
initial rejection, the parole commission agreed to a medical parole.

Parker is pretty well resigned to his fate. Near the end of our short
visit, he said to me, "I've spent most of my life in prisons, so it's no
big deal to die in one. I've lived long enough anyway."

He turns back toward the TV as if he's growing tired of our conversation. A staff member approaches the cell to tell me I have to
leave. At the door, I turn back to watch him lighting another Camel
as the TV showers his balding dome with a greenish glow in the
dim light of the cell.

"I'll see you later, Burt," I tell him as I depart.

"Okay, Red," he replies. "Hey! Send me a spy book."

"I'll do it," I tell him.

It's difficult to describe what Burton Parker and the way of his
death means to convicts like me.

He's from what we call the "old school." In prisons years ago, we learned to keep our mouth shut, pay our debts, keep our word, and never inform on anyone or hurt friends and family.

Convicts from the old school respect themselves and those around them. But there aren't many of our school left now, and as the alumni die off, they are like dinosaurs who can't be replaced. Parker lived by his code, and he's dying by it. There's no way this old con would sock his wife with his cost of dying.

Two of Parker's old friends here have offered to put up $1,000 each to retire his wife's debt. There's also a plan to take up a collection among the general prison population, but we don't know whether the rules allow it.

I sent him the spy book, but I won't be able to see him again.

All my phone calls here are monitored by the authorities. On Saturday, February 26, I talked about Parker with the editor of "Sunday Punch." When I went to see the dying convict again the following Monday, his section of the hospital was locked up tighter than a drum.

I was told by a hospital staff member that I wasn't to be allowed to interview Parker again.

But if he doesn't live long enough to read the story, he will know for sure I wrote it. I gave him my word that I would.

---

With that story, Dannie and I tried something new. We needed a broader perspective—from outside the joint—so we decided that I should interview Burton Parker's wife. Her story ran as a sidebar to Burton's.

---

# A TOUGH THREE MONTHS ON THE OUTSIDE

SAN FRANCISCO, CALIF. (MARCH 12, 1989)—Day after day, her husband sat heavily medicated in front of the television, with "nothing to do, nothing to plan for—just sit and wait to die."

"He'd been asking a lot about the financial situation," said Burton

Parker's wife. "He's no mathematician, but he knew the bills were mounting and I couldn't handle it. . . . It was eating him alive."

Parker's wife, who asked not to be identified further, was describing in a telephone interview the tense three months she spent with her dying husband before he did "the only thing he could do to get back in [prison] without committing a crime."

Like so much that happened with Parker during that stay, his wife has ambivalent feelings about his return to prison, which she did not oppose when she found out about it later. "In some respects, it's something of a relief to know he's back safe and sound and getting medical care I can't give him," she said. "But I miss him, and I wish he was here."

In addition to the financial problems caused by his expensive medication, she said, Parker was "bored to tears," and he was housebound by his cancer, his severe arthritis, and his physical inability to drive. She says her husband was also perhaps unable to "handle things outside—he was institutionalized" after his many years in prison. She is unable to say how much each factor contributed to his decision to return to prison.

At the time he left home to return to prison, they were down to the last $10 in the bank account until her next paycheck arrived.

Parker's wife said his medications were costing $400 to $600 a month. "I just don't make that kind of money," she said.

She said her husband was not eligible for Medicare or Medicaid. "We couldn't get any state or federal help of any kind." Parker had never worked long enough to qualify for Social Security, and his wife's salary—however inadequate for his medical needs—was too high to allow them to qualify for financial assistance.

"You talk about Catch 22," she added. "This is it."

The couple had started to talk about divorce so that he could get the kind of medical assistance he needed without her salary being considered.

And down the road, she said, was the specter of his increasing dependence. Soon, she said, "he'll need someone with him all the time, and it was troubling him."

Parker's wife said she was prepared "to quit work, go on welfare, and go bankrupt" in order to care for him, but she hadn't yet discussed that with her husband, who "likes to think he's independent" and definitely did not want to be dependent "on a woman, of all things."

Although Parker had talked with her about the possibility of returning to prison, she was unprepared when she got home on February 15, her birthday, to find her husband gone. She was angry. Her children were coming over for a birthday celebration, she said, "and what have I got to show them but an empty house." Later, she felt a mixture of emotions—relieved, yes, "but it hurts like hell."

She was not allowed to talk to her husband for three days after he turned himself in, and when they finally talked on the phone, they did not discuss his reasons for returning. "There was no need," she said.

The ambivalence remains. She believes that he made "a very noble gesture in going back," but she adds in the next breath: "In a way, he really did go home."

---

After Dannie's story appeared, security was increased at the prison hospital, and Dannie was never able to see Burton Parker again.

He tried unsuccessfully to keep up with the story inside the prison. "The warden let me know he doesn't want me quoting him about Burt Parker," he wrote me. "I guess his superiors would get mad if they knew he was talking with me." But there was a silver lining: "I am getting a bit more respect nowadays from officials. I believe they have realized I'm not out to 'get them.' "

Word did get back to the *Chronicle,* however, that Burton Parker subsequently had a change of heart and was willing to rejoin his wife for his final months. Mrs. Parker told a *Chronicle* reporter that her husband "decided he had made a terrible, terrible mistake. He really wanted to be home, but he didn't know what to do about it. He was very upset. He felt very bad about having left."

In May 1989, Burton Parker went before the U.S. Parole Commission, which was delighted to overlook his technical violation and re-release him. The only catch was that the Parkers had to divorce in order for him to qualify for public assistance as an indigent, single man. "Don't worry," he reportedly told his wife. "It's only a piece of paper."

Meanwhile, Dannie's readers kept up their dialogue with the prisoner. They were curious about his life. They asked questions, and when enough people asked the same questions, Dannie took up the challenge.

---

# A DAY IN THE LIFE OF A PRISONER

PHOENIX, ARIZ. (APRIL 9, 1989)—"What's it like in there?" I've been asked repeatedly. "What do you do in there?" "What's it look like?" "How do the days go by?"

Might as well ask me to describe the color and shape of boredom, or the sound and fury of ennui. Time in here is as inexorable as it is in the desert that surrounds us.

This is no granite-rock dungeon—public sensibilities would be offended by a Bastille in the high desert. The architecture, for lack of a better name, is néo–Motel Modern. The Bureau of Prisons' version of a dude ranch minus the females, the cowboys, and the happy trails to explore.

Indeed, our trails are a maze of concrete walkways that run to and fro among our units, the mess hall, and the many shops required for prison maintenance.

The most traveled walkway leads to UNICOR, Federal Prison Industries, where each of us criminals, if we so desire, can spend eight to sixteen hours a day as an employee in a government factory. The pay isn't bad for a prison—tops is $1.10 per hour—and the jobs afford some chance for economic stability upon release.

The trails I prefer lead to the mess hall and the recreation yard. Unfortunately, the rules say all convicts must work, and that includes me, an aspiring, middle-aged writer. So I've found myself a job close to home as an outside unit orderly, tending the local patch of dirt. My paycheck is $5 a month.

We live in modules—or units—a new look in cellblocks. Each houses about 130 convicts. This prison was constructed a few years ago to hold some five hundred men in single cells. Now there's over a thousand of us here, and the cells are doubled up.

We refer to our cell partners as "cellies." My cellie and I live on the second tier of a two-tier module. Below us, on the first floor, is a dayroom that contains a pool table, four card tables, a Coke machine, and some easy chairs. The unit guard has a small office near the outside door of the dayroom.

Our cell is about six feet by twelve feet, with a wooden double bunk at the rear, next to a large window that looks out onto the compound. The window has four thick vertical bars that frame and section our view of cactus and dirt.

The solid door at the front of the cell is metal with a three-inch-wide, eighteen-inch-high window made of some type of Plexiglas. The door is blue, the walls are off-white cinder block, and the window bars are chocolate brown. The floor is sparrow-egg tile over cement. The ultimate in neo–Motel Modern.

Two large fiberboard lockers, one with a writing desk attached, and a sink, toilet, and mirror complete the furnishings. My pinups of beautiful wahines in the sunshine and lush South Sea islands adorn the sides of one locker and the writing desk.

My cellie is a bank robber who received seven years for two bank robberies in the Los Angeles area. Like me, he's a former drug addict. I received thirty-three years for two bank robberies in the Washington State area. That gives us plenty to talk about.

We argue a lot about the elusive nature of criminal justice. But we both agree that Washington State federal judges take a much dimmer view of bank robbers than do Los Angeles judges.

My cellie gets up this morning and goes to breakfast at 6:30. I never go to breakfast. Nine years of identical breakfast menus have destroyed my morning appetite. I awaken when he returns.

I wake to the music of water gurgling in a cheap gooseneck drain and the sound of his toothbrush going *shuka shuka shook shook shuka.* The toothbrush sounds compete with gunfire echoing off hills nearby. The guards have a firing range right outside the prison.

At 7:30, my cellie leaves in response to a blaring loudspeaker: "Work call! Work call! All inmates to your job assignments! Work call!" I'm up and dressing as cons tramp off to work. Doors slam, feet stomp, and cons yell at one another.

Summer is here early, and it's nice outside. The front of our unit is landscaped in dirt, cactus, and a few pathetic petunias that struggle for life in the shade of the building.

My job is raking out of the dirt the footprints that were left by night security patrols and convicts going off to work. I also water and care for the sparse foliage.

I spend close to an hour and a half raking the dirt around the unit. As I work, a warm wind blows. The guard is inside, and it's peaceful and quiet except for the gunfire. I enjoy the solitude.

As I rake near the double fences and rolled razor wire, I think of my junkyard. My goal in life is to own a junkyard. No cars and grease, just a *Sanford and Son*–type of place with old and used things. I spend a lot of time designing it in my mind.

At nine o'clock, a ten-minute movement period is announced on the speaker. These are held hourly for movement from the yard and other places. Anyone leaving the unit—except for meals—must get a pass signed by the officer, and it must be signed again before it is returned to the issuing guard.

I'm finished raking—there are only so many footprints out there—so I ask the guard for a pass to the yard. "I've run out of passes," he tells me.

This happens often, and until he gets more, no one can go anywhere. Another bureaucratic foul-up that we learn to live with in here. Still, it makes me grind my teeth and take a few deep breaths.

Back inside, three cons are seated at a table in the dayroom. I join them for some talk. The guard now has a heavy rubber mallet in his hand, and he's going from cell to cell beating on the bars. The bars make a different sound if they've been sawed.

The table talk is about Ted Bundy's recent execution in Florida. It's one-sided talk. Everyone despises the guy—mainly because we convicts are further tainted in the public eye by his monstrous deeds.

No profound insights here. There's much more brawn than brain at our table—mainly weight lifters stranded by the pass drought. The guard walks by with his hammer in his hand, eyeing us to see if anyone is smoking. Smoking isn't allowed in the dayroom.

Guards are always close by, but they seldom join our conversation.

When the subject of Bundy is safely disposed of, I make my way back to the cell to do some writing. But the banging on the bars distracts me. So I make a cup of coffee and sit for a while designing my junkyard. At eleven o'clock, I hear the speaker calling the prisoners in the shops to lunch. Our unit eats last, so we won't go until about noon.

Some twenty cons are gathered in the dayroom now, waiting for lunch. The talk is of two recent stabbings here and other assorted mayhem. Boredom seems to breed talk of violence. Our dialogues continually drift toward violent acts and monstrous deeds. So much so that the talk becomes a form of monotony in itself.

Many convicts become steeped in that way of thinking and completely lose their sense of humor. When they attempt to smile, their mouths are as rigid as the coin return on a Coke machine. Many guards suffer from that syndrome, too. It's a sure symptom of the cage beginning to swallow its prey.

After an interminable wait, lunch is announced for our unit. We tramp down a sidewalk toward a mess hall done up in pastel colors. The outside walls are glass, and it looks like a deformed hamburger stand.

Off to the left is a sidewalk leading to the recreation yard a half mile away. Other sidewalks run to the isolation unit, visiting room and education buildings, laundry and maintenance shops. A few bushes and forlorn cacti "decorate" the bare dirt between the walkways. No one is allowed to walk in those expanses. It seems a terrible waste of space in a crowded prison.

The mess hall, built for half the population we have now, is crowded and noisy, with spoons hitting plates and people yelling and talking in several languages. Lunch is pretty good today. A recent one-meal food strike has helped a lot.

Various bigwigs, including the warden, stand against the walls and watch us eat. Convicts pushing carts of dirty trays and others bringing clean silverware yell to each other, "Get out of the way!"

As we progress down the serving line, a young man in front of me decides he wants just spinach. A server piles his plate with spinach until water runs over the edge onto his plastic food tray. A woman guard stands at the end of the line, protecting the desserts. She looks at his tray as he passes and says, "Hello, Popeye."

We sit four to a cramped table. A few loudmouths bellow across the room, their voices bullying out over all the regular noise. Miss Manners would be appalled at this culinary anarchy.

The idea is to eat fast and get out. As I leave the dining room, a guard I call Robocop beckons me over for a shakedown. Lying around his feet are extra oranges and napkin-wrapped sandwiches that he has confiscated from convicts. As he digs his fingers up in my crotch, I ask in a loud voice: "Hey, if these shakedowns are random, why do I get one every day?"

He doesn't reply, just goes on patting and squeezing.

Back at my unit, there are passes to be had now. I head out to the handball court in the recreation yard. Halfway there, I meet one of the people I call derelict personalities. "DPs"—in my personal shorthand—are people who have been defeated by the cage or life itself. They don't fit anywhere and are just barely able to mimic those of us who believe we do fit. I collect them, but not in a snobbish way. More like a ship collects barnacles.

This one is on psychotropic drugs and shuffles along slowly. He's a nice fellow with a warm smile. He bums a cigarette, and as I light it for him, a female guard walks by us wearing a pair of tight uniform pants.

I turn facing his direction as we both watch her hip movement. I'm a bit ashamed of this blatant display of male chauvinism, but her hips have the same visual effect on us as would an unidentified flying object.

Off to my right, I notice a large saguaro cactus with one limb raised skyward. It reminds me of an eternally stranded hitchhiker. An appropriate backdrop for a derelict personality and a sex-starved convict—descriptions that would fit many of my fellow prisoners.

It's a workday, and there are only a few people on the recreation yard. Most of them are lifting weights, while a few run the track, shoot baskets, or play handball. I'm addicted to handball, and an older man invites me to play a few games.

My old friend Leroy comes along. Leroy is an elderly longtime convict who steered me toward writing many years ago in another prison. We sit on the grass in the warm sun talking writing, parole dates, women, and freedom. The last three are common topics in here.

At 3:45 P.M., the loudspeaker blares out. "Recall! Recall! All inmates return to your living quarters! Recall!"

As we walk back to our units, guards stand alongside the sidewalks watching us. Squarks and snarls blare from their two-way radios. They remind me of vigilant sheepherders.

At 4:00 P.M. each day, we are locked in for a standing count. We must remain on our feet until two counting guards go by. This is to prevent the dummy-in-the-bed trick.

Mail call is immediately after count, and we gather around the pool table as the officer calls names.

Then we settle down to wait an hour or so until our unit is called for supper. We spend a lot of time in here waiting for doors to open.

After supper, I head to the yard for my evening phone call. There's a world-class sunset above me. Heavy pearl-gray clouds hang low over a still desert. Their flat bottoms are suffused with a deep cherry-purple glow. All are connected by shards of soft yellow sun rays. The hills and cacti glow a deep purple, waiting in illicit reverence.

At the phone room in the yard, I turn in a slip to reserve a phone call the following day. We are allowed one collect call of fifteen minutes each evening. Appointments are made a day in advance. When my turn comes, I make my call from one of fifteen phones on the wall in a small room. Beside me, fourteen other convicts babble in English, Chinese, Farsi, and Spanish. It's no place for sweet nothings, but a phone call is an important link to the free world.

Back in my unit, I shower in one of two showers on my tier and wander down to the dayroom to relax awhile. It's 9:15 now, and lockup is at 10:30. A newly arrived convict takes the chair beside me and asks for a cigarette. I hand him one. He lights it, leans back, and lets out a sigh that sounds like a truck tire going flat.

Oh no, I think to myself, here it comes!

Sure enough, he begins talking. The courts trampled on his rights. His lawyer sold him out. His wife is doing him wrong. The parole board is corrupt. On and on he goes for a half hour and never mentions any crime he committed.

I rise in the middle of his monologue—it's one I've heard thousands of times in places like this—and say: "Well, buddy, I'm tired and I'm going to bed."

Tomorrow, I'll get up and do the same thing all over again.

---

Dannie and I had nearly finished editing that story and planned to talk again in a day, but the call never came. I got the sinking feeling I always got when something unpredictable happened on the other end of our tenuous line of communication.

Faced with a deadline, I wrote around the remaining few minor questions and scheduled the story for publication. But before it ran, Jeff Leon managed to get in touch with his client, and a letter arrived a few days later for me with the same message:

Well, they have once again locked up your prison correspondent. I haven't the foggiest notion of what the hell is going on. After some loud yelling on my part, my writing materials were returned to me. But I'm still in Isolation. . . .

I tell you—this deal worries me because they surely wouldn't have the nerve to just lock me up for the drill. So they must be devising some kind of charge that they think will stick. The fact they haven't asked me if I did or didn't do something tells me that they plan to just lay some violation or other in my lap. They don't *want* any feedback from me.

I've been as careful as possible not to infringe on any rules, so it will be interesting to see what they come up with. . . .

I'm pretty sure that under their rules they can hold me up to six months in seg on a "pending investigation" charge. So maybe they've just decided to do that in order to keep down my contact with the outside world. . . .

In mid-letter, Dannie was called up for an FBI interrogation about gambling at the prison. Like most prisoners, he had periodically bet a pack of cigarettes on a football game—although that's something he would never tell a prison official—but he had done no wagering, he assured me, on any scale that would interest the FBI.

Although a gambling investigation may not have been the real reason for the detention—rumors of other charges swirled through the special lockup—it helped Dannie to have a concrete reason beyond the official "pending investigation."

"I feel better knowing what the game is," he wrote. "Not much I can do, but at least I know."

Once again, I and other allies were compelled to rush to the convict's defense; it was becoming a well-practiced drill. And once again, despite his intentions, the story Dannie had to tell was his own.

---

# WAS IT A CASE OF CRUEL AND UNUSUAL CHECKERS?

*PHOENIX, ARIZ. (APRIL 30, 1989)*—"Would you mind telling me what this is all about?" I asked, as we waited for a guard to open the door from the inside of the detention unit.

"I feel like putting you in the hole," said the lieutenant.

"Do you have any special reason for feeling like that?" I asked.

"I need to lock you up," he said.

Before the summons came, I had been working on an article for "Sunday Punch." At around nine o'clock Tuesday morning, an officer arrived at my cell. He told me to go to the lieutenant's office immediately. I walked over there with some apprehension, because a summons to the lieutenant's office is never good news.

When I arrived, the lieutenant stood there with a pair of handcuffs in his hand.

"Turn around, Martin, and put your hands behind your back," he said.

I obeyed, and he placed the cuffs on my wrists, then grabbed hold of them with a firm grip.

"Let's go."

When the door to the hole opened, the lieutenant left and a guard ushered me into a room and told me to strip. When I was naked, he looked into all my body cavities and handed me a pair of red coveralls. He cuffed my hands behind my back again and led me up a flight of stairs and down a corridor with cells on both sides.

We stopped in front of Cell B-14. The light was off inside the cell, and the guard flipped the outside light switch as he opened the large metal door for me to enter.

A convict was sleeping on a top bunk over against the back wall of the cell. The guard slammed and locked the door behind me.

"Bend down and stick your hands out!" he yelled through the door.

There's a food-tray slot on the door about knee high. It's locked from the outside. The guard opened it as I stooped down backward and shoved my hands out. After what seemed an interminable amount of fumbling, he got my cuffs off and slammed the opening shut. I'd recommend that procedure to anyone who enjoys pain.

The guard switched the light off as he left, and the cell once again became dark as a cave while I fumbled my way to the lower bunk.

"How you doing, Red Hog?" the man on the top bunk said as I lay down.

"Fair to middlin'," I replied.

He went back to sleep as I lay there in the darkness trying to figure out what I had been locked up for. I was lying on a thin plastic-covered mattress with no pillow. The bed was hard. The springs were a steel mesh screen spot-welded to the metal frame of the bunk.

I'd been there an hour or so when an arm drooped off the top bunk, and a pillow hung down by my head.

"Need one of these?" a voice asked me out of the gloom, and I realized the voice was that of a youngster I know as "the kid," who has been in the hole for five months.

I put the pillow under my head and asked him to get the light turned back on. After a few minutes, a guard walked by and the kid yelled, "Hit that light!" A fluorescent light in the ceiling came on and illuminated my surroundings.

I made my bed with the two sheets and blanket the guard had thrown in when I arrived. I began to survey my surroundings. It didn't take long.

I always look first at the graffiti on the walls. This cell of cinder block and concrete is the largest I've ever seen for a detention cell.

There are very few graffiti here for an isolation cell. A swastika with the two lightning slashes of the SS is drawn on the wall. It hangs just above a small metal stool and table hooked to the wall at the end of the double bed.

There's been a swastika on the wall of every isolation cell I've ever been in, and I've spent time in more of them than the average convict. I've never been able to understand a prisoner's lingering fascination with Hitler's Germany. There aren't that many Nazis in prison. Maybe one convict out of three hundred.

But as I look at this macabre symbol hanging suspended in time on the wall, I have an insight into the puzzle. Perhaps all these swastikas don't represent a convict's political beliefs as much as they are put up to remind us of the ways of our keepers. This one certainly reminds me of someone.

Scratched into the paint on the cell door are mementos of past occupants. "Weasel," one reads. Another proclaims: "Hell fire! J.D. was here!" On another wall is written: "What about Steve." No question mark.

There's a large window with four vertical bars next to the top bunk. But the view is totally obscured by heavy wire mesh screens and a strip of canvas just beyond them.

About the time I'm adjusting to my new environment, the food slot opens and two trays are inserted into the cell along with two Styrofoam cups of Kool-Aid. The kid and I each take one. Lunch is a roast beef sandwich and a scoop of turkey dressing. The dressing is on a little microwave tray covered by a plastic wrap sitting on the food tray. Our food is precooked and reheated by microwave over here in segregation. Just as we finish and slide the trays back out, the guard wants to know if we want a shower. We kneel down again as he cuffs us. He opens the door and we walk down the hallway to a single stall shower with a barred door across the front. Inside the shower, he uncuffs us through the bars.

After the shower, he cuffs us again. Back to the cell, kneel down, uncuff. I'm really starting to get the feel of the place.

Sometime during the afternoon, they cuff us again and march us downstairs to a small recreation yard. It's fenced into small sections, and they put us four to a section.

Back in the cell, the kid and I are trying to figure out what I'm in here for. He was put in here for insolence toward a staff member. After three months, they offered to release him back to general population. He refused. There are only three years left on his five-year sentence, and he's decided to do the rest of it here in the hole.

"I can be insolent over here anytime I feel like it," he says. "What else can they do?"

I have a hard time sleeping the first night, and early in the morning the food slot pops open and two trays appear. The microwave tray contains three pieces of burnt French toast and a big slice of turkey salami. The smell of the turkey salami has been cooked into the French toast by the microwave oven. After one bite, I decide to wait for lunch.

After the nonbreakfast, I tell the kid we'll do some push-ups. We'll do 150 today and add fifty each day until we get up to a thousand. He accepts the challenge, and we do six sets of twenty-five each. I'm silently hoping I didn't let my mouth get the better of me. He does push-ups a lot easier than I do.

Sometime Wednesday afternoon, my writing materials are returned to me, as guaranteed under a federal court order. As I sit down to do some writing, a guard appears outside the cell holding a pair of handcuffs and says I'm wanted downstairs.

When I walk into the lieutenant's office, I find him standing there with a well-built black man who wears Levi's and running shoes. He has the look of an athlete, but as I sit in the chair he's pointing at, he shows me a gold badge and his FBI identification.

He reads me my rights and says: "Martin, I'm investigating gambling here at the prison, and I need to ask you a few questions."

"Our conversation is over with," I reply, as I stand up to leave.

The lieutenant escorts me out, and as we wait for a guard to come get me, I ask him: "Am I locked up pending his investigation or yours?"

"A combination of both," he replies.

"These 'combination investigations' could stretch out for months or even years," I comment.

"That's right," he responds cheerfully.

I'm outwardly calm, but my heart is pounding in my chest—the FBI always gets its man.

I'm the checker champion here at the prison—probably in the town of Phoenix as well. Recently, an older convict arrived here from Leavenworth penitentiary. He was the champion there and immediately looked me up.

I played him for fifty push-ups a game and won ten in a row. Now I'm wondering if there's such a crime as "cruel and unusual checkers." Whoever informed about the checkers will probably be put in the witness protection program and given a new name along with relocation and living expenses for a few years.

An orderly comes by sweeping the corridor and calls me. He says that the stoolie over on "protection row" told him that he didn't accuse me of gambling. He says the stoolie accused me of taking some documents from the hospital. The documents are supposed to concern a story I wrote recently about Burt Parker, a man who had returned to prison to die of cancer.

Now I'm extremely confused, because the prison grapevine these days is laden with liars, and you can't believe a word that arrives on that route. That is, unless you are a lieutenant.

Some time later, the lieutenant says that I'm being investigated because a convict accused me of threatening him with great bodily harm. Who knows the real reason?

The kid is a tattoo artist, but he's also good at sketches. He sits around drawing all day, and some of it is quality art. He drew us a checkerboard on white paper and made us some checkers out of cardboard. I'm teaching him the finer points of the game.

We're up to 350 push-ups a day now. We get three showers a week and three hours on the recreation yard each week. The only legitimate complaint we have is that they won't bring us a mop or broom to clean the cell.

But things are generally looking up. I've been thinking that I may just tell them to go to hell when they come to let me out of here. But I can't afford to be as brave as the kid.

Technically, there are twenty-four years left on my sentence. That's a lot of push-ups.

---

This tour of duty in Isolation began on March 28, 1989, and ended a week later. Once again, the *Chronicle* city desk assigned a reporter to the story. The news story noted that Dannie and I had been in the middle of editing an article together and quoted me as pointing out that the preliminary injunction guaranteed Dannie's right to continue writing for the *Chronicle*. Even if it were not the intent of the special detention, I told the reporter, the effect was to circumvent the court ruling because Dannie was incommunicado. And *Chronicle* attorney Lisa Zinkan was quoted as saying the newspaper might make a motion against the prison for contempt of court.

Journalism organizations, several of which had by then given us awards, passed resolutions reflecting what I had been arguing: Dannie should either be charged with something or released to the general population. The resolutions were a demonstration of the kind of helpful visibility that the awards had given him.

Once again, calls of concern from Dannie's readership came in almost as fast as they could be fielded.

Dannie later told me that he was visited in Isolation by his unit manager for his "three-day review." The unit manager didn't know what was going on either, but his visit did tell Dannie something: "The man they locked up with me didn't get any kind of 'review' at all," he wrote me. "By that I figured you and Jeff must be putting some heat on [the prison]. I'd never heard of a 'review' before."

On April 3, Dannie was released back to the mainline. No charges were filed, nor did he ever receive adequate explanation of why he had been isolated to begin with. By then, prison officials were saying that he was in the hole because another inmate had accused him of making threats. No evidence was found that Dannie had threatened anyone, and the other convict remained in Isolation, prison officials told both Dannie and the news people who inquired.

All the outside attention appeared to have had some effect within the prison. The lieutenant who let Dannie out of the hole "was acting *real* nice," Dannie said. "A complete turnabout in attitude from when he locked me up."

A secondary effect of the special detention was that once again Dannie's cell—including his notes, manuscripts, and legal mail—was searched by guards. Some legal documents were missing. When he got back to the cell, Dannie was told that guards had stayed there for two hours and then called in the investigating lieutenant, who was there another hour. Jeff Leon was quoted as saying he believed the entire episode was a ruse to search the convict's papers.

Legal mail is privileged correspondence entering and leaving the prison, but, it seems, not after the letters reach the convict's cell. The missing attorney-client correspondence concerned the lawsuit against the very same BOP whose officials were apparently reading the letters.

One final irony of the episode: It was on Dannie's third day in special detention that Kevin Sherbondy, whose vindication was the greatest tangible result of Dannie's writing, was finally released from prison.

Dannie's next *Chronicle* story set off as much of a tempest as did his article on Sherbondy.

---

## LONG DAY'S JOURNEY INTO DEATH

*PHOENIX, ARIZ. (JULY 2, 1989)*—The little chapel here at the Federal Correctional Institution in Phoenix was filled to overflowing on Tuesday, June 13. Convicts shuffled in out of the hot sun, holding their caps in their hands. They were attending a memorial service to pay last respects to fellow prisoner John Chaffee, thirty-two. He had died the day before in a Phoenix hospital.

Chaplain James Rivett led off the service by playing "Rock of Ages" on a guitar as the cons sang along. After the old hymn of comfort, the chaplain began speaking:

"I've been approached by many convicts, and I know there's a lot of anger among you," he said, "but this anger can destroy you."

He went on to say that he had been in contact with John Chaffee's father in Chico, California, and that the father was grateful for the concern of fellow prisoners and the excellent medical care provided to his son by prison authorities.

At this point, the solemn atmosphere turned restive.

"Who told you to say this shit?" an angry voice asked from the crowd.

"Nobody put me up to it!" the chaplain exclaimed defensively.

He then launched into an anecdote about how his own father had died of an undiagnosed liver ailment. He ended by saying that nothing could have been done to help John Chaffee anyway.

"Did they put your father in the hole for complaining?" another voice yelled out.

"I don't have to listen to this bullshit," another convict muttered as he put on his cap and stalked out.

Most of the two hundred or more mourners stood up and followed him out. It was a pitifully small group—probably about forty—that heard Rivett play "Amazing Grace" at the close of the eulogy.

A froth of anger and frustration brewed among the convicts who milled around in front of the chapel. Chaplain Rivett had already been nicknamed "Dick Tracy" by many convicts because of what they feel is his tendency to act like a rigid cop. But the consensus was that he'd outdone himself this time.

John Chaffee's death was a prolonged, undignified affair that unfolded like a Stephen King horror story. Everyone here, including some staff members, are tainted by the shame and guilt of watching it happen.

It doesn't help that in spite of being a first-term convict serving a short sentence for bank robbery, Chaffee was a nice guy. He was deeply involved in Alcoholics Anonymous here and was eager to learn a trade and turn his life around.

Top officials here don't like to be interviewed by convicts, so their detailed views on John Chaffee's lengthy death agony are not available to us, but here's how the young man's last months looked to his fellow convicts:

Chaffee's medical problem first became apparent in late February. He had signed up for a morning class in heating and air conditioning. He also worked afternoons in the kitchen. The class takes about seven months to complete.

A week or so into the first phase of the class, he began showing up late, sometimes as much as an hour late. Many of those mornings, he seemed disoriented and unfocused.

A convict instructor who initially thought he was drinking or using drugs pulled him over and told him that if he didn't shape up, the staff instructor would fire him. He even offered to purchase Chaffee an alarm clock to help him get up in the morning.

"That's not the problem," Chaffee told him. "I can't sleep at night. I'm having these headaches, and there seems to be pressure on my brain. I'm getting to where I can't remember things very well."

He began going to sick call at the prison hospital here. But in order to see a doctor, one must first convince a physician's assistant (PA) that something is seriously wrong. Chaffee wasn't able to convince anyone.

When a convict complains of severe pain, medical staff members usually think he's trying to con them out of drugs or malingering to escape a work assignment. The fact that Chaffee was a former drug addict probably didn't help him at all.

One PA—who likes to tell convicts that he is a doctor—listened to Chaffee's complaints and told him his illness was "psychosomatic." When Chaffee asked him what that meant, the PA replied: "It's all in your head."

By the end of March, he was seen many times emerging from his cell in the mornings crouched over, holding his head in his hands, and staggering like a drunk.

He began to pass out in the cellblock, and each time he went to the hospital he returned and said they told him he was malingering or that his problem was "psychosomatic."

On March 8, he took a job in construction mechanical services (CMS) because he could no longer cope in the class on heating and air conditioning or in the kitchen. For a while, he received excellent work reports in CMS. His boss said he was a very good worker.

Around the beginning of April, his problems caught up with him there also. He'd lost more than twenty pounds of weight and was looking haggard and haunted. His memory was failing completely, and he could no longer perform his duties.

His boss went to the hospital and told them that Chaffee had been a good worker and that there was indeed something wrong with him. At that time, he was finally granted a "medical idle," which allowed him to miss work.

A cell partner began complaining about him moaning all night, and Chaffee was moved to another cell with a more understanding cellie who gave him a bottom bunk and did what he could to comfort him.

During his long ordeal, Chaffee was prescribed several drugs. Sinequan—a mood-altering drug often prescribed for anxiety—was prescribed for a while. A friend of Chaffee's said that Chaffee later received prednisone and some type of tranquilizer.

By April, Chaffee was telling friends that the PAs in the hospital were getting mad at him for being a nuisance. Several times, when he arrived late for medication, they told him they were closed and he had to return the next day.

He began approaching prison lieutenants and custodial staff, begging them to help him. Convicts passing by became embarrassed about hearing him beg and whine. But most understood and sympathized with him.

Typical of the official responses is what I heard a lieutenant tell him in front of the mess hall one day: "Well, just get on back to work and go to sick call in the morning."

By the end of May, his situation became intolerable. He was passing out regularly in his housing unit and stumbling and falling as he made his way down the sidewalks outside. At times, he was bent over like an arthritic old man, holding his head in his hands and moaning.

Convicts—many of them angered or scared by his pain—began to berate him.

"Stand up for your rights, man!" they yelled at him. "They can't do this to you!"

He agreed, and sometime near the end of May he went to the hospital, determined to get some help. No one saw him for a few days after that because he was locked up in Isolation.

He was released from the isolation unit on June 2, and during the few more days he remained with us, he told his friends that he couldn't go back to the hospital. He said they told him they would lock him up if he complained again.

When someone suggested that he see the warden, Chaffee explained that he had already talked to him and that the warden had promised to have a neurosurgeon examine him.

Chaffee had reached the end of his rope and unknowingly was very near the end of his life. By this time, even many convicts were convinced that he had a brain tumor or aneurysm of some kind.

On June 5, at the noon meal, he was holding a food tray and staggering, trying to make his way to a table. A convict who thought he might be drunk took him by the elbow and told him to cool it before the lieutenant saw him.

Chaffee looked at him out of bleary, unfocused eyes and replied: "I wish, man. I wish."

It's about a fifth of a mile from the mess hall to Navajo A, the cellblock where he lived. The mess hall here has glass walls. After Chaffee finished eating lunch that day, many of us watched him walk back to the cellblock. It was a pitiful sight.

His legs were stiff as boards, and his head and neck protruded at a strange angle. He would take a lurching step or two and then stop and wave his arms, as if to recover his balance. It took him more than twenty minutes to cover the distance to his cellblock.

Chaffee was walking his last mile, and considering the pressure and his unrelieved pain, he made an admirable job of it.

The next morning, June 6, he collapsed in the cellblock, and a wheelchair was dispatched from the hospital to pick him up.

Two convicts who work in the hospital said that Chaffee was pushed through the waiting room to the trauma room at the rear of the hospital, where he sat in the wheelchair all day, slipping in and out of consciousness, until a mobile CAT-scan unit was called in at about 4:30 P.M.

An evacuation helicopter came in after dinner and flew him to an outside hospital. He died on June 12 of complications from a brain tumor.

The day after the aborted memorial service, several of the convicts who had walked out of the chapel were summoned to the lieutenant's office, where they were told that if anything happened over the Chaffee matter, they would be transferred.

One convict told me that a lieutenant told him he would "be history." He already is.

On Friday, June 16, about thirty convicts here were gathered up in the afternoon. By the time dinner was over, they were on a bus and gone. Their personal property was still in their cells here when they left. Among that bunch were some of those who had been summoned to the lieutenant's office, along with some of Chaffee's best friends.

There's a lot of paranoia in the air here now. Convicts are asking: "Who's next to roll?" It's a hard blow to be placed on a bus without your property and shuttled from prison to prison. I've been that route a few times myself.

But it's effective. Convicts who were once willing to talk to me now clam up when I ask for details about Chaffee's final days. I know of unit staff members who tried to intervene with the hospital for Chaffee during his painful last months. They refuse to discuss it with me. Several guards also were sympathetic but apparently were unable to get anything done for him.

Most of what I've written here I observed myself. Chaffee had told me that his boss at CMS intervened at the hospital to get him a "medical idle." He asked me in May if I could possibly write something about his plight. I told him the public wasn't really interested in a convict's medical problems.

The PA was right. It was all in his head.

Chaplain Rivett may have been able to convince Chaffee's father that he received "excellent medical care." It will be a cold day in hell before he convinces anyone around here.

———————

The story of John Chaffee's lingering death reverberated for many months both inside and outside the prison walls.

Several prisoners who mailed Dannie's article home said their letters arrived but not the enclosed clipping. One man told Dannie that the day after he sent a copy of the Chaffee article to his mother, he was summoned to the lieutenant's office and asked if he was "some kind of agitator." Not long afterward, the man was transferred to a prison in Texas.

That kind of reaction to an article published in an outside newspaper and then mailed back to the outside world was reminiscent of Lompoc officials' response after publication of "Mr. Squirrel." And it raised the same question: From whom was the article being kept, the convicts or the public?

The *Chronicle* distributed Dannie's story through a wire service, and within days·it had been reprinted in papers across the country, including the local *Phoenix Gazette* and *Arizona Republic,* both of which gave it top-of-page-one treatment. The *Chronicle,* as well as both Phoenix papers, assigned a reporter to follow up on Dannie's story.

Also doing follow-up reporting was Olive Talley, a tenacious reporter for the *Dallas Morning News* who had just completed a year-long investigation of medical care in the federal prison system. Talley was later named a Pulitzer Prize finalist for her investigation. Her exhaustive series, published the week before Dannie's article on Chaffee, documented serious deficiencies in medical care at federal prisons, including faulty diagnoses, botched surgery, and unnecessary suffering and deaths.

*Chronicle* reporter Gary Swan located and interviewed John Chaffee's father, who told of receiving a letter from new Phoenix Warden O. I. White saying that John had become very ill on June 2. "He was immediately transferred to our health service center," the warden's letter said, and "that same day, he was transported to St. Joseph's Hospital." But the hospital spokeswoman confirmed to Swan what Dannie had written, that Chaffee was not admitted until June 6.

The warden and the prisoners also differed by months on when John Chaffee first brought his medical problems to the attention of the prison medical staff. The warden's spokesman maintained that Chaffee's prison medical care was "given in a timely manner and was appropriate."

Meanwhile, harrowing new reports surfaced of the treatment accorded Chaffee while he was alive. Many of the reports came from the men who had been transferred out of Phoenix, apparently because of some real or presumed association with Chaffee. Through their parents, friends, and lawyers, Swan and I tracked down many of those convicts.

They provided details of their highly unusual middle-of-the-night transfer. They had been summoned unexpectedly by loudspeaker to the lieutenant's office, where they were relieved of watches, other personal items, and locker keys and immediately chained. They were stripped and given traveling clothes. (In a normal transfer, prisoners are given time to return to their cells and pack their belongings.) The convicts were informed only that they were "going for a ride."

On board the bus, the outcasts searched for clues to their unexpected fate. They discovered that many of them had crossed paths at some point with John Chaffee; that was all they seemed to have in common. The convicts learned their destination late that night by watching the freeway signs.

When they arrived at Terminal Island prison in Long Beach, California, well after midnight, the weary transferees were met by a large contingent of armed guards and by video cameras recording their arrival. They were processed and sent immediately to a block of isolation cells that had been cleared for their arrival. There they remained for months, without charge and with just two words of vague explanation for the emergency transfer: "administrative reasons."

For those unexplained reasons, the convicts—many with years-long clean records—lost cherished jobs and educational and vocational training programs. All this, as one of them wrote the *Chronicle,* "for the heinous crime of simply being John Chaffee's friend." They were subsequently dispersed to federal prisons throughout the country—two to an institution. Some whom we traced ended up far from loved ones, in places like Talladega, Alabama; Butner, South Carolina; Lompoc; and Oxford, Wisconsin.

Those men, at some risk to themselves, helped fill in the blanks in the story of Chaffee's last days. One, Walter Nusz, was located in Memphis through another transferee, whose mother had written me. Nusz had been Chaffee's cellmate for three days in Isolation, and he gave me a chilling firsthand report of the desperate efforts to get medical help for the dying convict.

Nusz said Chaffee was unable to get out of his bunk and spent his time "crying like a little kid" and pleading with his cellmate: "Can you help me, Walter? I keep telling them there's something wrong, but they won't do anything." Whenever a staff member passed the cell door, Chaffee, "his hand held out like a baby," begged from his bed, "Please help me. Please help me."

On the second day, Chaffee fell out of his bunk. He lay on the floor for hours, apparently unconscious. Nusz says officers came by to look at him but "wouldn't even put him back in the bunk." Nusz himself finally maneuvered the helpless man back into his bed, where he gave him what nursing assistance he could.

Nusz tried to feed Chaffee, because his cellmate seemed uninterested in food, but his greatest triumph came after Chaffee asked him to rub Ben-Gay on his sore neck. Nusz was reluctant at first ("I don't like to do that to guys"), but he did. Chaffee, as a result, finally found enough relief from his pain that he fell asleep for a few hours.

Meanwhile, Nusz tried frantically to get his cellmate medical assistance. On the second day, Nusz wrote a "copout"—a formal request for staff assistance—but received no reply. He continually rapped on the cell door and begged for medical help.

Finally, a medical team came by to examine Chaffee briefly while Nusz, locked in the shower, shouted out: "He's sick, do you understand? He's sick." Although Nusz says the medical team had little more in the way of diagnostic gear than a stethoscope, they left the cell saying, "There's nothing wrong with him . . . he's faking it." Nusz was also told that Chaffee was in the hole for "observation" because officials thought he was walking around drunk. Replies Nusz, "Anyone could tell the dude wasn't drunk."

When Chaffee left the isolation cell on the fourth day, Nusz helped him get dressed and instructed him to get to the yard with whatever energy he could muster and beg for help there.

I asked Nusz—three months after Chaffee's death—if he had been interviewed by a BOP investigative panel about his experiences with Chaffee. "No one's talked to me about nothin'," he replied. But if investigators did question him, "I'd just tell them what I told you. That's all I know."

■

An investigation into John Chaffee's death was in fact requested three days after publication of Dannie's article—and several weeks after Chaffee's death—by Phoenix Warden White, who had arrived on the job after the death. In an apparently unprecedented response, the BOP sent a team of its medical experts from around the country to Phoenix to review Chaffee's treatment. Although a prison spokesman said the warden initiated the probe, he told the *Phoenix Gazette,* "I don't think it would be totally out of line to think that in the backs of people's minds it [Dannie's article] didn't have something to do with it."

Reports from convicts indicate that whomever the medical investigators interviewed in their day or two at the prison, it wasn't inmates. Nor, apparently, did they talk to Chaffee's boss, who had interceded with medical staff on the convict's behalf. There were so many signs of either a cover-up or a lax investigation that the medical panel's report was apparently discarded at BOP headquarters in Washington in favor of an internal Justice Department probe.

Stymied in their efforts to receive results of the official investigations, the *Chronicle,* the *Dallas Morning News,* and the *Phoenix Gazette* cooperated in a largely unsuccessful Freedom of Information Act request for all records relating to the investigation of Chaffee's death.

Dannie later summed up the BOP's investigation into John Chaffee's death: "It went into a black hole." But BOP Director J. Michael Quinlan, in an interview with Olive Talley six months after the appearance of Dannie's article, did summarize the bureau's conclusions. In what Talley called "a rare confirmation of inmate complaints," Quinlan conceded that Phoenix staff members had been insensitive to Chaffee's medical needs, but he said that nothing they did or didn't do would have altered the progress of the fatal tumor.

Quinlan admitted that Chaffee "was in administrative detention for four days on the mistaken belief by the staff that he was possibly intoxicated when seen walking across the compound. In retrospect, he was not intoxicated." The BOP chief refused to divulge whether any staff members would be disciplined as a result of the investigation, but he said that "a combination of things are being planned in terms of sensitivity training."

One of the reasons sometimes cited for the medical-care crisis in federal prisons is overcrowding. With the runaway expansion of the prison population, some BOP institutions were running over 200 percent of capacity at the time; systemwide, the figure was 155 percent of capacity. Figures such as those portend serious troubles for society years down the road, but, of course, the first to feel the effects are the men and women packed into the institutions, as Dannie made clear in his next article in "Sunday Punch."

# REPORT FROM AN OVERCROWDED MAZE

*PHOENIX, ARIZ. (SEPT. 3, 1989)*—A man was stabbed in the chest in a noisy mess hall as we ate lunch one day in Lompoc penitentiary in California. He ran by the table where I was eating with three other men. Dark arterial blood was pumping out of his chest and splashing onto the floor within three feet of our table.

We watched him leave the dining room and then finished our lunch. After the meal, I remarked to one of the cons I'd been eating with that it seemed to me we should at least have lost our appetite.

"I don't see why we should've," he replied. "It was his problem, not ours."

I had been in prison for seven years at that time, and I began to realize that something drastic had happened to me. I had divorced my feelings from the things I could see about me, and my senses had withdrawn to a world that had nothing much to do with my environment.

As I pass the nine-year mark this month, I wonder how wide the chasm between my vision and my senses will be in two more years, when I am due to be paroled.

It isn't a reassuring line of thought. But I also understand that while living in a crowded cage awash in a sea of noise, I must acquire a caged mentality or I won't survive.

The two most devastating aspects of modern prisons are noise and overcrowding. Prisons are noisy places anyway, but when they become overcrowded, as most are now, the noise becomes unbearable, and there's no escape from it.

The din of an overcrowded prison puts a heavy burden of stress on us all. We become, among other things, tense, irritable, introverted, bitter, paranoid, and violent.

A study of overcrowding done on a colony of laboratory mice back in the '50s uncovered many types of abnormal behavior. Cannibalism, self-mutilation, aggressive behavior (to the point of attacking any moving object), sexual ambiguity, and introversion. Those characteristics were brought about by overcrowding, not by deprivation of food or other necessities.

Looking about me, I can see stark examples of those mouse aberrations manifesting themselves in closely confined men. Much of that overcrowding results from legislative changes, and the effects on individuals can be painful to behold.

A twenty-year-old man came here recently from the East Coast. He was sentenced to fifteen years with no possibility of parole under the new federal sentencing code. He was convicted of bank robbery, and it's his first trip to prison. The new sentencing code allows very little credit for good time, and he will have to serve about thirteen years before his release.

Not long after he arrived here, he was placed in Isolation by mistake when the authorities confused his name with that of a notorious stool pigeon. Soon after that incident, he was assigned a cell with a weight lifter twice his size who tried to force him into a homosexual act, then beat him within an inch of his life when he refused.

He approached a guard with one eye swollen shut, and through mangled, swollen lips, he mumbled that he'd like a cell change.

"There's no room," the guard replied. "You'll have to stay where you were assigned."

The young man then violated another rule so that he could be put back in Isolation in order to get a cell change and a new cell partner.

"I never thought prison was this bad," he told me in the yard when he was released from Isolation.

I assured him that this prison is not as bad as maximum-security prisons like Leavenworth and Lompoc. He didn't seem to take much consolation from that fact.

Stories like that young man's will become more common as bewildered newcomers and cage-wise cons are pressed ever tighter because of tough new sentencing laws.

The small cellblock I live in was designed for sixty men in single cells. There are more than 120 of us in here now, with all the cells doubled up. We don't choose our cell partners. When a bunk becomes vacant, another convict is moved in.

When you live in a small cell with another convict, his presence is always there, whether you're using the toilet, writing a letter, or reading a book. It's a much closer relationship than a marriage. But it's between two people who usually don't want to live with each other.

Outside the cell, the lines and lists go on forever. We stand in a long line three times a day in order to eat. At the prison store, we wait in a raucous crowd until our name is called. We stand in line to be strip-searched before visits with people on the outside, then stand in line to be strip-searched after the visit. We line up at the laundry and line up to sign up for a phone call.

Anyone who wants to work in hobbycraft finds there's a three- or four-month waiting list for a hobby card. When the prison is over-crowded, all the lines and lists are longer.

I've seen convicts go crazy while standing in a line; they begin hitting and kicking everyone they can reach. For someone with an aversion to lines, this aspect of prison is hell on Earth.

Many prisoners in this pressure-cooker environment develop antisocial coping mechanisms.

When people tour a prison, they see convicts nonchalantly making their way to jobs, or standing patiently in chow lines waiting to eat. In the cellblocks, they see us playing pinochle or lying in a cell reading a book. They go away thinking that we live a calm existence.

But the real world of convicts lies hidden from the view of a tourist. These crowds of seemingly uniform prisoners are banded together in groups that work against the laws of the prison system itself.

Some convicts like to drink, and four or five of them will get together and make wine regularly. Others gamble and run betting pools. Stolen food and government merchandise are bought and sold. Drug users band together in schemes to obtain their drug of choice.

The guards don't see much more of our real world than the tourists, unless they happen to stumble upon someone using drugs or gambling.

We've developed codes and signals to protect our world. I can look at a convict across the building from me and put my right index finger under my eye, and he will nod his head and remain standing where he is while I go back into my cell.

I've just told him to watch for the guard, and he will stand there and watch until I come out and signal him that I'm finished with whatever I'm doing. A convict will do that for someone he doesn't even know, and we all know the signal. It's only one of many we use to communicate in our own world.

By nurturing our hidden life and being loyal to it, we find some relief from the crowds and the noise. Even if it's only a drunk, a high, or an exciting wager, it helps. The best of it all is that it's hidden from view and belongs to us alone.

Naturally, some of this goes on all the time in all prisons, but overcrowding encourages the climate of lawlessness; it spurs us to develop our subterranean activities.

When a sixty-man cellblock is made into a 120-man cellblock, there is still only one guard. His job becomes twice as hard, even as the extra convicts help to develop more schemes.

The overcrowding pushes us further toward introversion, secretiveness, clique mentality, violence, and deceit. Those aren't the traits society wants to foster in a man headed back to the "free world" someday.

The new federal sentencing law, approved by the Supreme Court early this year, is adding another dimension of madness in already overcrowded prisons. Because of the "get-tough" legislation, judges will no longer have much of a say in sentencing. Whatever the circumstances of the crime, the sentence is definite and final. Parole is abolished. The basic unfairness of those harsh new sentences is hard to believe.

Every week, people are coming in here with twenty-five- and thirty-year sentences with no chance of parole. Many of them are as young as nineteen and twenty. They are more abusive toward guards and violent toward fellow convicts. They don't have anything to lose. The courts have tattooed the term "criminal" on the foreheads of young men who might still have had a chance to take other routes.

Recently, at a 4:00 P.M. standing count here, a guard walked by a convict's cell and told him to stand up.

"Fuck you!" was the reply.

The guard asked him again to stand up.

"I said fuck you!" the man replied and remained sitting down.

After the count, some guards came and led him off to Isolation. A few days later, when he was released from the hole, I asked him why he had done that.

"I have a ten-year sentence with no parole," he told me. "I only get one year good time, so I have to do nine years if I'm a good boy. Well, I'd rather lose that year of good time right now and do ten years my way than nine their way. I'll stand up when I feel like it, and I meant exactly what I said: Fuck him!"

Older convicts are in a state of shock right now because of the heavy impact on them of the new sentencing law. A forty-five-year-old man whom I've known for years just received a thirty-year sentence for possession of a gun. His prior crimes were two second-degree burglaries and an assault that didn't involve a weapon. He will have to serve twenty-five years in prison before he's eligible to be released.

"I can't believe this," he says. "People don't do this much time for murder. If I do survive this sentence, I will be seventy years old when I get out."

"What if you do live through it?" I asked him. "What will you do at that age when you are released?"

"Man, if I have to do all that time and finally get back out, the only thing I'll want to know is if that judge and that prosecutor are still alive," he replied.

A man here from Seattle pleaded guilty to a conspiracy to sell cocaine. It was a plea bargain, and he received twenty years, of which he will have to serve eighteen years in prison. He is forty-seven years old.

I told him I couldn't understand how someone could plead guilty in exchange for eighteen years in prison. I would take my chances in court.

"They held back another charge," he said. "If I refused the plea bargain, they were going to add that charge as well and give me thirty years."

Members of gangs from the inner cities are already arriving here in large numbers. Most of them were sentenced to long, nonparolable terms under the new sentencing guidelines. These are kids who grew up in ghettos bumming quarters to play Pac Man machines.

They've heard the slogans "War on Drugs" and "War on Crime" used so often that now they believe it. When people go down on their turf, they are war casualties to them, not victims.

They wear their gang colors in prison yards now, and their young eyes burn with an old, hard look of having nothing much more to lose. It's as if they are saying: "Well, you got tough on us. Now what?"

Not long ago at Phoenix, the isolation building became so full that convicts had to be put on a waiting list to go to the hole. Often, when a man finishes his isolation time, he has to languish in there another two weeks until a mainline cell comes open.

I sometimes wonder what happened to those deranged mice when the overcrowding study was completed. I doubt they were turned loose to roam in an innocent colony of field mice.

But most of these convicts with unnaturally long sentences will survive and eventually be released. After fifteen or twenty years in a noisy, violent, overcrowded prison, some of them are going to make Freddy Kreuger look like an Eagle Scout.

---

Dannie's message got through to at least a few of those who most needed to hear it—through the good offices of the sheriff of San Francisco.

Sheriff Michael Hennessey runs the San Francisco County jails, and in fact Dannie was a resident of one of Hennessey's jails during the trial of our lawsuit. Despite his position on the other side of the bars from Dannie, the sheriff testified in our behalf at the trial, just four months after publication of Dannie's article on overcrowding, and the article figured in his testimony:

I just happened to see [Martin's piece] one Sunday and was very impressed with how clear he was and how descriptive he was about what jail overcrowding does to the psyche of the people who live and work there.

And I was unaware that this case was going on at that time. So it has no relation to this case. But I brought it to work with me the next day and Xeroxed it and sent it to every member of my Board of Supervisors. I sent it to the mayor [and] deputy mayors in charge of criminal justice. . . . I thought that here was a perspective that would get lost in bureaucratic arguments over money and construction issues and jail internal issues. . . . And I . . . used it in an attempt to make changes in our jail.

▬

**A** few months before his trial, Dannie started feeling the heat at Phoenix. He was called in more frequently for urine tests, and guards shook down his cell more often—sometimes as frequently as twice a day. "So it looks like they are aware the trial is getting close and are desperate to get something on me," he said in a letter, "but I damn sure won't help them on that."

After still another urine test he wrote, "Maybe they think settlement negotiations would go better if they could add eight months on my time. I'm not using any drugs or alcohol, so they will have to find another way."

Dannie arrived without further misadventure at the San Francisco Hall of Justice jail several days before the start of our trial on December 4.

# IV

## A TIME OF TRIAL DECEMBER 1989 — MAY 1990

> The real issues, I believe, are: (1) Does a convict have a First Amendment right to publicly define himself and his surroundings? And (2) does the public have a First Amendment right to hear a prisoner's viewpoint. . . .
>
> Any permanent harm that comes to us all won't be because of what we talk about. It will come from what was passed over in silence.
>
> —*Dannie's open letter to a forum on the First Amendment*

■

On September 14, 1989, on a *Nightline* show devoted to our dispute with the BOP, then U.S. Attorney Joseph Russoniello said, "We have the regulations because obviously the *San Francisco Chronicle* doesn't use the good enough judgments to be able to restrain itself from publishing a person and what he has to say that might cause disruptive activity in a controlled environment. So the Bureau of Prisons has no choice but to impose regulations against those it has control over."

Russoniello's comment, three months before our lawsuit went to trial, illuminated the government's attitude toward prisoners and the media as much as anything that happened in the courtroom itself. The fundamental issue, it now appeared, was not bylines or compensation. As San Francisco's top federal prosecutor saw it on the eve of the trial, the government's target was the newspaper. The *Chronicle* won't submit to prepublication censorship—known to lawyers as "prior restraint"—so the government punishes the prisoner-writer instead.

Russoniello's comment was especially revealing because other federal prison regulations permit, even encourage, prisoners like Dannie to write "for private use or for publication . . . without staff approval" and to send manuscripts to the news media unopened through "Special Mail" procedures.

Warden Rison himself has said: "We do not control the content whatsoever. The inmate is [free] to write with whoever he wants to, with respect to the manuscript." Indeed, the sheets of yellow legal paper on which Dannie wrote his manuscripts reached my desk unimpeded and uncensored. The violation—*his* violation—occurred when the *Chronicle* published them.

■

One other government action helped set the stage for the trial. In late November, the Justice Department submitted to the court proposed new regulations governing federal prisoners' relations with the news media. The draft regulations, it said, were to be published in the *Federal Register* six days before the scheduled opening of the trial. Why the hastily drawn and often contradictory regulations were submitted to the court was unclear: We were challenging existing regulations, not whatever the government might put into effect in the future.

Also puzzling—but more revealing—were the actual provisions of the proposed regulations. They maintained the prohibition against "compensated byline journalists" that we were challenging as illegal, and they added further restrictions on the media. What both sets of regulations had in common was the attempt of a public agency to control how the media report on that agency.

Under the new rules, the BOP would have required that "a representative of the news media, as a condition of any face-to-face interview granted by the Bureau, shall provide authorized staff of the Bureau of Prisons an opportunity to respond to any allegation that might be published or broadcast." The penalty for violation of the regulation was loss of access to the prison for journalists or their news organizations.

In practice, that rule would have foreclosed use of prisoner sources in sensitive news media investigations.

The new regulations would also have restricted the frequency of convicts' interviews with the media and expanded the warden's discretion in denying media access. A warden would have been permitted to deny a journalist's interview request if "the Bureau has received objections from other government agencies which have expressed an interest." That last provision would have given all federal agencies unprecedented veto power over potentially embarrassing news investigations.

No press release heralded the new regulations, and the likelihood was negligible that they would have been noticed in the *Federal Register*'s sea of small print. So I alerted the *Chronicle*'s city desk, and the newspaper published a page-one story on the rules.

Among the reporters I subsequently notified was the *Washington Post*'s Eleanor Randolph. As it happened, her story appeared hours before Attorney General Richard Thornburgh put in a rare appearance at the daily Justice Department press briefing. Reporters, alerted by the *Post* story, sharply questioned Thornburgh about the rules. The attorney general defended them as part of a departmental review of all public-information policies in order to control unauthorized "leaks."

Several hours later, Thornburgh issued a statement withdrawing the draft rules he had just defended: "This proposal was submitted prematurely and without my personal review. It will be subject to further review before resubmission." The rules have not subsequently resurfaced.

███

*Dannie Martin and the Chronicle Publishing Company* v. *R. H. Rison et al.* finally came to trial on December 4, 1989. Dannie and I welcomed the trial. It was, first, an opportunity to defend ourselves and explain our intentions. For Dannie, it was also a rare opportunity to testify in court without lying; he enjoyed the feeling.

Throughout the trial in San Francisco's Federal Building, we sat opposite each other at the plaintiffs' table, passing notes on our observations. It felt almost like a normal working relationship.

But, although the trial took place in a court of law, there were repeated reminders of the prison, not least in the treatment accorded Dannie. He sat at the counsel table in an orange jumpsuit, surrounded by a regiment of tailored business suits. Hovering a few steps back was a marshal assigned to guard him. One marshal warned him not to smile, wave, or speak to anyone but his attorney. "Not even hello," said Dannie in a note. "But he can't stop me from smiling or nodding."

When some of our witnesses paused coming off the stand to shake the convict's hand, federal marshals waved or scowled them off. John Conrad, a criminologist and former BOP chief of research, was grabbed by a marshal, who hissed, "Get out of here." But when Clair Cripe, the BOP general counsel and a government witness, stopped to greet Dannie, he received no such rude brush-off.

During the trial, Dannie and I shared the camaraderie of original participants as the lawyers, who outnumbered us by as much as four to one, imposed logical theories on our three and a half years of unpremeditated actions. We were also bound together by the use of our monitored phone conversations, which had been transcribed and studied for hours by lawyers and legal aides and were then bandied about in debate, interpreted in lawyers' briefs, and finally misquoted to our detriment in the judge's ruling.

Even our friendship became an issue at the trial, with the government attempting to portray me as a naive, "loose-cannon" journalist personally biased by friendship with this convict. On the stand, I was quizzed by government attorney Mark St. Angelo about whether I had sent birthday cards and presents to Dannie. It was a tactic that I believe was calculated to distance me from the presumed respectability of the *San Francisco Chronicle,* which the government had earlier tried—and failed—to remove as a co-plaintiff.

Until rebuked by Judge Legge, government attorneys also lost no opportunity to call attention to Dannie's criminality, and they repeatedly and unsuccessfully tried to get Dannie to name fellow prisoners— anonymous sources, friends, and others whose names, as the judge ruled, had no relevance.

During and immediately after the trial, I had frequent opportunities to visit with Dannie in his temporary quarters at the county jail atop San Francisco's Hall of Justice. The visiting conditions were more primitive than at the federal prisons—chatting over a frequently malfunctioning phone, with a thick glass barrier between convict and visitors. But the jail was close enough to my home that my wife and daughters could also visit for the first time with my colleague, who had been such a big part of our family because of his often daily dinnertime phone calls.

He also got to meet many "Sunday Punch" readers who had been corresponding with him regularly. This network of long-distance friends that he had built up over his years of writing was to be the nucleus of his support system after his ultimate release. They were his San Francisco family.

■

Through the five weeks of intermittent court days stretching over the Christmas and New Year's holidays and then in final arguments in early February 1990, witnesses and lawyers walked and rewalked through the controversy—one foot in the abstractions of constitutional law, the other in the contentious events of a year and a half earlier in Lompoc penitentiary. It was fascinating, if at times surreal, to watch as lawyers untangled the roots of mighty American principles in the soil of our personal experience.

Specifically at issue in the trial was the regulation barring federal prisoners from publishing under a byline or for compensation or "acting as [a] reporter" *in the news media.* But the broader issue was the balancing of the sometimes conflicting interests of prison, prisoner, and press: Dannie's and the *Chronicle's* First Amendment rights of free speech and free press and the prison system's responsibility to assure the security of its institutions.

Much of the testimony bore on the supposed threat posed by a prisoner's bylined, compensated writings. The Bureau of Prisons maintained that bylined articles in the news media are dangerous in theory and that Dannie's "Gulag Mentality" was dangerous in practice, as well.

In theory, BOP witnesses said, a byline in the news media gives a prison writer the status of "big wheel" or "spokesman" among the prisoners, which destabilizes the institution. And the money a prisoner could earn as a free-lance writer, the warden said, would permit the writer to "solicit support from other inmates to do whatever the money will allow him to do, for example, pay other inmates to move narcotics into the institution, or pay inmates to act as strong men in an effort to control the flow of contraband in the institution." Hence, convicts are not allowed to write for the news media under their own bylines or for compensation.

On the big-wheel issue, our attorneys countered that convicts could achieve status within the prison in countless other ways, often with the support of the prison; that the problem of inmate influence derived from gang leaders and not from bylines in free-world publications read by few prisoners anyhow; and that in any case, prisoners were allowed to have bylines in books, pamphlets, and even prisoner union newspapers, but not in general-circulation newspapers and magazines.

In fact, Dannie never sent me a bylined story; *I* wrote "By Dannie Martin" on the top of his stories, following customary editorial practice. In my testimony, I argued that it is, finally, up to the *Chronicle*'s readers to decide how much credibility they will give to feature stories in the newspaper, and one of their best guides in making that evaluation is the author's identity—the byline. That is especially true when, as in Dannie's case, the article is a uniquely personal hybrid of opinion and observation by a nonstaff writer. Indeed, the absence of a byline generally suggests that the piece is a news account by a staff writer.

And, of course, it would be irresponsible to run a first-person commentary without a byline. The reader must know who this "I" is who's talking.

Other testimony revealed that no state prison system had found need of a similar byline regulation to safeguard security in its institutions. Several prison experts testified that an *anonymous* article by a convict poses more of a danger to institutional security than one whose source can be identified by both fellow convicts and administrators.

Many prisons have inmate-run publications that include bylined articles by inmates, apparently without breaching security. The federal system itself had such newspapers until they were terminated in the early '80s. The reason they were abolished was "totally budgetary" and not a result of security concerns, according to former BOP Director Norman Carlson, a witness for the government.

In some prisons, convict newspapers are valued highly by penal authorities. One such publication is the *Angolite* at Louisiana State Prison in Angola, recipient of numerous national journalism awards. The work of Editor Wilbert Rideau and Associate Editor Ron Wikberg (now released), both murderers with a combined fifty-four years behind bars, has turned their own lives around. It has also influenced state legislation and prison administration, and it has provided prisoners with a valuable safety valve.

■

The prohibition on compensation for convict-writers was challenged by our attorneys partly on the ground that prisoners could and often did earn in prison industries or through handicrafts programs hundreds of dollars a month—many times the $100 or $150 that Dannie earned for an essay in "Sunday Punch." The same prison administration that forbids the sale of writings to newspapers helps a prisoner sell his handmade wallets or paintings through art fairs or display cabinets in prison visiting areas.

Convicts can also receive money from family and others on the outside. That money is routinely sent from the mailroom to the inmate's account at the commissary—just as a newspaper's compensation would be. The prison limits monthly expenditures from commissary accounts. There was no adequate explanation of why those legitimate sources of prisoner income do not pose the danger to security that was said to be posed by the *San Francisco Chronicle's* money.

Both sides in the dispute argued that their positions on compensation were crucial to the functioning of their institutions. The *Chronicle* said that both bylines and compensation are important editorial incentives, attracting free-lance writers and helping to assure the quality and accuracy of their work.

For their part, BOP officials maintained that compensation contradicts the intent of imprisonment. "The rationale behind this regulation," said BOP Director J. Michael Quinlan in court papers, "is simply that continuation of a business from behind bars is inconsistent with the nature of incarceration. . . . The fact that the sentencing judge opted for incarceration means that he expected certain consequences to flow from that decision, including cessation of the defendant's regular employment affairs."

It was not easy to square Quinlan's argument with the facts of our case. Dannie was not continuing an outside occupation; he was developing a new and potentially sustaining talent. And one of his sentencing judges was impressed by his writings, which were forwarded to him by attorney Schwab, and urged him to keep it up. In an unusual gesture, when the judge had visited Lompoc penitentiary he sought out Dannie in his cell to visit with him. There was no evidence that he opposed compensation.

Representative Robert Kastenmeier, then chair of the congressional committee that oversees the BOP, had made clear in another context that Congress had no such intent either. Kastenmeier, in a 1983 letter to the bureau's general counsel, had argued that prohibiting prisoners' sale of creative works "may chill inmate expression," and he cited a Senate report on another piece of legislation: "The Committee does not intend that the felon be prohibited from selling his ideas."

■

$T$he third part of 540.20(b) was the most bewildering. It prohibits "acting as [a] reporter," which—like "byline" and "compensation" and "conducting a business"—is not defined in the regulations. As the only professional journalist to take the stand at the trial, I testified that I had no idea what it meant to "act as a reporter."

Government witnesses defined the phrase in varied and divergent ways. Some said they thought it refers to "regular" or "semiregular" or contractual employment by a newspaper or magazine. (Dannie himself was a free-lance writer with no contract and no regularly scheduled column.) Others suggested that it applies to publication of "news" or "facts" or "verifiable facts"—as if opinion could exist independent of facts.

Because of its ambiguity, the prohibition against "acting as a reporter" is a wild-card clause that appears to give prison administrators a tool to punish writers of articles they find distasteful—even if those articles are unbylined and uncompensated—according to standards that are never spelled out, in print or otherwise.

So vague is the regulation we sought to overturn that the government's own attorney, speaking at our first emergency court hearing, told the court: "I'm not sure the regulation is 100 percent clear what kind of publication or what kind of status of authors it refers to on its face. . . . I don't know what the official interpretation is."

From everything we later learned, the attorney's confusion was understandable. There is no "official interpretation."

■

$W$hen government witnesses at the trial pointed to the dangers of prisoner writing, their arguments were largely hypothetical. Carlson, for instance, asked to comment on one *possible* threat to the "security" and the "orderly running" of a prison, tiptoed through the following answer: "It would be speculative on my part, but I could envision a scenario by which that [information disclosed from the special housing unit] could cause problems with other inmates."

Other government witnesses speculated that a byline *could* result in breaches of prison security, mostly because other convicts *might* elevate the writer to the status of "spokesman" for his fellow prisoners. On the other hand, there *could* be a danger to the writer from prisoners resentful of his role as spokesman. "Inmates don't like having spokesmen for them," said one government expert.

The theorizing perplexed Dannie, who was the only one in attendance with the personal experience to evaluate the dangers a prison
writer faces and the influence he wields. He asked me in a note passed
across the counsel table: "How can I represent the population and be
in danger from them at the same time?"

Theories aside, no witness could recall any prison disturbance that
had ever been caused by a prisoner's writings in an outside newspaper.

Legally, to suspend the prisoner's and the newspaper's access to First
Amendment rights, the BOP had to come up with convincing institutional imperatives—how convincing depended on which legal standard of proof applied, and that was at issue. Security was the BOP's
all-encompassing justification. But in prisons, the people deciding which
publicized information is a security threat are often the very officials
who stand to be embarrassed by press disclosures.

As Patrick McManus, former top-level penal official in Kansas and
Minnesota, testified, security "tends to be a defense that all of us in
corrections pull out rather rapidly . . . and I think people who don't
hang around prisons tend to have to take that on face value . . . so it
becomes kind of a nifty way to . . . defend practices that maybe oughtn't
to be defended."

Several witnesses testified that, in the words of San Francisco State
University Professor John Irwin, "prison administrators don't like to be
criticized for their work . . . they're particularly thin-skinned because
they have been historically immune from criticism because they have
been so remote." The problem, then, is to distinguish between a real
threat to the security of the prison and a threat of embarrassment to
prison officials.

Certainly Dannie's "Gulag" article was embarrassing to prison officials, but there was no evidence that it provoked any disturbance at
the prison. A far greater threat to prison security, several witnesses
said, was the warden's unpopular action in isolating Dannie for his
writing. As McManus testified: "I think the [warden's] response to the
article in fact created the situation I suspect that brought us all here
today."

That "security" is a malleable concept was made clear by Carlson,
who reviewed a previous important press-prison case from the 1970s,
*Saxbe* v. *Washington Post Co.* The issue was policies prohibiting face-
to-face media interviews with federal prisoners, with the BOP arguing

that more liberal media access rights would be a threat to security. Carlson—a defendant in that lawsuit—testified at our trial that the BOP "purposely waited" until the Saxbe case was decided in its favor in the Supreme Court and *then* changed its regulations to increase media access, as it had decided to do before the high court acted.

Clearly, the peril to security that the BOP had cited in the Saxbe case was not so compelling that it couldn't be overlooked once the case was won. Stated another way: Despite its testimony, the bureau didn't really need the challenged regulations to preserve security.

No one wants to be a party to a prison disturbance, but there are many ways of avoiding such disruptions. One effective one, our witnesses suggested, is to increase, not decrease, communication between the public and the prisoners. As Irwin said: "Prisoners are extremely frustrated when their grievances are not responded to by the prison administration. They are greatly mollified when they believe that they are reaching someone outside."

Conrad, the former BOP chief of research, speculated that Dannie's "Gulag" article "enhanced security by 'letting off steam' and forcing prison authorities to explain their actions to the inmates and the public."

—

**M**uch of the trial testimony centered on the specific context in which this dispute arose. Many prison officials had read Dannie's bylined articles and even discussed them with him prior to the crackdown. One who was aware of his bylined writing for years was Williford, the regional director of the BOP who formally ordered Dannie's transfer to Phoenix. Yet Dannie had been allowed to write about twenty articles under his byline before the crackdown—which came, surely not coincidentally, two days after he published an article criticizing his warden's policies and naming the warden.

Prison officials insisted at the trial that the "Gulag" article in itself posed a severe security threat. As evidence of that threat, three prison officials in succession testified that in the days following publication of the article, there was an eerie silence in the prison, and that such a preternatural silence often precedes a riot.

Lompoc Associate Warden Thomas Curd said the inmates were "standoffish . . . the institution seemed a little quieter than normal . . . something was wrong." Security chief Brew went to the mainline after Dannie was released from segregation to "check the mood of the place":

It was awfully quiet. Not as much noise as you normally hear. I know that may sound funny, but in a prison when inmates are not making noise, we have found over a period of years that that indicates that they are pretty tense, that something may be getting ready to happen.

Dannie's ACLU attorney, John Hagar, summarized Brew's concerns by remarking to him, "The institution was so calm you were concerned there may be a riot."

But the eerie-silence issue collapsed when two later witnesses—both prison officials called by the BOP to testify on other issues—stated on cross-examination that Dannie's writing caused "a stir" and "a buzz" in the prison, that the noise level went up for a couple of weeks. Lompoc Unit Manager Edward York summarized the threat: "There is a great concern to us when the place becomes abuzz, with everybody talking all of a sudden. It's a security concern."

The reaction of the courtroom spectators to this testimony was more riotous than anything that occurred in Lompoc penitentiary during June or July of 1988.

Clearly, the business of assessing security threats is not yet a hard science. According to the prison paralegal, security chief Brew based his assessment of a security threat after Dannie's article on his observation that "there is something out there . . . we can't put our finger on."

Warden Rison provided another illustration of just how tenuous were the signs that prison officials interpreted as security threats. Rison testified in his deposition that "another *major piece of evidence* [emphasis added] I recall was Paul Hofer," the prison's acting spokesman and also the staff psychologist. "We had picked up information," Rison said, "that Hofer had been all but totally ostracized, *which was a major sign of disruption* [emphasis added]. Inmates had totally avoided him in group therapy."

Why were the prisoners avoiding the prison psychologist? For the answer, one need look no further than Hofer's own declaration to the court. He said that "approximately a dozen inmates" had "ventured into my office [and] chosen to discuss my role in the Martin case and how it has destroyed my credibility with the inmate population." Hofer was the spokesman who had announced that Dannie was sent to the hole for his own protection.

■

As the trial unfolded, it became clear that the prison system and the newspaper were in fundamental conflict over the newspaper's right to control its own content. Charles LaRoe, executive assistant to the warden at Lompoc, posed the issue bluntly when he referred in a deposition to "our policy concerning what inmates can submit *and how it's to be published*" (emphasis added).

Warden Rison was equally direct when he expressed his concern in an early press release that "these articles by Mr. Martin were not published as strict 'Letters to the Editor' but were carefully developed with assistance from the editorial staff of the *Chronicle.* . . ." Prison regulation 540.20(b), as interpreted by prison officials, made an exception of letters to the editor. That is, the same material that violates the regulation on one page of a newspaper or magazine is permissible on another.

In practice, Dannie's articles would not have fit in most newspapers' letters-to-the-editor column, even if that were a proper editorial format for such writing. Space constraints limit the depth and substance—the content—of what a letter writer can say.

But why is a convict's name on the letters page less dangerous than on, say, the Op Ed page? The government's intent in framing the letters-to-the-editor exception was apparently to undercut the credibility of prison writers. BOP General Counsel Cripe was surprisingly candid on this issue. Here's how he described the effect of a byline:

> . . . being published with a recognition by the paper of his special status [is tantamount to saying] "looky here, readers, you should pay special attention to this because this isn't a column with no name on it. This isn't a letter to the editor where we get every kind of kook writing in about every kind of thing" (and sometimes I think they're established just for humor). "This is something we established that you should pay attention to because we published it in an article under a byline."

Another government witness, anthropologist Mark Fleisher, said that publication of prisoners' writings might be reasonable "if there were some way of saying that, well, what this inmate is writing is a fun story, and it isn't a reflection of reality in this particular place at this particular time."

In short, prison officials wanted to control how prison writings appeared in newspapers so that those accounts would not be believed by the paper's readers. And the sanction they chose to control editorial placement was punishment of the convict-writer.

But the journalist's right to edit and place articles has been endorsed by the Supreme Court. As former Chief Justice Warren Burger wrote, press freedom "includes the right of a newspaper to arrange the content of its paper, whether it be news items, editorials or advertising, as it sees fit."

■

If none of the current rationales for 540.20(b) makes sense to an outsider, the historical intent was less obscure. Norman Carlson, who was BOP director when the regulation was drafted, explained its political origins in the tempestuous 1970s.

Carlson recalled that during the height of the anti–Vietnam War campaign in this country, Catholic priests Daniel and Philip Berrigan "were kind of figureheads, if you will, of a large group of dissidents who were serving time in federal prison. They were, I guess it's fair to say, anti-establishment in every sense of the word, and there was obvious concern that they were trying to use their contacts in the community to reinforce this whole notion while they were serving their sentences."

Asked about the origins of the inmate-reporter prohibition, Carlson said, "As I recall, we did modify our policy as a result of that era. I don't think we have to say the Berrigan brothers, per se, but there was, as I say, a number of inmates in custody who were extremely anti-establishment, in every sense of the word. And we felt that there was a need to tighten up to insure that they did not have access to the media on a regular basis. . . ."

Thus, government suppression of "extremely anti-establishment" views appears to have been the regulation's purpose from the beginning.

If Dannie had written for the *Chronicle* about sports or recipes, it is a good guess that he would not have been charged with any offense. Many federal prisoners had written about uncontroversial subjects—with bylines and for compensation—in newspapers and magazines, without any hassle from their keepers. One of them was the Detroit Tigers' onetime Cy Young Award–winning pitcher Denny McLain. While doing time in a federal prison, the former baseball great wrote monthly columns for *Sports Fans Journal* and *Metropolitan Detroit*.

McLain testified in a declaration in our behalf that both his writing and his outside income were well known to prison administrators. In fact, his unit manager told him that "as long as I [did] not chop up" the prison administrators in his columns, "no one would say anything."

Testimony such as Carlson's and McLain's called into question the original intent and the subsequent enforcement of the regulation we were challenging. In final arguments, our attorneys asked that such historical circumstances be considered in the light of one overwhelming principle: The First Amendment at the very least demands an extraordinary skepticism toward any set of publication restrictions that *specifically singles out* "the news media."

■

In the long hours between court sessions, Dannie kept doggedly to his writing, which he viewed as the ultimate measure of his success— both in prison and upon his release. He liked to call it "laboring in Warden Sussman's salt mines."

During this time, we were able to edit his manuscripts in person, and he wrote several stories during his stay in San Francisco, including one on a subject dear to the old-time convict's heart.

## THE ZOO ZOOS AND MUSH FAKES OF YORE

*SAN FRANCISCO, CALIF. (DEC. 24, 1989)*—The old ways of convicts are disappearing at a rapid rate. There's a new age of criminality usurping our old social systems.

No one knows what motivates the new breed of convicts. Their values are few, and they refuse to adopt the traditional rules and customs of prison life. I can't explain modern prisoners because I understand them less than anyone.

The most glaring difference between the new and the old is that today's prisoners are more apt to plead guilty and to inform on their associates. Many of them—especially captured high-level drug dealers—see themselves as failed businessmen rather than criminals. It's an attitude that often leads to confession and informing.

Old-school cons never plead guilty, and to them, informing is a craven sin.

As that old tribe of convicts becomes extinct, they walk around prison yards like old, slow dinosaurs. I know something about these relics of antiquity because I happen to be one of the clan.

Their demise is tinged with sadness, if only because a way of life is passing away from a society that was never truly known by anyone except its own members.

It wasn't a glamorous group by any means, but it was the oldest minority group known to man that was never fully studied by a cultural anthropologist. Experts have lived among apes, lions, wolves, and the tribes of darkest Africa, trying to learn their habits and customs. I don't know of a one who ever lived among and studied convicts.

In lieu of the real thing, I've decided to play cultural anthropologist for a day and take a look at some of the rapidly expiring habits and mannerisms of the tribe. They can be put into three categories: vernacular, custom, and etiquette.

Some of the terminology is being absorbed by society at large—words and phrases like "homey," "homes," "home boy," "zoo zoos," and "off the wall" are a few that come directly to mind.

Before 1958, there were no racial prison gangs in California; there was no Mexican Mafia, Aryan Brotherhood, or Black Guerrilla Family. All the cliques in prison were neighborhood groups. The biggest towns in the state had the biggest and most powerful cliques.

If someone was from your town, he was a "homey" or "home boy," unless for some reason no one wanted to claim him. If he was from the same area and you associated with him outside prison as well, he was a "road dog." The term "home boy" has been incorporated into society's vocabulary, but "road dog" never made it that I know of. "Zoo zoos" and "wham whams," convict slang for candy and sweet edibles, have found life beyond the walls.

Those prison walls are filled, and always have been, with obscenities and graffiti, most of them bitter and contemptuous and satirical. As long as decades ago, a convict spouting scatological absurdities would be told that he was talking nonsense, or that his words were "straight off the wall." Years later, when hippies began describing things as "off the wall," older cons smiled knowingly.

Other words from old convict societies aren't even used in prison anymore. "Mush fake" is one such word. It meant handmade goods—often contraband.

Everyone smoked in the old days, and convicts made picture frames and purses out of woven cigarette packaging. People made cardboard shelves and curtains for their cells. It was all mush fake. Now and then a guard would say: "You have too much mush fake in this cell." The meaning was that if you didn't get rid of a good portion of it, he would take it all.

Another dead and gone word is "rumpkin," which was the convict equivalent of "airhead."

The first convict custom that comes to mind is tattooing. Most convicts wear tattoos that are laden with symbolism—strictly macho statements in a macho world.

They don't like color in their tattoos; it's all basic black ink. Anything else is considered sissyfied. We call tattoos "tacks." If someone has a lot of tattoos, we say he is "tacked back."

What tattoos say more than anything is: "I'm an outlaw and don't care who knows it." Some tattoo "White Power," "Brown Power," swastikas, and other Nazi symbols, adding a further dimension to their statement.

There are some convicts—despite the macho image they project—who have deep feelings of fear and insecurity in this violent environment. They wear their tattoos as camouflage.

But tattoos are also beginning to disappear from the prison yards. There's an influx of Third World prisoners now, and most of them wouldn't dream of getting a tattoo. The practice simply has no place in their culture.

Their attitude toward body decoration is that if one is going to be an outlaw, he's better off if no one knows about it—an attitude so obviously correct that even some white convicts are beginning to catch on.

Another custom in all prisons is walking counterclockwise around the perimeter of the exercise yard. It's done that way in every prison I've been in or heard about. Even as a pseudo-anthropologist, I'm at a loss to explain that custom.

Often I feel that since we are all fighting time, we walk that way to defy time itself as represented by the clock. But that sounds more like metaphysics than anthropology.

Nowadays, prisoners are seen standing around laughing and joking with guards. In the old days, that simply wasn't done. Anytime a convict had to talk to a guard, he would approach the nearest convict (whether he knew him or not) and have him stand by and listen while he talked to the guard.

That was the custom when I was in Soledad, San Quentin, and Folsom in the early to late '60s. A man could lose his life for getting too cozy with the police. That custom, too, is all but dead and gone.

Prison mess halls usually seat four to a table. Often a con eats a meal with three people he doesn't know. When someone is finished eating, he will close his fist and bang his knuckles once on the table before he departs. Everyone at the table feels the vibration of the knock.

It's the way we say "Excuse me." I'm not sure if it's etiquette or custom, but I know how the practice originated. In the 1800s and the early part of this century, convicts weren't allowed to talk in prison mess halls. Knocking the table was the only way to say "Excuse me." We still do it—it's one of our tricks that even the newcomers have picked up on.

Another form of etiquette that old cons adhere to is a rule of conversation. Two men are talking together and a third walks up and joins them. If the two fall silent, it means it's a private conversation, and manners demand that the third man leave.

When a new-breed inmate walks up and two convicts fall silent, he begins to exclaim: "Hey, how you guys doin'? Huh? Huh? Sure is a nice day, huh? Huh? Isn't it, huh?" He may do that for fifteen minutes while they stand there and stare at him.

There are many other mannerisms and customs that we jailbirds live by. I've pointed out a few in an effort to show that there are strong tribal bonds among a captive population of old scofflaws.

When I use the word "convict," I don't mean only the ones in jail. The term also refers to those who are outside the walls marking time until they come back. I've often heard a convict on his way home tell a friend with a long sentence: "I'll see you when I get back."

Another eccentricity that most convicts share is a hatred and fear of hard, honest labor. If you see a convict walking along a hallway in a building and yell "Work!" he will usually jump out the nearest window without even looking to see what floor he is on.

There's a world of difference between the attitudes of the old-style convicts and the new, but that's a story for another day. Suffice it to say that these new boys have fewer scruples about senseless, unprovoked violence and crimes against children.

The old ways may be going, dust to dust, but what's replacing them doesn't look to me like much of a bargain for society. What was once a spurious cliché now seems to be the general rule: There's no honor among thieves.

---

Dannie followed that a month later with another story on guards. It represented the flip side of the story he had told in "The Prisoners on the Other Side of the Bars." This article was written at San Francisco County Jail and published soon after Dannie was returned to Phoenix.

---

## THE HACKS WAR

*SAN FRANCISCO, CALIF. (JAN. 21, 1990)*—A woman in San Francisco wrote a letter to me at the prison in Phoenix, and it got lost. When she called the mailroom to inquire, the mailroom guard said to her:

"Oh, this must be Mr. Martin's fiancée."

"Nope," she replied, "just a would-be pen pal."

"I'm sorry," the guard replied, "but you sound like his fiancée. I thought you were her."

When I arrived in December in San Francisco for my trial, the same woman called the Bryant Street jail for information about my visiting hours.

"One to three," the deputy told her, then added, "But you know what he's in for, don't you?"

"Yes," she replied, "he's in for bank robbery."

"Well, that and beating up his girlfriend," he told her. "Actually, not his girlfriend but his cohabitant, who was female."

The woman, who hadn't met me yet, was beginning to have second thoughts about making my acquaintance. But she persisted, and I was able to explain to her that I have no fiancée and I didn't beat up any woman.

I also explained to her that we were minor casualties of a war that has been going on forever between convicts and their keepers. It's a war that society never sees and one in which the guards always have the upper hand.

I think of it as the "Hacks War," because most convicts call prison and jail guards "hacks."

Some guards can't continue working in this cloistered environment without acquiring an abiding hatred for convicts. When they talk among themselves, they refer to us as "thugs," "dirtbags," or "slimeballs." They use the most profound degenerates among us as a paradigm for hating us all.

It's a form of chauvinism found only in institution-related work. Most prison guards are ex-military men, and they find a certain esprit de corps in the pursuit of hating and punishing thugs and slimeballs.

Of course, not all guards exhibit that type of behavior, but many of the ones who don't drift over to administrative jobs, leaving the front lines and trenches to the convict-haters.

Not long before I left Phoenix, a convict approached me in an extremely agitated state. His tale of woe was all too familiar.

He had been writing his wife and also writing a girlfriend that his wife didn't know about. The girlfriend wasn't aware he was married. In prison, all letters must be dropped unsealed into a mailbox. The guard on the midnight shift reads and inspects the letters, then seals and mails them.

This fellow had written his wife and girlfriend on the same evening. The night guard switched the letters so that his wife received the girlfriend's letter and vice versa.

I wasn't surprised that it happened, but it was surprising that he'd been in prison more than two years and didn't know better than to mail a letter to his wife and girlfriend on the same day.

Most convicts live by a rule that is written in concrete. One doesn't write to two women on the same day, because some guards will automatically switch the letters if you do.

The making of prison wine, or "pruno," as we call it, is another activity that is played out in the trenches of the Hacks War. Pruno is usually made in plastic bags or jugs using orange or grapefruit juice as the main ingredient. Sugar, water, and yeast are added, and it's left to work in a warm place for three to four days.

Convicts display great ingenuity in finding hiding places for their wine, and guards spend a lot of their time searching for it. When they find a batch, the normal procedure is to pour it down the nearest drain. But the guards involved in serious war games don't operate according to normal procedures.

What they do—especially if they find the booze at night when everyone is asleep—is open the bag and urinate in it. The bag is then closed and carefully placed back where it was. Wine that has been urinated in several times is far too presumptuous, even for a convict's palate.

Cell shakedowns and the packing of personal property when someone is sent to the hole are prime opportunities for rabid guards to get their licks in. A shakedown can be performed in a methodical way that leaves the cell pretty much as it was. Indeed, some guards are so good that you may not realize you've been shaken down.

Others leave the cell looking like a tornado hit it dead center— toothpaste squeezed onto personal effects and your Tang and instant coffee mixed together in one container, best clothing confiscated while the oldest rags are left in the locker.

The moves in the hidden war run from petty cruelty to serious skirmishes that can—and often do—result in serious injury or loss of life.

Guards who transport prisoners often put handcuffs on in such a way that they cut off circulation to the hands for hours at a time. Federal Bureau of Prisons guards are notorious for this practice because they use a plastic device called a "black box" over the handcuffs. I once complained about a savage handcuffing and was told by a lieutenant: "You wanna play, you got to pay."

A man I knew was stabbed to death in San Quentin because of a document "leaked" from his central file by a prison guard. The memo stated that he had informed on an unsuccessful escape plot.

That happened in the mid-'60s, and to this day I believe the document was a fake and a forgery. Others who knew the man feel the same way. He was a victim of the Hacks War.

During the turbulent '60s, there were guards being assaulted and killed, and their war became especially ugly as they retaliated in diabolical ways.

It's mellower now—just garden-variety harassment like switching letters, sabotaging wine, and shooing off prospective girlfriends.

If you notice a tattooed man in the local tavern sniffing carefully at the bouquet of his draft beer before he drinks any, it's a pretty good bet he's a veteran of the Hacks War. If he gets drunk, he can probably tell some war stories that would rival those of a Vietnam vet.

---

While Dannie was in San Francisco for the trial, he was interviewed frequently; it was the first opportunity for much of the local press to visit with him. But even upon his return to Phoenix after the trial, he was less isolated than he had once been. The trial increased the visibility of the legal principles at stake and of the man whose writing ignited the controversy. Increasingly, the world came to the prisoner who couldn't travel himself.

The only traveling he did was back to Phoenix, but it was not the kind of trip you write about in glowing postcards to the guys back at the office.

## AS THE CROW FLIES

PHOENIX, ARIZ. (FEB. 11, 1990)—The three kinds of stories that people seem to like to tell most are stories of war, of successful operations, and of "post-traumatic, long-flight stress syndrome," better known as jet lag. The following is my contribution to the latter genre.

Last November, Judge Charles Legge of the U.S. district court in San Francisco issued a writ ordering my presence at trial. I was hustled out of the prison here at Phoenix and accompanied by two marshals on a United Airlines flight to San Francisco. I wore a pair of loose handcuffs, but the trip was pleasant and mentally refreshing.

After a lengthy trial, the judge ordered me back to the prison here at Phoenix. No duration was set. The trip was relegated to the Bureau of Prisons for what I knew would be transportation on a jet that convicts call "the BOP Crow."

On Saturday, January 13, a jailer in the San Francisco Hall of Justice (who turned out to be a pretty good fellow) woke me up at 4:00 A.M. and told me: "Roll your things up, Dannie. The feds are on their way."

After being carefully strip-searched, I was placed in a holding cell with two other prisoners to await the arrival of the marshals. They came in around 5:00 A.M. One of them, a woman, told me I could take nothing along. Not even a comb or a piece of paper.

Chains were then wrapped mummy-fashion around our waists, with our cuffed hands cinched to our belly buttons. Leg irons with a short connecting chain were attached to our ankles so that we could take only short hippety-hop steps. Thus shackled, we were led to an elevator and taken to the basement garage of the jail, where a three-seat van awaited us. Before I reached the van, the leg manacles had begun to gouge into my ankles, and I hoped the trip wouldn't be a long one.

It was dark and drizzling as we drove to the new federal jail in Dublin, a town about an hour's drive from San Francisco. Along the way, the leg irons began to bite my ankles. The connecting leg chain pulls down on the inside of the shackles, and as it draws them down, the outside iron catches like jaws against the protruding ankle bones. My feet were already going numb from loss of circulation.

We finally parked at the rear door of the Metropolitan Detention Center in Dublin and waited until six more convicts came trudging out, all similarly shackled to the nines. After the new arrivals squeezed into the van with us, we drove to an Air Force base in Sacramento.

A Boeing 707 waited on the tarmac. U.S. marshals stood sentry around the plane holding sawed-off shotguns and M-16 rifles. As we hobbled up into the plane, the rasp of the leg irons against my already sore ankles felt like torture.

The plane was almost full of shackled convicts, and we were ushered to seats near the front. A lit sign said, "Fasten Seat Belts," but no one bothered. With my hands grafted by shackles to my waist, I couldn't reach for my seat belt anyway.

As I gazed around the plane's dim interior, I noticed there was every type of prisoner on the flight. Young convicts, some probably going to their first prison, older ones changing prisons, and even older, infirm men heading for the prison hospital at Springfield, Missouri. Six women prisoners sat forlornly in the front section. All of us were chained in the same manner.

During the flight, six marshals stood and sat around the plane, like German shepherd police dogs, staring at us. When someone inquired as to our destination, another replied, "I don't know."

When we finally descended through the cloud layer to land, I saw trees and mountains, but no one knew for sure where we were. A few convicts got off and more boarded. The plane was now filled to capacity. An elderly man who sat down beside me told me we were in what he called "the beautiful environs of Portland, Oregon."

Our next stop was Salt Lake City, where the same process was repeated. The hundred or so convicts in the plane sat mutely in their seats. There was no chatter. Everyone was nursing his own private misery with the chains and manacles. Up front, a woman tearfully sobbed something to a marshal who kept shaking his head no.

The old man beside me told me that he had severe diabetes and circulatory problems and was worried about the loss of blood to his hands and feet. I began to feel ashamed of myself for dwelling on my own misery. I thought about the story of the man who had no shoes meeting the man who had no feet.

It was near dark when we landed again—at El Reno, Oklahoma. By then, the shackles on my wrists and ankles felt like tourniquets, and both my feet were asleep. I was wishing my brain were asleep also, but it was wide awake and feeling every nuance of the pain.

The women were put in a van to be taken to the local jail while we headed for the federal prison near El Reno. An hour or so later, we pulled up at the old prison and were led out of the buses once more and lined up between the double fences in what was now a bitter-cold wind. We stood there shivering, some of us in T-shirts, for the fifteen minutes it took to count us again, and only then did we hobble into the prison.

An area below my left ankle bone was swollen to the size of a half-orange. A physician's assistant took me up to the hospital, where two more PAs examined me. They initially thought it was phlebitis and told me to keep my leg elevated and soaked in hot towels.

We were all led into an old cellblock called Arkansas Unit, consisting of four tiers of cells. The double cells run down the middle of the building. Between the cells and big windows are walkway areas that convicts call "the freeway." It was 1:00 A.M. before we got in there.

Another surprise awaited us. No cells were available, and orderlies were placing folding army cots for us, side by side down on the freeway. We were issued two sheets, a blanket, and no pillow. There was one toilet for sixty of us.

By the time I sat on my cot, twenty-two hours after I left San Francisco, I was totally exhausted and disoriented. I hadn't smoked in four months, but I took a look at my surroundings and told the fellow in the next cot: "Give me a cigarette."

Four large heating fans hung right above our cots, and they sounded like a jet gaining altitude as they ran all night. It seemed only a few minutes until a raucous buzzer announced breakfast, and doors on tiers above clanked as they were rolled open.

I was a miserable, headachy, tobacco-poisoned wretch as I mingled with the moving crowd and greeted the cold, dark morning. We left the building as cattle leave a holding pen. The dining room was crowded and served the worst food I've encountered in a federal prison. At every subsequent meal I attended in El Reno, they were out of glasses and silverware before my unit got there. Cons ran around borrowing glasses and spoons from friends who were finished eating.

Sunday evening, a few of us new arrivals walked to a recreation room that contains two large TV screens. The high point of my trip back to Phoenix was watching the 49ers leave big, muddy footprints all over the Los Angeles Rams.

Arkansas Unit was like Grand Central Station, filled with convicts headed in every direction. Each night around midnight, doors began clanking as convicts rolled out and left for parts unknown. A guard told me that at any one time, the federal government has five thousand prisoners in temporary holding status or in transit.

At midnight Wednesday, I was rousted out for the final leg of my trip. By the time about seventy of us had completed the strip search and chaining-up process and left the prison, it was 6:00 A.M. When we boarded the plane again, I noticed that the emergency exits had steel bars bolted across them so that they couldn't be opened. I wondered if the Federal Aviation Administration had approved this measure. But then, we were only convicts.

When we sailed into another cloudy dawn, I felt good about being on the last leg of the trip. But I began to hear grumbling from those who were going to prison hospitals and didn't seem to be getting anywhere. One man was chained up and carrying crutches.

We stopped at Denver, San Diego, Long Beach, and Lompoc, and from there we finally flew on to Phoenix. By the time we got here, it was late evening. When I left the plane, my ankles hurt so bad that when a guard frisked me and pressed down on them I screamed. He looked at me as if to say, "I'm only doing my job."

About fifty of us were put in a bus, brought here to the prison, and placed in another cage to await processing. Two PAs came in to ask routine questions about our health.

At nine o'clock Thursday evening, I was released back to the general population. My trip from San Francisco was over, five days after it began. I was elated to be off "the BOP Crow." A hot shower was pure luxury. As I showered and shaved, I thought about an old convict named Frank Coppola and what he once said to my old friend Leroy.

Frank was a man with serious heart trouble. He was doing time here at Phoenix and had served thirty years in prison without being paroled. He filed a writ alleging that thirty years was enough and he should be released.

A judge back East agreed and ordered him returned to the court there, so that he could be formally released. The day he left, he walked up to Leroy, shook his hand, and said, "I'll be all right now if I can survive the airlift."

In a way, he did. He got all the way to a holding cell in the courthouse there, where he died of a massive heart attack. After being on the airlift five days myself, I wondered how he made it as far as he did.

The tortuous route certainly isn't as the crow flies. More like a government chicken with its head cut off.

Take my advice: Fly the friendly skies of United.

---

Dannie spent the following months in Phoenix with one ear perpetually cocked in the direction of San Francisco. As the wait for a verdict stretched on over the months, he wrote to a friend to ask him "to check the obituaries for me and see if that judge is still living. Haven't heard a peep out of him."

Meanwhile, Dannie continued his exploration of his environment. The most significant of his essays from this period was a package of three pieces on a Supreme Court decision that created scarcely a ripple among the commentators of the free-world press but set off a wave of apprehension behind bars.

# A PRESCRIPTION FOR TORTURE

*PHOENIX, ARIZ. (MARCH 18, 1990)*—On Tuesday, February 27, the U.S. Supreme Court rekindled the convict's worst nightmare.

The court, by a vote of six to three, gave prison officials sweeping power to force convicts to take psychotropic drugs against their will. The ruling may have played well on the street, but it cast a dread pall over the feelings of many of us convicts.

To those of us who have watched convicts being plied with drugs that made them total zombies, the decision was maddening. It's true that some convicts need to be medicated, but we have seen others who don't need the drugs being forced to take them by incompetent and tyrannical bureaucrats.

Justice Anthony M. Kennedy, writing for the majority, said: "Given the requirements of a prison environment, the state may treat a prison inmate who has a serious mental illness with antipsychotic drugs against his will if the inmate is dangerous to himself or others and the treatment is in the inmate's best medical interest."

Justice John Paul Stevens said in dissent that a mock trial before a prison tribunal doesn't satisfy due process and that a competent individual has a constitutional right to refuse antipsychotic medication.

Many citizens will no doubt agree that medication should be forced on violent or mentally ill convicts. But there's much more at stake. It is our observation that psychotropic drugs are also used to quell what prison officials view as "troublesome" prisoners.

I'll let prison officials give their side of the story independently—they don't give official comments to convict-writers anyhow—but prisoners have simply too many credible stories of psychotropic drug abuse in the prisons to discount them all. Here's the way it looks to many convicts:

The drugs we are talking about are sometimes used in here as exquisite forms of long-term torture. Some of these mind- and body-paralyzing chemicals are Prolixin, Haldol, and Thorazine. They are brand names for a class of major tranquilizers based on the drug phenothiazine, which is widely prescribed for schizophrenia and other severe mental illnesses.

Such is the power of these drugs that I have seen men do things under their influence that almost defy description. One man on an antipsychotic drug at Lompoc penitentiary climbed a roll of deadly-sharp razor wire, oblivious to the danger, and got hung up in the wire about halfway up. A guard fired a warning shot. The convict was then hauled off the wire by other guards.

It's no secret that federal and state prison officials have for years been forcing convicts to take these drugs. But knowing we had recourse to the courts, the officials used discretion about whom they forced them on. Now that we are stripped of access to outside courts, things look grim for our future.

In the mid-1980s, the director of the Bureau of Prisons, Norman Carlson, came to Lompoc for a tour of the prison. About the time he showed up, a friend of mine disappeared from the yard.

I heard a rumor that he had been locked up because a staff member overheard him threaten Carlson. When he showed up on the yard some eighteen months later, he told me about a most chilling journey.

He said he had been taken to the basement of the isolation unit in Lompoc, where the dark cells have solid iron doors and rings on the floor. He said he was chained to the floor and pumped full of Prolixin, and he remained there until he was bundled onto a plane for a trip to the dreaded 10 Building, the psych ward at the Springfield, Missouri, prison hospital.

When he arrived at 10 Building, he told me, he was chained to his bunk in a cell and given more Prolixin. He said of the experience:

"Man, it was pure torture. My eyes would pop open sometimes at midnight, and I'd be wide awake until morning. My mind would be racing, but my body wouldn't function. It was like when you dream you're trying to run and can't move.

"When I defecated on myself, the orderlies would sometimes wait two days to clean me up. It wasn't long before I begged them for some relief, and once I began begging, the staff began to lighten up some.

"I stayed in 10 Building for nearly eighteen months and was kept on heavy doses of Prolixin the whole time."

Other convicts have disappeared into the maw of 10 Building at Springfield and not been heard from for five years or more. I don't know if they remain there, but no one I know has seen them at other prisons. There's a persistent rumor that a member of Detroit's infamous Purple Gang spent thirty years in 10 Building.

Every federal prison has men shuffling around hallways and cell-blocks as if they are walking in slow motion. There are some here at Phoenix. It's common practice in federal prisons to heavily medicate those who are perceived as a threat to staff.

But, as I and other prisoners can attest, there are even more violent men who regularly kill fellow convicts. These types are transferred to another prison after they kill someone, and they often do it again. Many of them aren't ever medicated with psychotropic drugs. As long as they are no threat to staff, they continue their murderous sprees. This sends us convicts a pretty clear message.

The people who are medicated become defenseless in the convict community and are often seriously abused by predatory fellow convicts. They are physically unable to defend themselves, and that fact increases their paranoia manyfold.

A little-acknowledged aspect of chemical straitjackets is the direct threat they pose to law-abiding society.

A violent man at Lompoc who was nearing the end of a ten-year sentence was kept heavily dosed with antipsychotic drugs. He'd done every day of his sentence because of lost good time. I used to watch him trying to run the track. He ran as if he were under water. It took him fifteen minutes to complete a lap that I ran in three minutes, and I'm no speed demon.

He was so disagreeable, paranoid, and violent that no one wanted to approach him. When his sentence was finished, the guards walked him to the front gate and shoved him out into the free world—no halfway house, no parole—and I doubt he went off to a psychiatrist and got a prescription to continue on psychotropic drugs. I've often wondered what happened when he regained his physical momentum after ten years of suppression by disabling chemicals.

Another convict who comes to mind is murderer Gary Gilmore, the subject of Norman Mailer's book *The Executioner's Song*. Gilmore was once strapped to a bunk in the Oregon State Prison for five weeks during the early 1970s and injected with massive doses of Prolixin, according to another convict. A man who was there at the time told me that after the ordeal Gilmore completely lost his sense of humor and became "extremely morbid." All this was several years before the savage murders for which he was ultimately executed.

It's apparent that Gilmore had insufficient, if any, follow-up treatment after his release, and what he did and how he did it are more than obvious.

Federal parole was recently abolished. Most of the men who are forced to take psychotropic drugs will one day be released on their own. Meeting and greeting one of them will be like dealing with a pit viper.

Prison guards now have the power to force drugs on them and chemically sedate them, but they will be pulled off those drugs before release, and their rebound—not to mention their hatred and lust for revenge—will be acted out in the arena of unsuspecting citizens. One can only hope they don't get their hands on a weapon before entering a convenience store late at night.

A man here at Phoenix who takes antipsychotic drugs can be seen around the yard jerking like a puppet. He can't be still, either sitting or standing. I once watched him in a TV room, and he stood up and sat back down in his chair twelve times in three minutes.

He moved into a cell here with a man who didn't know he was on psychotropics. At 3:00 A.M. on his first night there, the drugged man awoke and began pacing the cell. His cellmate woke up and watched him with some concern until breakfast at 6:30.

The following night, when the drugged convict fell asleep, his cellie used a roll of tape to secure him in the top bunk. He accomplished that by winding the tape around the man's legs and chest and bringing it all the way around the mattress. The convict woke up again at 3:00 A.M. and, finding himself bound, began screaming so loud he woke up the entire cellblock.

The same man was also forced to take antipsychotic drugs at the Oregon State Prison. He robbed a bank in Portland two weeks after his release while still wearing the dress-out clothes he left prison in.

Another problem with administering psychotropic drugs in here is that dosages are mixed and dispensed by physician's assistants who convicts seriously doubt are qualified to do that. Looking at some of their patients reinforces that doubt.

There's an extraordinary amount of grumbling and disgust in here about the Supreme Court ruling. A man I talked with today pretty well summed up our feelings when he said:

"They already had permission to put on rubber gloves and dig around in our bodies lookin' for drugs. Now they have the power to dig around in our brains as well."

■

The first of two sidebars that ran with that story related the experiences of one of Dannie's fellow prisoners.

## 16 DAYS OF HORROR IN 10 BUILDING

*PHOENIX, ARIZ. (MARCH 18, 1990)*—Federal convict Miguel Valdez, fifty-seven, tells a story of beatings and forced drugging at the infamous 10 Building, the psych ward at the Springfield, Missouri, prison. In light of the February Supreme Court ruling on the drugging of convicts, his story takes on new significance.

In 1986, Valdez formed a group in Portland, Oregon, called Mexican-Americans for Social Justice. The group supported boycotts by Cesar Chavez's United Farm Workers and demonstrated frequently over Hispanic social issues. They became a considerable thorn in the paw of the local establishment.

Valdez was arrested in January 1988 and jailed without bail on a drug conspiracy charge. Because of his political bent, he says, he was kept in segregation at the Portland jail. His jury trial commenced in March 1989 before U.S. district court Judge James Burns.

On the third day of his trial, an incident occurred that brought an exotic form of misery into his life.

"As I entered the courtroom, my little boy, who was eighteen months old at the time, came running up to me. I stooped down to catch him, and a marshal ran up and pushed me while yelling: 'Get away from that kid!'

"Before I could think, I hit the marshal with my fist. More marshals came and carried me to a holding cell, where they beat the hell out of me. The judge dismissed the jury and told them I was mentally incompetent to continue my trial right then."

That, Valdez says, was only the beginning of his ordeal:

"After they beat me until both eyes were swollen shut and my ribs caved in, they put me in the hole for three days, then chained me up and put me on the airflight to Springfield, Missouri.

"When I got to E Block at Springfield, the guards shackled me to my bunk by hands and ankles. They gave me intravenous shots of Prolixin and forced liquid Thorazine down my throat. I lay there shackled for two nights and days with no food or water. All they gave me was Prolixin and liquid Thorazine."

He says that by the third day, his tongue had swollen up and was sticking to the roof of his mouth, and he was thinking he might die of thirst. Valdez says his condition was probably exacerbated by his diabetes.

The solid door on his cell had a small peephole. When two guards looked in, Valdez said he began yelling at them: "Hey, give me some water!"

"Shut up, asshole!" one of them reportedly replied. "You don't have anything coming."

But, Valdez continues, "I kept on yelling for water, and those two came in and beat me up again while I was shackled. A nurse named Bertha, who appeared to be Puerto Rican or Cuban, came in not long after they beat me. She ordered them to take off my shackles after I told her I had been without water or food for two days and nights. She gave me some water and juice, and it was the best I've ever tasted."

Valdez says he spent sixteen days in 10 Building's E Block on Prolixin and Thorazine. Seven days of that time, he was shackled to his bed.

"The judge was calling them, wanting me back for trial, but I was so beaten and marked up, they couldn't bring me back right then," he says. "They began giving me big doses of antibiotics to heal the cuts and bruises."

When he returned to Portland after his stay in 10 Building, his trial resumed before the same jury, and he says he was given Thorazine twice a day for the duration of the trial.

Valdez was convicted, and in July 1989, he was sentenced to thirty years in federal prison and sent back to 10 Building at Springfield. But this time, he says, he was taken off Thorazine and put in another section.

"I was only in E Block two days before they put me in F Block and gave me a job as nurse's attendant and orderly. It's obvious I'm not violent or crazy. I've never had, or needed, psychiatric treatment in my entire life."

He worked in 10 Building for six months before he was transferred here to Phoenix. As we talk, he shows me the deep scars left by the shackles on his wrists and ankles.

He says that last September a tour of about twelve men and women came through 10 Building at Springfield. "Before they arrived, the guards were running around taking the shackles off of everyone, and they had me cleaning up their cells."

Valdez says that as long as he lives, he won't forget 10 Building or what happened there. "It's a pitiful place. Two or three times a week, you can hear convicts pleading and whimpering like animals as guards shackle them, beat them, and force medicine into them."

---

For the other sidebar, Dannie relied on his own past experiences.

---

## PAYING YOUR DUES

Phoenix, Ariz. (March 18, 1990)—While approving the forcible administration of antipsychotic drugs to convicts, a majority of the high court addressed civil-liberties concerns by deciding that a hearing before a prison tribunal satisfies one's constitutional right to due process.

Well, I know about those prison hearings.

Often, a convict is hauled up before a prison court and found guilty on the word of a "confidential informant." No other evidence is required, and the informant is never produced or identified.

Due process, in other words, requires about as much evidence in here as "a little bird told me."

In that type of proceeding, a prisoner could be forced to take antipsychotic drugs on the word of a confidential informant that he had threatened a staff member or that his actions were bizarre and potentially violent.

In 1982, I left a cellblock in Lompoc penitentiary on my way to dinner. A convict in the hallway ran at me with a ten-inch knife in his hand and tried to stab me in the neck. I grappled with him and finally wrenched his knife away, breaking my thumb in two places in the process.

When guards arrived, the man I was struggling with ran, and I was observed with the knife. They charged me with possession and conveyance of a weapon. When I appeared at an institution trial, several witnesses came forward, and all corroborated my version of the melee. No one said anything to the contrary.

The captain told me that what happened didn't matter. I was charged with having a weapon, an officer observed me with the weapon, so therefore I was guilty. I served 120 days in Isolation and lost 180 days of good time. Fortunately, the captain didn't take a mind to drugging me to protect my fellow convicts.

Prison justice is a law unto itself, and often facts aren't allowed to get in the way.

The high court may call it "due process." Convicts call it "paying your dues."

---

The important story Dannie told in those three essays had been on his mind for years, and the Supreme Court decision finally gave him an occasion to discuss the issue. In the years we had been corresponding, Dannie had returned frequently to the subject of excessive prison use of heavy-duty tranquilizers.

At one time we even tried to put together a *Chronicle* investigation of psychotropic drug usage in prison, but the project foundered, as have so many similar investigations, when the BOP refused to hand over to the paper its statistics on the use of such drugs. Our Freedom of Information Act request ran into a bureaucratic wall.

The frustration of discussing prison issues through individual feature articles is that whatever injustices are briefly exposed disappear again behind the massive and impenetrable facade of the prison bureaucracy. If abusive drugging has been going on in federal prisons—and the dimensions of the problem are unknowable at this time—it is presumably continuing unabated. But now, to the press blackout has been added the secrecy assured by court-sanctioned closed hearings.

■

Old-time cons like Dannie, to survive years in prison, develop an ability to roll with whatever punches are thrown at them, real or metaphorical. They know that festering resentments only make the time go harder. So, characteristically, for his next "Sunday Punch" piece, Dannie once again got in touch with his inner imp.

# BLACK TIE AND SHACKLES

PHOENIX, ARIZ. (APRIL 8, 1990)—In his quest for a kinder, gentler nation, President George Bush has finally extended the hand of friendship inside prison walls. Many convicts were alarmed that the negative Willie Horton ads he ran during his campaign signified a tough-on-crime policy. After the election, Bush stopped federal furloughs for drug dealers.

But in an astounding display of political diplomacy, the president has eased our fears by writing a personal letter to a notorious convict serving twenty years on a drug conspiracy charge. He has invited John (Big John) Walters, fifty-seven, to an evening of dinner and dancing in the capital.

"I'm really happy with the invite," Big John says. "It shows that President Bush understands we are all human. But I am really having problems trying to get the trip approved by my counselor."

The letter, dated March 13, 1990, and sent to Big John at his prison address, congratulated the convict on his acceptance for membership in the Republican Inner Circle after his name had been placed in nomination by Senator Phil Gramm. It went on to say that the president and Barbara look forward to seeing Big John in Washington on May 3, 1990.

"The counselor says no way am I getting a furlough for this, so I guess I'll have to fire off a letter to someone and get my travel plans straightened out," Big John says.

When asked how he came to be nominated to the Republican Inner Circle by Senator Gramm, Walters replied:

"When I was arrested back in 1985, in Newark, California, the FBI took $503,000 in cash from my car and turned it over to the government. I never got any of it back, so I guess it was considered a political donation. That should put me right up there with the cream of the crop of political donors."

When he was informed that the money was probably given to a drug task force and was an unlikely source of his nomination, Big John said:

"The only other thing I can think of is an incident that happened in a sushi bar in Houston back in 1982. I'm sitting there enjoying a bit of sushi when this tall, slim guy wearing glasses and a jogging outfit jogs in and orders a bunch of sushi to go.

"Four guys wearing dark suits and wing-tip shoes jogged in and stood there running in place while he ordered. When the order came, he'd forgotten his wallet, and the four men with him didn't have enough money between them to pay for it.

"I love sushi, and I couldn't bear to see a man have to return his order, so I graciously picked up the tab. He thanked me and told me he would invite me to dinner one of these days. I'm not certain who the man was, but who knows? This could be it!"

That story is more plausible—well, barely more plausible—because it's a documented fact that Big John does love sushi. The U.S. marshal who finally arrested him after an eighteen-month manhunt was mad because he hated sushi and had been in every sushi bar on the West Coast while following Big John.

It isn't often that a fellow convict is invited to an intimate dinner and dance with George and Barbara Bush. A lot of us are shaking John's hand and congratulating him. We are hoping that he can raise some issues in Washington that are of grave concern to us all.

"Smitty," the head jailhouse lawyer at the law library here at Phoenix, voiced his legal opinion when asked about the ramifications of the president's invitation:

"He definitely won't get a furlough to attend that dinner. The rules are very clear on that—no furlough. But that don't mean he can't attend. What will happen is he will be picked up by two U.S. marshals, handcuffed and shackled with leg irons, and delivered to Washington, D.C., via the 'BOP Crow' for the dinner."

Big John became visibly upset when the procedure was explained to him.

"No way!" he exclaimed. "Forget it! I'm not going to sit down and try to eat with handcuffs and leg shackles on. Besides that, how would I look dancing a waltz like that? If that's how it's going to be, they can forget it, I ain't goin'!"

Walters also received a personal letter from Senator Bob Dole at his prison address. The senator's letter informed him that he had been nominated by Senator Gramm because of his "accomplishments and commitment to our nation." But neither Dole's letter nor the president's said anything about handcuffs or leg irons.

Dole's letter also said there would be discussions on trade, monetary policy, crime and drugs, and the environment. This led some of us to believe that perhaps they want Big John to make a speech on the issue of drug smuggling.

"I couldn't help them much there," he says. "There were no drugs involved in my case. The DEA got a business associate of mine to call me up and ask to borrow a quarter of a million dollars to buy some cocaine to help rescue his failing business, and I said yes. They got the conversation on tape and arrested me for conspiracy to import cocaine. I could explain to them how you can get twenty years for talking about drugs on a telephone."

"Gee," he added, "I hope they don't renege on the offer when they find out I'm not a bona fide smuggler."

There's not much sound political expertise to be found on a prison yard. The John Walters invitation has the tint of a quid pro quo, and I queried the nearest thing we have in here to an expert on Republican politics. He's a sixty-four-year-old convict named Leroy who bills himself as president of the Committee of Old Republican Prisoners (CORP).

"I can't speak for George Bush," Leroy said, "but I can speak for the Republican Party, and I guarantee you this is no quid pro quo."

Convicts feel good about the letters Big John received because they could be indications of political changes of some magnitude, although with all the speculation and rumors, it's difficult to decipher their true meaning. But, with all the talk, I did get up the courage to ask Big John something that up to now convicts have been afraid to ask him.

While he was on the U.S. marshals' most-wanted list, one of his aliases was D. Cooper. There's been a persistent rumor over the years that he is the infamous D. B. Cooper, who extorted money from an airline and parachuted out over Washington State. I went ahead and popped the question.

"Get outta here!" he replied. "Look at me, man! If I was D. B. Cooper, I would have needed two parachutes and a good spare. I weigh three hundred pounds. You want to talk politics, fine, but I don't know D. B. Cooper from a bale of cotton."

There's a lot of talk here at Phoenix now about setting up an etiquette class to teach convicts which spoon to use if they ever get invited to dine with the president. But it's still hard for us to imagine anyone at a black-tie Republican dinner wearing handcuffs and leg shackles.

———————————

Dannie published several other articles in the *Chronicle* over the next few months—a book review and a few topical pieces—and he had another package of stories on my desk and almost ready for publication when we received word of the court ruling that once again changed the course of his troubled new "career."

# V

# HE SHALL REMAIN
# NAMELESS
# JUNE 1990 –
# OCTOBER 1991

Waterloo! 6–26–90

*Dear Peter: I couldn't help but feel sorry for you when you gave me our verdict. You sounded pretty sad, buddy. But I feel this is only the opening shot in this war. . . . Law like that makes me feel that now even jurists view me as less than human.*

*If we can't shake up a mind-set like that, we can't write a lick. I believe our most important task now is finding some way to mount an appeal. . . .*

*I feel very bad about all the time and energy you put into this. You were the motor that drove the whole vehicle, and I guess now you feel like you've thrown a rod or dropped an oil pan. . . . We'll get back on the highway. I feel it in my bones. . . .*

*I feel I'm still in pretty good shape in here. My main protection wasn't the court order, it was this pen in my hand. It still is. . . .*

*My mother used to say, "They can kill you but they can't eat you." Hopefully Legge didn't legalize cannibalism some-*

*where in that fifty-two-page frame he built around five words,*
*"overriding need for prison security." Indeed.*

*Well, hell, I still feel good about things. All this episode will*
*do is force me to work on honing my writing skill. I'm not tak-*
*ing this shit lying down. I'll come back like a hog out of a mud*
*wallow.*

*I've got your help, so there's not much else I really need.*
*Things will get better before they get worse.*

*Your #1 pal,*
*Dannie*

Judge Legge had handed down his ruling, an assistant city editor
informed me in a solicitous voice. We had lost on all points; the judge
said prison security comes first.

When that call came from the city desk on June 26, 1990, I did
indeed feel as if I'd thrown a rod, although I would not have put it
that way.

I called Jeff Leon to inform him of the ruling. For the longest time,
the lawyer who was never at a loss for words was dead silent. But his
numb disbelief was almost audible. Neither of us had expected such a
ruling.

Of the major figures in our lawsuit, the least disturbed by the ruling
was Dannie himself. He was also the one with the most to lose. Dannie
was sustained by his indomitable confidence in the justice of our case.
But also, as a convict, he always expected the worst; he was used to it.
And he was used to waiting and to having no control over events. Even
when he allowed himself to hope, as he did with our lawsuit, his guard
was always up. Practice had taught him that that was the only way to
survive half a lifetime in prison.

Judge Legge prefaced his ruling with praise for Dannie's writing:

Martin's articles are entertaining and educational. Some of them appear
to have actually produced worthwhile results. Martin's writing style
is light, concise, and easily readable. Many legal writers, scholars,
attorneys—and yes, judges—could well imitate his style.

He continued—in words a prison reformer might have used—by lauding the role Dannie's writing had played both in prison and in the free world:

> Writing by prisoners also appears to be worthwhile for rehabilitation, particularly if a prisoner such as Martin is able to use it as a base for a future career outside the prison. Writing is a healthy use of time. The writing of published articles could provide a good role model for other prisoners. And such articles, even if critical of the prison system, may provide a nonviolent means to defuse tensions within a prison. The public appears to be interested in the subject of life in prison; and light and air, literally or figuratively, are generally healthy to any institution.

I couldn't have put it better myself, although I could certainly have wished for better than what followed. Legge held that 540.20(b), the "byline / compensation / acting-as-a-reporter" regulation that Dannie was accused of violating, was constitutionally valid, justifiable because of the unique security needs of a prison. So was the use of the "conducting-a-business" regulation against freelance writers, and so, too, were the actions taken against Dannie in the weeks following publication of "The Gulag Mentality."

The basis of the judge's reasoning was that "in recent first amendment cases, the [Supreme] Court has extended considerable deference and discretion to the decisions of prison administrators." Indeed, twice in his opinion Legge left the balancing of First Amendment and prison security entirely to the BOP, seemingly abdicating *any* judicial role:

> Defendants' primary objective is prison security. . . . There are other valid penological interests, such as rehabilitation, which would weigh in favor of looser control by the prison authorities. But as long as prison security is a valid interest, *the order of priority of the penological interests is for the Bureau of Prisons and not this court to decide.* [Emphasis added.]

And again, balancing "the potential dangers" of prisoners' writings against "the benefits of more public awareness of prisons," he wrote: "These are questions which are *not within the power of this court to decide* [emphasis added]. They are for the Bureau of Prisons to decide."

He did not specify who has the power to evaluate the legitimacy of the prisons' claimed security needs, which are so easily confused with institutional embarrassment. Nor was it clear from his ruling who beyond the prison walls could weigh security judgments against the First Amendment rights of press and public. In the words of a *Chronicle* reader who wrote to us, "Who is able to police the police?"

But the judge did conclude that his ruling "is not *carte blanche* for the Bureau to restrain opinions which it does not like. In a civilized society governed by the rule of law, voices of dissent cannot and should not be suppressed." He then warned the BOP against the very power he seemed to have given them earlier in his ruling:

> When those [First Amendment] rights [of prisoners] conflict with a genuine concern for prison security, as in this case, restraint can be imposed. But the word "security" cannot be just a label invoked to shield all actions from scrutiny.

As for whether any actual breach of security resulted from publication of "The Gulag Mentality," Legge concluded that "dangers and threats [of violence] occurred in Lompoc prison." Alluding to the noisy-prison / quiet-prison conundrum, he wrote:

> Many witnesses testified to changes in the mood of the prison population at the time of the publication of "Gulag," Martin's administrative segregation, and then his release into the general population. The changes in mood were variously, and perhaps inconsistently, described. But the testimony was consistent that there were changes, and that changes are an indicator of potential difficulties within the prison.

In other words, some said the prison was noisy and therefore dangerous; some said it was quiet and therefore dangerous. So it must have been dangerous.

Similarly, citing other indications of disquiet in the prison, Legge wrote:

> There is some question whether these events and the prisoners' statements were motivated by the article or by Martin's being placed in administrative segregation. But in either event, there were indications of a security problem.

Such reasoning sidestepped the question of whether Dannie's "Gulag" article *caused* a security problem. But Legge did cite evidence to suggest that Dannie and I were likely to cause a future problem. "The tape-recorded conversations between Martin and the *Chronicle*," he wrote, "indicated that further articles would be written 'to keep pressure and heat on' the warden."

Issues of fact usually are omitted when such constitutional cases go up on appeal, but for the record: We never planned to pressure the warden with "further articles," and repeated searches through the tape transcripts have failed to turn up the words quoted in that sentence of Legge's ruling.

The judge also wrote, "The recordings disclosed that Martin intended to write an article about the high security unit within the prison and about the inmates there." The reference is apparently to "A Report from 'Solitary' "—in which Dannie wrote about the treatment he received in the hole—and to prison officials' mistaken assumptions of what was going to be written in that article.

■

In his opinion, Legge glossed over the *Chronicle*'s and the public's interests, in the apparent belief that they were not affected by the rules we were challenging:

> The regulations do not inhibit the content of what is printed by the *Chronicle*. They do not authorize the Bureau of Prisons to tell the *Chronicle* what can or cannot be printed, and the Bureau has not attempted to exercise such a power. The *Chronicle* is free to publish whatever it wants. . . . The restraints which the regulations place on Martin as a prisoner do not prohibit the *Chronicle* from publishing anything that he sends to them.

Except, of course, that the prisoner can be punished for editorial decisions made by *Chronicle* editors—byline and page placement, for example.

Months later, the director of the BOP demonstrated that he did not share the judge's—and the Justice Department's—interpretation that the regulations are not directed toward what the *Chronicle* can publish.

In sum, Legge's ruling gave the government unprecedented power to "edit" the nation's newspapers and magazines, determining the manner of presentation of prisoner writings—even the page on which those writings may appear—and forbidding monetary incentives for convict manuscripts. And it left the scope of that power unclear because of the undefined prohibition against "acting as a reporter."

Ambiguity about which writing is punishable would, of course, be a signal to other convicts to refrain from the very dissent and institutional scrutiny that Legge warned had to be preserved.

Two days after Judge Legge's ruling, the *Chronicle,* in an editorial, picked up on the jurist's parting warning to the BOP. "In keeping with the injunction to allow voices of dissent to be heard," the editorial said, "the *Chronicle* will continue to carry firsthand reports about conditions in federal penitentiaries."

But it was not as easy as that. With the guarantees of the preliminary injunction removed, protecting Dannie from punishment became our first consideration. I held up publication of the articles I had in hand while discussing the issue with Dannie and the attorneys.

We also had some legal housekeeping to attend to. First, Dannie needed a new attorney. Leon had changed firms, and his new firm could no longer bear the extraordinary expenses of the pro bono representation. To replace him, we were fortunate to find Bill Turner, a San Francisco attorney who specializes in prison and media law and who was willing to represent Dannie pro bono. There were also changes in the *Chronicle*'s legal team, with Zinkan and Neil Shapiro passing the torch to Jim Wagstaffe and Marty Kassman, who had been assisting at the lower-court level.

Then there was the question of a possible appeal. Making the decision a great deal easier were the hundreds of supportive letters that Dannie and I received from *Chronicle* readers. One message expressed again and again in those letters, in almost identical words, was: Appeal the decision. As one writer put it: "I sincerely hope you continue to fight this one out—for yourselves as an institution and for us, your readers."

Many prisoners wrote to tell us of the impact of the decision behind bars. They linked the self-respect of all prisoners to Dannie's fate. As one federal prisoner said, the BOP is "afraid of inmates such as Dannie Martin because he restores the individual inmate to a higher degree of self-worth than the BOP would allow. He is no threat to the Bureau of Prisons, only to the idea that we, as inmates, are subhuman to the rest of humanity."

There had never been any schedule for the appearance of Dannie's articles in "Sunday Punch." I printed them as they came—or as they were accepted and edited—but over time he had settled into a pattern of a story every month or two, and his readers got used to that frequency. Now, as we considered the impact of the court ruling, some of Dannie's more ardent fans demanded to hear from him. "Dear Editor," wrote one, "What has become of Dannie Martin? Why have you allowed him to vanish from your pages without explanation? . . . Don't let him disappear into a dark hole."

There are many dark holes. My priority was keeping Dannie from some dark hole of punishment within the prison. In stories following the court ruling, one assistant U.S. attorney held out the continuing threat of discipline for "The Gulag Mentality." And U.S. Attorney William McGivern showed how little rope they planned to give the writer in the future: "If he just wants to get his views known, he can always write a letter to the editor."

**Within** six weeks of Legge's ruling, the *Chronicle* and Dannie's new attorney filed notices of appeal. The appeal itself was accompanied by an amici curiae (friends of the court) brief in which many national news organizations seconded the *Chronicle*'s right to control bylines and placement of stories it publishes. The amici brief was undertaken with seed money from the Society of Professional Journalists, the nation's largest and oldest organization of journalists, and was prepared under direction of SPJ's constitutional counsel, Bruce Sanford. The Associated Press, the world's largest newsgathering organization, and the American Society of Newspaper Editors were among the groups joining in the brief.

Turner also filed—unsuccessfully—for an emergency stay to restore the protections granted in the preliminary injunction, pending an appeals court ruling. With the request denied, the immediate problem in conforming with 540.20(b) was to try to figure out what behavior was prohibited. Legge himself had conceded that "the terms here, whether describing the writing or the writer, are not ones of precise definition or consistent usage," and he said he was relying on "common sense meaning" and "general intent."

The key question was: If we published Dannie's writing without compensation or byline, would he nonetheless be vulnerable for "acting as a reporter"? After reading and rereading the judge's ruling, we still didn't know what activity that phrase prohibited. Dannie expressed his understanding of the words in an interview with the Associated Press: "I don't know what acting like a reporter is. I guess they do. When they get ready, they'll bring that hammer down on my head and say that's what I'm doing."

Although the penalties for "conducting a business" are light—and none are listed for "acting as a reporter"—the real threat would come from whatever action the parole board might take based on Dannie's violation. The convict's time was starting to look tantalizingly short—less than a year and a half. But because he was tentatively scheduled for parole eleven years into a thirty-three-year sentence, the members of the parole board had twenty-two years to "play with" if they saw fit.

**I** informed Dannie in a phone call of the options. Among them was to wait out the appeal process, which I suspect would have pleased at least some of our attorneys, although they were far too committed to the First Amendment to have pushed such a course. If Dannie kept appearing in print—even though it was at some unknown future risk to himself—it would be harder to convince an appellate court that he was being muzzled.

I asked Dannie what he wanted to do. He replied that it was up to me, but I let him know that this decision was not one I could make. It was his ass on the line, and the decision whether to place himself in jeopardy had to be his alone.

"Well," he replied, "then I want to keep on publishing."

It did not surprise me.

Before settling on a format, I fleetingly considered several bizarre options that would appear to be legal under Legge's ruling. Perhaps we could have put a "Letters to the Editor" logo over anything Dannie wrote, creating a letters section with enough room to contain his essays. We could also have used *my* byline over his stories and begun each with: "Dannie Martin told me the following."

But I rejected these options. Although all such formats would have highlighted the flaws of the regulation we were challenging, I did not want to appear to taunt the judge or evade his ruling through glib technicalities.

Nevertheless, Dannie's next essays, and all subsequent essays in the remaining fourteen months of his imprisonment, appeared in a format unprecedented in journalistic history—a format more suggestive of South

Africa than of the United States. The writer's name appeared nowhere on the essays. In place of his byline were the words "By a Federal Prisoner," and an accompanying box explained:

> This story is by a convicted bank robber and prisoner at the Federal Correctional Institution in Phoenix who has been a frequent contributor to "Sunday Punch." Under a recent court ruling now being appealed, federal prisoners may not have their writings published in the news media under their bylines. Therefore, in an attempt to protect the convict-writer from further disciplinary action, the *Chronicle* has chosen to publish this story anonymously.

The decision to adopt this peculiar format was mine, with input from Dannie and the attorneys and with approval from my superiors at the *Chronicle*. The wording of the box seemed the best possible compromise between what *Chronicle* readers had a right to know about the author and what the court had ruled was permissible. I hoped the wording would show that the *Chronicle* has the power, under the First Amendment, to choose what it wishes to publish but that our choices were nevertheless limited by the punishment that Dannie could face.

And, of course, the convict was not compensated for any articles published after the court ruling.

The ultimate importance of the anonymous byline may lie less in the legal implications than in the social import. The convict who began publishing to make a name for himself lost his name. And there, in 11-point type, was the repudiation of much that he had tried to accomplish in his writing: humanizing prisoners so that the public could deal with them as individuals rather than as ciphers.

---

**W**hen the Ninth Circuit court of appeals finally heard the case in late August 1991, Justice Department attorney William C. Brown was subjected to insistent questioning from the three-judge panel trying to clarify apparent inconsistencies in regulation 540.20(b). The judges grilled him about what a byline is and why a convict's byline is dangerous to prison security when it appears in the news media but not in a possibly bigger publication that isn't a news outlet.

Finally, Brown cut his argument close to the bone. The Bureau of Prisons, he said, "had to draw a line somewhere. They chose to draw it in a way that goes after the news media. . . ."

As one *Chronicle* attorney remarked after the hearing, "I have only one thing written down on my pad: 'They chose to go after the news media.' "

■

While constitutional arguments ricocheted through the higher reaches of the court system, "a federal prisoner" wrote some of his most powerful pieces. Although his works appeared anonymously, the author was anything but anonymous. Only to newer and more forgetful readers was he nameless.

The first package of two stories that were to run without Dannie's byline had sat on my desk until the request for a stay was rejected and he decided to risk punishment by publishing anonymously. Two months late, we published the story of the prison drug war.

## THE BOTTLE WARS TURN UGLY

PHOENIX, ARIZ. (AUG. 26, 1990)—The drug war has reached fever pitch behind prison walls. It began during the early '80s as an effort to slow down drug use by convicts. As the decade passed, the war evolved into a frenzied spasm of hard sanctions and witch-hunts, yet there are more drugs and drug abusers in here than ever before.

The crackdown began with random urine testing of suspected drug users, and as soon as administrators began testing us, convicts began playing a game called "beat the bottle." By the end of the decade, the lighthearted bottle games had taken on a far more troubling tone.

In the early '80s, a counselor was likely to hand someone a bottle and tell him to go into the rest room and fill it. Cons would regularly carry a bottle of clean urine and substitute that for their own.

It wasn't long before guards began accompanying us to the rest room and watching closely as we gave the sample; thus began the season of adulterants. People who knew they would "test dirty" deposited all sorts of foreign substances into the bottle. The most popular additives were table salt, ammonia, baking soda, bleach, and Ajax cleanser.

Soon after the advent of the adulterant era, the guards began shaking us down carefully and making us wash our hands thoroughly before each test, and convicts began "flushing." Flushing is accomplished by drinking enormous amounts of water prior to giving a sample—usually more than a gallon in a ninety-minute period—and sipping regularly after that until test time. Those test samples can be as clear as bottled spring water, and some of them pass with flying colors.

But nowadays, even flushing has its drawbacks. Last year, a lieutenant here in Phoenix looked at samples given by two convicts and said, "Lock them up in Isolation. These bottles are too clear."

Added to the paranoia on both sides is the firm belief among prisoners that serious mistakes are made at the labs where the samples are sent for scrutiny. Many apparently reliable convicts say they are clean and receive positive readings; others confess that they've been dirty yet received negative readings.

Convict Dean Rose came here on a disciplinary transfer from the federal prison at Pleasanton in Northern California. In January of this year, a lieutenant found a "white powder substance" in a glass ashtray on Rose's locker in his Pleasanton cell. The substance was dropped into a test kit and turned brown, which indicated methamphetamines.

The "substance," Rose says, was a Top Ramen soup mix that contains beef bouillon. Concentrated beef bouillon, of course, also turns brown when water is added.

Rose spent sixty days in Isolation, lost thirty-two days of good time, and was given a disciplinary transfer here to Phoenix, with a recommendation that his parole date be delayed. So far, his appeals and entreaties have been unsuccessful.

A man I know who had been using amphetamines was called in for a test. The guard turned his head, and the man filled the bottle from the clear, flushed water in the toilet bowl. The sample was accepted, and it came back positive for morphine. These unusual incidents occur with such regularity that we've become convinced that testing procedures are fraught with error.

There's a lot at stake in the bottle wars. In the early '80s, if a test came back positive for drugs, the parole board could delay a convict's parole date up to four months for each positive test. That sanction usually followed a stay of up to thirty days in Isolation.

Things are a lot worse now. The incident report given now for a positive drug test is a "100 series" offense. We call a disciplinary write-up a "shot." A "100 series" shot is in the category with murder and assault on a prison guard. The parole commission can now take away a parole date for one dirty drug test. The shot can mean that a convict must serve every day of his or her sentence—and that can mean decades of added prison time, without the legal representation or other guarantees of a trial on the outside.

In the ten years of escalating vigilance and sanctions by authorities, I don't know even one drug abuser who stopped using drugs in prison because of a fear of added time or punishment. The attitude in here seems to be exemplified by the words of an acquaintance:

"Hey, man, I robbed banks and took a chance on getting twenty-five years to get money for drugs. I don't know how they think I'll quit [because I'm] worrying about a few more months. I need them drugs worse in here than I did outside."

The tests are said to be random, but the surest way to get one is to be targeted by a "note dropper." Notes are written to staff—often anonymously—by inmates who claim that so-and-so is using drugs or committing other rule infractions. A note accusing a convict of using drugs will get him a urinalysis for sure.

A note dropper can also get a person locked up in Isolation, without a hearing, if he charges that a convict has threatened someone or is a threat to someone. Much of the time, the information is erroneous and the target of the note is released after a lengthy investigation.

Modern-day prison security relies heavily on note droppers, and when some hideous character has a personal ax to grind, he will drop a note on someone who gets visits. The note will say the person is bringing drugs into the institution. This earns his victim a trip to the "dry cell" (see related story below).

The dry cell here at Phoenix is in the isolation unit. A bright light burns twenty-four hours a day. There's no apparent ventilation, no running water, and no blanket. The room appears to be heated continuously, with the temperature hovering around a hundred degrees. It's a virtual torture chamber furnished only with a bowl to defecate in and a rubber mattress to sleep on. The guards stationed outside never take their eyes off the suspect.

His bodily wastes are meticulously inspected over several days before he is released from the cell. If this procedure weren't so disgusting and degrading to all of those involved, it would be wryly humorous. It's a well-known fact among convicts that many if not most of the drugs in prisons are brought in by guards who need to supplement their meager income. When found out, they are usually quietly dismissed. They never make the dry cell.

The saddest aspect of the procedure is that convicts are usually taken to the dry cell from the visiting room, stranding friends and loved ones who may have traveled thousands of miles.

In my two years here at Phoenix, I've known several convicts who have had to endure the ordeal. Not a one of them was discovered to have drugs inside him. But the numbers add up to many bowls of stinking effluvium, hot days and nights of stench and uncleanliness, shabbily treated loved ones and indelible images of hatred branded on the minds of cons and their keepers.

Those of us in the trenches of the drug wars are beginning to suffer a unique form of shell shock. There won't be any heroes returning from these battles. Everyone who is even remotely involved is a casualty.

---

Two sidebars ran with that story. The first was also by "a federal prisoner."

---

## 'THE MOST PAINFUL HUMILIATION'

PHOENIX, ARIZ. (AUG. 26, 1990)—David (Curly) Ayala, thirty-eight, received a long-anticipated visit from his wife, Caroline, on Friday evening, June 1. The weekend ended in a nightmare he could never have imagined.

Caroline Ayala drove to Phoenix from Los Angeles, intending to visit Friday evening and all day Saturday and Sunday. After the Saturday visit, unbeknownst to his wife, the convict was handcuffed and led off to the dry cell; his Sunday visit was canceled.

"I couldn't believe what was happening to me," he says. "They handcuffed me, and four guards surrounded me. I was frog-marched to Isolation, stripped, and put in the dry cell, and all the while I'm telling them I have nothing inside me and I don't smuggle drugs." At the time, Ayala had no idea what prompted officials to suspect him of drug smuggling.

His protests were to no avail, and he says that when he was pushed into the dry cell in a pair of boxer shorts, the heat felt like a sauna. He says there were no vents in the concrete cell and no air circulating. As he walked around the cell trying to orient himself, he noticed that it contained only a rubber mattress and a bowl shaped like a large dog-food bowl, which he was to use as a toilet. A guard was stationed on the other side of a sheet of Plexiglas that covered the door, watching every move he made.

"Keep your hands where I can see them at all times," the guard barked at him.

Ayala says he walked around the bowl looking at it and wondering to himself: "Now, how in the world am I supposed to have a bowel movement in that?" The bowl was large enough, but the logistics were daunting.

At dinner Saturday night, he was handed a sack lunch that contained two baloney sandwiches. Knowing he would have to have several bowel movements before his release, he began complaining that he couldn't do it on sack lunches. He was told that a Lieutenant King had ordered him on sack lunches.

He requested laxatives to help him along and was told he could have nothing.

"They would give me a glass of water, but I had to beg for it and then wait while the guard told another guard on the two-way radio to bring one up. If the other guard was busy, I waited."

It was after midnight when he had his first bowel movement, and after he'd figured out a way to approach the bowl and begin his business, the guard got frantic:

"I can't see!" the guard yelled through the Plexiglas. "Hold everything up out of the way so I can see, and keep those hands in plain sight!"

In a low voice, Ayala tells me, "That was the most painful humiliation I've ever experienced." He's obviously uncomfortable talking about it.

When he finished his bowel movement, he says, they wouldn't

give him toilet paper to clean himself with. There was no paper of any kind in the cell, he said. He passed the bowl through the slot in the door, and the guard looked into all his body cavities before cuffing him and removing him briefly from the cell so it could be searched.

A woman lieutenant named Smith arrived with wooden tongue depressors and began probing around in the bowl as he was put back into the cell. He asked her if she would please let him have some toilet paper to clean himself with.

"I figured that since she was a woman she might have more sympathy than the robots I was dealing with," he says.

She ordered the guards to bring him a wet towel and washcloth so he could clean himself and hand it back out. Afterward, he asked Smith if someone could meet his wife when she arrived on Sunday morning and explain things, because he knew she'd be worried when told that she couldn't see him. Smith told him she would "take care of it."

(Ayala's wife, Caroline, told the *Chronicle* in an interview that no one told her anything when she showed up for her Sunday visit. She said she had even bought sandwiches from the vending machines for her and her husband to eat when he was brought out.

(Caroline Ayala said that after about an hour in the prison she began asking the visiting-room guard where her husband was. "He's being paged," was the reply.

(She said she was finally told by a duty officer named Delaney that she couldn't see her husband because he was in administrative custody and under investigation.

(To any other questions, Delaney replied that he couldn't answer and that she would have to get answers from her husband in three to four days, she said. Caroline Ayala became alarmed about his condition, but she was assured by Delaney that her husband was safe, was in perfect health, and had all his possessions.)

When David Ayala finally dozed off on the rubber mattress, in spite of the light that shone around the clock, he was awakened by the guard yelling through the slot, "I can't see your hands. Keep them in plain sight!" David says he finally went to sleep with his hands hanging off the end of the mattress.

The following Tuesday, after seven negative bowel movements, Ayala was released from the dry cell. He says that a Lieutenant Hoskins finally told him on Wednesday that he'd been placed in the cell because his name had been mentioned in some "snitch notes." But that explanation doesn't sit well with the convicts here in light of Ayala's prison record.

He came to prison in October 1985 with a fifteen-year sentence for bank robbery. He has worked in a prison factory for three years.

The only "incident report" he ever received was for heating coffee in his cell in 1986. He's had many urinalysis tests, and they all were negative for drug use. By anyone's definition, he's a model prisoner.

When I talked to him right after his release from the dry cell, his actions reminded me of a person suffering from "jet lag." He was dehydrated and disoriented and looked to be in mental and physical pain from his ordeal.

"It's strange being in there for three days and not knowing if it's night or day or how many times you'll have to use the bowl before they are satisfied," Ayala says. "The only times I got to clean myself was the midnight-to-eight shift when Lieutenant Smith was on."

On Friday, June 8, Frank (Smiley) Morales, forty-two, was cuffed and led from the visiting room to the dry cell. His girlfriend had driven here from Utah for a weekend visit. On Saturday, she was told that her visits were canceled and she'd have to leave.

Morales stayed in the dry cell until Monday night. By that time he'd had six negative bowel movements. He says they did give him toilet paper to clean himself with. He also stated that some of the guards told him they hate the procedure as much as we do but that "orders are orders."

Otherwise, his experience was the same as Ayala's, and he asked me one probing question:

"I wonder if they just built that cell for Mexicans?"

---

Part of the story took place outside the prison—and the reaction appeared to be continuing. For that reason—and because the alleged conditions in the dry cell were so horrible—Dannie and I felt we needed some response from the prison administration. So, once again, I made a few calls and wrote a reaction sidebar to accompany the "federal prisoner's" stories.

# A WIFE SPEAKS OUT FOR
# HER HUSBAND

*SAN FRANCISCO, CALIF. (AUG. 26, 1990)*—David Ayala's stay in the Phoenix dry cell did not end his nightmare, according to his wife, Caroline, but a prison spokesman denied charges of mistreating the convict and others in the dry cell.

In a telephone interview with the *Chronicle,* Caroline Ayala said that since convict-writer Dannie Martin spoke with her husband, David Ayala has been charged with having a dirty urinalysis test— the first of his prison term—and sent to "the hole" (disciplinary segregation unit) for two weeks. He was later convicted of the charge, she said, and is trying to appeal the decision.

She believes those "positive" test findings resulted from his speaking with Martin. The result, she said, is that her husband's parole date has been delayed for two months, and his family visits have been suspended for ninety days.

David Good, press spokesman at the prison, called the charge "utter nonsense." He said the Bureau of Prisons does not tamper with test results and that a certified lab tests and retests all positive urinalyses. He said there is no chance of a mistake or of a mix-up in samples.

But Caroline Ayala insists that the prison is "trying to railroad" her husband. She said he was told when he got out of the dry cell "that he got away with it that time but they'd be watching him" and giving him frequent urine tests.

She said she and her husband had discussed over a monitored phone line Martin's request to discuss with him his experiences in the dry cell. Her husband, she says, is "not a prison troublemaker— he's always kept a low profile." But he wanted to speak with Martin both to protect him from further retaliation and because the couple were worried that someone would die in the dry cell sometime if he didn't speak up about his experiences.

The urine that tested positive was taken on May 21, Caroline Ayala said, and the lab received it on May 30, according to papers her husband saw. The report on the test was received back at the prison in Phoenix on June 7, nearly a week after David Ayala's stay in the dry cell, she said, but it was not until June 18 that Ayala was written up for an offense.

According to Caroline Ayala, prison regulations require that the convict be written up within twenty-four hours after a dirty urine test result is received at the prison, but prison spokesman Good said there is no such requirement—only that action be taken in "a reasonable time."

Good added that Ayala was sent to the segregation unit for investigation. After the disciplinary hearing, he said, he may appeal.

Good also disputed some of David Ayala's charges about the dry cell. He acknowledged that convicts use a bedpan in the cell and are under observation twenty-four hours a day, but he said that it is otherwise a normal cell, with normal bed and linens, normal prisoner clothing, and the same ventilation and air conditioning as the rest of the prison.

Good said toilet paper is available as usual, and the only difference from a regular cell is the replacement of a toilet with a bedpan. Asked if a light is on twenty-four hours a day in the cell, Good said that "it depends on the circumstances," that the light can be kept on around the clock but "needn't be." He said there is no requirement that a convict's hands be visible at all times.

Nevertheless, Caroline Ayala maintained that convicts "are tormented in this cell" and treated "like dogs."

At one point after David Ayala's release from the dry cell, he was told by a prison investigator, according to his wife, that it would be a waste of time and money for her to get an attorney to protest his treatment. The investigator told him, "We do things by the book. . . . You can't touch us," Caroline Ayala said.

"Well," she continued, speaking of his experience in the dry cell, "I want to see the book that says they have the right to do what they've done to my husband."

---

**I**nterestingly, the prison spokesman's denial of conditions reported by Ayala was more sweeping when I began my interview with him than when we ended it. At first, Good told me that there was a normal toilet in the dry cell but that it wasn't hooked up to any plumbing. Later, after conferring with someone who apparently was located near his desk, he revised the answer, saying it wasn't actually a toilet but more like a bedpan.

But there was another and far more significant twist to the sidebar I'd written. All three stories had been edited and ready to run at the time Legge handed down his ruling. After our unsuccessful stay attempt, I set about modifying the stories for publication. I removed Dannie's byline on both of his stories. Needless to say, my name remained atop my sidebar.

But in the process of expunging Dannie's name wherever it occurred, I unthinkingly took it out of the text of my own story, where Caroline Ayala spoke of the consequences of her husband's interview with "convict-writer Dannie Martin." I am a *Chronicle* journalist and not a prisoner, and of course there was no legal reason why I could not mention Dannie's name in the text of my own article.

Ashamed at my initial, instinctive change, I restored the reference to Dannie. In doing so, I did not intend to twit the judge. Dannie's name was a legitimate part of the accusation I was reporting; to have omitted it would have been to submit to a more direct and despicable form of censorship of a *Chronicle*-written story than anyone had suggested during the trial.

But the irony of the juxtaposition did not escape me. My reaction story in which Dannie was named indirectly as the author of the "dry cell" articles appeared beneath the convict's own anonymous essays, illustrating unintentionally how ineffectual censorship is in an otherwise open society.

■

With the pipeline open again, Dannie sent me a story about the effects of new sentencing laws. It wasn't the first time he had written about the subject, but the issue is at the core of our current crime-and-punishment debate and Dannie's reformulation was so eloquent that it has subsequently been widely reprinted and anthologized.

## A MOUNT EVEREST OF TIME

*PHOENIX, ARIZ. (OCT. 7, 1990)*—The big prison story these days is the story of Patrick Grady and Gordon Brownlee and Kevin Sweeney and Curtis Bristow. They all made serious mistakes, and they will all have decades to brood over those mistakes.

Grady, forty-two, has been a close acquaintance of mine over the past two years. He's a Vietnam veteran who wears a mustache because a Vietcong fragment grenade slightly disfigured his upper lip and part of his cheek.

He was also wounded in the leg by gunfire and decorated repeatedly for valor in combat. Along with his wounds in Vietnam, Grady picked up a drug habit. When he returned to his hometown, Seattle, he began selling drugs to support it.

In 1988, he was convicted of numerous counts of conspiracy to possess and sell cocaine. It was his first felony charge. A federal judge in Tacoma, Washington, sentenced him to thirty-six years in prison. He will have to serve thirty-one years before he can be released.

Grady has a wife and a four-year-old daughter and professes shock over the severity of his sentence. "I can't believe that the system of government that I put my life on the line for could do this to me," he says.

"I may be naive, but I've always thought a person could recover from one mistake. I grew up on the old cliché about a 'three-time loser.' Now I've made a mistake, and my wife will be seventy when I get out and my daughter will be thirty-four. That's the end of my family. I can't ask them to wait that long."

Grady doesn't say much about his sentence, but I can see in his eyes a form of terror and despair akin to what was probably there when he saw a fragment grenade land nearby. A few days ago, he asked me a question.

"How is it that I get thirty-six years in prison for selling cocaine when people who rape a woman, bash her head in with a rusty pipe, and leave her for dead only get ten years? Am I supposed to be four times more evil than them?"

The bitterness and numb disbelief of Patrick Grady are mirrored in the minds of thousands of men and women in the federal prisons, and the numbers are increasing at an alarming rate.

In 1989, there were 44,891 criminal cases filed in federal courts, according to a U.S. judicial report. That was almost triple the 15,135 cases filed in 1980. Those numbers, more than anything, represent the escalation of the drug war in the past decade. More than one-fourth of all criminal cases filed in district courts are drug cases, according to the same report.

But there's a darker side to those statistics, because many people sentenced under new federal drug laws aren't ever getting out of prison. Some who will get out may be so old that they won't remember coming in.

Even prisons such as the one here at Phoenix that are designed for medium-security prisoners are experiencing a large influx of men who have been sentenced to nightmarish terms of incarceration.

Since 1987, federal sentences have been nonparolable. The maximum good time that can be earned is fifty-four days a year. Thus, a person with a twenty-year sentence will serve about seventeen years if he or she is a model prisoner. It used to be that a twenty-year sentence would result in seven to twelve years of "real time."

Many people outside applaud the big numbers and harsh sentences. But those I see in here who are weighed down by the years are not gun-slinging stereotypes; they are real, hurting people, and they have families outside whose lives, like their own, are devastated. The people who support those new sentences should at least look at their effect on the people I meet in here.

A former college professor from the Bay Area whom I met here at Phoenix got life without parole for possession of seven kilos of cocaine. A Sacramento man who is forty-five years old received twenty-seven years for conspiring to manufacture methamphetamines. They both have wives and children who hope they will get out someday.

Now that most of the power is in the hands of prosecutors, long sentences are no longer oddities—they have become the norm.

Gordon Brownlee, a San Francisco native who lives down the tier from me, tells about the pressure a San Francisco prosecutor put on him.

"I was arrested in 1989 with one gram over five kilos of cocaine and charged with possession with intent to sell. Had it been under five kilos, the sentence range would have been five to forty years. But the extra gram made it ten years to life," he says.

"The only criminal record I had was a charge in 1982 for trying to buy marijuana from an FBI agent. The prosecutor told me that if I would become an informer I could get off lightly, but if I didn't he would use the 'prior' to enhance my sentence to twenty years to life."

Brownlee is forty-two years old and has a wife and baby daughter. On July 28, 1989, after a plea of guilty, he was sentenced to twenty years in prison. His release date is in 2006.

Few people in here, including those who were apprehended for drug violations, believe they should get a slap on the wrist or be let off lightly. But convicts believe that this country has entered an era of criminal justice when the punishment for drug offenses heavily outweighs the crimes, and the result in human terms is disastrous.

Bob Gomez, an elderly man who helps fellow convicts with legal work, contends that an oversight by Congress created most of the problem.

"A few years ago," he says, "Congress designed some harsh new sentences for drug offenses. Those terms were drafted with the thought in mind that offenders could be paroled in one-third or do the entire sentence in two-thirds of the total amount.

"When the new nonparolable sentences were approved, they simply grafted the big numbers onto the new sentencing code. No politician had the temerity to jump up and say: 'Hey, we're giving these guys too much time.' "

The problem goes beyond the sheer number of years people get under the new drug laws. Enforcement agents outside, spurred on by the public's drug hysteria, at times seem to be coercing crime as much as they are fighting it.

Kevin Sweeney, thirty-three, and Curtis Bristow, thirty-two, are both former residents of San Diego. They received twenty and fourteen years respectively for conspiracy to make methamphetamines. Their cases raise troubling questions about the "war" against drugs.

Sweeney and Bristow were jailed along with a hundred other defendants arrested in a four-year Drug Enforcement Administration sting operation in San Diego. One defendant was sentenced to thirty years. But the police operation itself had some ugly aspects.

A chemical store had been set up in 1985 by a man who was working with the DEA, according to a DEA agent. He began selling chemicals and glassware to would-be methamphetamine makers and turning their names and addresses over to the DEA, the agent testified. In the ensuing four years, according to trial testimony, he sold hundreds of pounds of ephedrine over the counter. Ephedrine is the key ingredient in illicit meth. It's illegal to sell in the state of California.

One of his customers was a fifteen-year-old boy. At the time, a DEA agent was also directly involved in the store's operation.

At the culmination of the sting operation in 1989, the store owner testified that he cleared $900,000 in one year from the sale of ephedrine that the DEA allowed him to keep in addition to money they paid him.

He also testified that he taught novices how to make the drug using the chemicals and glassware he sold them. A rough estimate of the amount of drugs he put on the street under the auspices of the DEA is mind-boggling.

Attorneys have appealed the charges as "outrageous government conduct," but given the political nature of drugs today, no one holds out much hope for relief.

Bristow, who worked for the government as a sandblaster, had no criminal record other than traffic violations. He was sentenced to 163 months for possession of the chemicals he bought from the chemical store.

Sweeney, with one prior felony on his record, got 240 months in federal prison.

It's easy for a judge to say "twenty years" or "thirty years." It takes only a few seconds to declare. It's also easy for the person in the street to say: "Well, this criminal has harmed society and should be locked up for a long time."

The public is unable to imagine what the added time does to a convict and what it does to his family.

Two years is a lot of time. Twenty or thirty years is a Mount Everest of time, and very few can climb it. And what happens to them on the way up makes one not want to be around if and when they return.

The first thing a convict feels when he receives an inconceivably long sentence is shock. The shock usually wears off after about two years, when all his appeals have been denied. He then enters a period of self-hatred because of what he's done to himself and his family.

If he survives that emotion—and some don't—he begins to swim the rapids of rage, frustration, and alienation. When he passes through the rapids, he finds himself in the calm waters of impotence, futility, and resignation. It's not a life one can look forward to living. The future is totally devoid of hope, and people without any hope are dangerous—either to themselves or others.

These long-timers will also have to serve their time in increasingly overcrowded and violent prisons. As I write this, authorities are building a prefab unit next door to my cellblock that will hold three hundred new convicts. Some two-man cells here already hold three people. There are twelve hundred of us in a prison that was designed and built for five hundred.

A more sinister phenomenon is the growing length of the chemical pill line daily at the prison hospital, the place where convicts go for daily doses of tranquilizers and psychotropic drugs such as Prolixin and Haldol. The need for these medications is a sign of the turmoil inside these long-timers.

Indeed, it is ironic that men who are spending decades incarcerated for illicit drug activities are now doped up by government doctors to help them bear the agony of their sentences.

Two years ago, the chemical pill line was very short. Now it snakes along for a good distance. Society is creating a class of men with nothing else to lose but their minds.

---

Statistics tell another side of the story that Dannie told in "A Mount Everest of Time." The federal prison population has more than doubled in the past ten years—during a time when the violent crime rate leveled off—and is expected to double again in the next eight years; there are now more than 1.2 million Americans in jails and prisons, at an annual maintenance cost of about $22 billion. Western Europe's rates of imprisonment are about a quarter of the U.S. figure, as is Canada's.

The apparent abuse of "stings" and informants under color of law enforcement is another element of this story that has been slow to reach the public. The *Atlanta Journal-Constitution* has reported that the U.S. government paid out more than $63 million to informants in 1989, with state and local governments adding $40 million more.

■

For his next story, Dannie again returned to a subject he'd begun to explore previously. It concerned another grievance that anyone associated with prisoners has heard repeatedly.

# PRISON MEDICAL CARE ON THE CRITICAL LIST

*Phoenix, Ariz. (Dec. 2, 1990)*—A prison buddy of mine has never been sick a day in his life, but, for the past year, his face has felt numb; he gets dizzy spells; he is frequently nauseated. And he is worried.

He has gone to sick call at least twenty times, he says, and he has begged the physician's assistants—PAs, we call them—to find out what is wrong with him. They took blood samples and told him there was nothing wrong.

But my friend knew better. He kept insisting that they diagnose his ailment.

Finally, after nearly a year, he had an EKG. It showed heart problems so serious that the prison doctor told him not to move, asked him if he was okay, and said he needed to go downtown for further testing. The following day, however, when he returned to the prison hospital, my friend says the doctor did not even recognize him. He reminded the doctor of what had happened the day before.

Later, when my friend again asked the doctor what was going on with his medical tests, the doctor said that the hospital trip had been denied by the captain. When my friend went to see the captain, he was told that for security reasons, he'd have to have the tests at the prison. That was several weeks ago, and the machines to conduct those urgent tests are still not available here.

My friend's story is not unique. There's a myth afoot that convicts don't have to struggle for medical care as ordinary citizens do. Actually, the search for medical care in here is more like a war between convicts and an army of PAs whose motto is: "We got it, you need it, try and get it."

Prison hospitals like the one at Phoenix are staffed with one doctor, one pharmacist, a bevy of PAs, and sometimes a nurse or two. With sixteen hundred convicts here, it is not easy to see the one doctor.

At Lompoc penitentiary in 1987, I fell in the shower and injured my rib cage. I was racked with pain and couldn't take a deep breath.

A PA at the hospital told me that I had "strained the cartilage between ribs" and time would heal it.

I requested an X-ray and demanded to see the doctor, to no avail. The PA informed me that he knew his business and that his say was final.

A year or so later, I was moved here to Phoenix and given a routine chest X-ray upon my arrival. A few days later, I was summoned to the lieutenants' office, where two lieutenants told me to remove my shirt and began examining my upper body for bruises and abrasions. "Have you been fighting?" one of them asked me.

When I asked what was going on, he said, "Your chest X-ray showed that you have a broken rib. We'll have to lock you up for a while until we find out if you've been in a fight with someone."

I explained that I had fallen in the shower a year earlier, and we proceeded to the hospital, where they checked my medical records and released me.

Similar stories can be heard everywhere in the federal prison system. A friend of mine at Lompoc whom we called Flappers because of his oversized ears complained one day of severe chest pain. After numerous trips to sick call and visits with PAs, he'd made no progress toward getting a competent diagnosis.

He had a long record of drug dependency and was accused by one PA of "faking pain to get drugs." Six months went by. Flappers lost forty pounds.

Finally, he bribed a convict who worked as an X-ray technician's helper to sneak him into the hospital and X-ray his chest. The helper was to ask the technician to read Flappers' X-ray when the technician visited the prison again.

The X-ray was taken, and when the technician arrived, he called Flappers in and told him he had a tumor "as big as half a grapefruit" growing on his rib cage. Flappers was immediately transferred to the federal prison hospital at Springfield, Missouri, where he died of cancer soon after his arrival.

Another man recently went to the hospital at Springfield for a back operation. While there, he noticed that a large number of convicts were dying from cancer, heart conditions, and HIV-induced illnesses. He got into a conversation about the high death rate with a doctor, who told him:

"The problem with this place is that by the time we see most of these patients, they are so far gone there's not much we can do for them."

Convicts as a rule aren't surprised by the stonewalling and the inefficiency of our medical care. Most of us come from poor families, and destitute people on the outside always have a hard time getting decent medical care. What rubs us the wrong way is the image created by the Bureau of Prisons that we get good treatment.

Calvin Robinson, who gained notoriety as the "Drug Tug Skipper" when apprehended beneath the Golden Gate Bridge a few years ago, has been trying to get treatment for a severely ulcerated foot for more than eight months. He echoes the sentiments of most of us:

"If they want to make bad medicine part of my sentence, I can live with that. But with a public out there paying, even if grudgingly paying, for decent medical treatment, and the BOP advertising that we get good care, where's it at? What happens between what the public thinks, what the BOP says, and what we get?"

The Phoenix prison was constructed five years ago on a patch of desert that belonged exclusively to rattlesnakes, scorpions, and tarantulas. As of now, the snakes, scorpions, and spiders haven't entirely conceded the land to human beings. We see fewer every year, but we still see plenty of them.

On September 12, Aldo Pablo was playing handball in our recreation yard when he was bitten on the finger by a rattlesnake that was in the grass beside the handball court. The snake bit him at 6:40 P.M.

A yard officer walked Pablo to the hospital. When they arrived there, the front door was locked. The guard called the PA inside on his radio and asked him to open the door.

Pablo says that once he got inside, the PA's initial reaction was amusement and skepticism about his story. The guard with him told the PA that Pablo had indeed been bitten by a rattler.

The PA phoned outside the prison for an ambulance. By this time, Pablo says, he was extremely nauseated, and his finger had swollen to the size of a "small banana." His arm was rapidly swelling toward the elbow.

When the ambulance arrived, Pablo says, the guards got into an argument with the driver over sending him downtown in his prison clothes. There was another delay while they located a prison jumpsuit, handcuffs, and leg shackles for him to wear in the ambulance.

He says he finally reached the hospital around 7:45 P.M. and only then began receiving anti-venom shots. He remained in the hospital four days, and at one point the doctor thought he might have to amputate the finger, he says.

"I know people have been bit here by rattlers in the past," Pablo says, "so why don't they have some of that anti-venom? Man, I thought for a while there that I was dead when I realized they had nothing. My heart was running about a hundred miles an hour."

When our current warden took over, he had a small fish pond installed in front of the hospital and stocked with goldfish. The pool is about two feet at its deepest. It's a nice oasis in our barren yard, enhanced by a little pseudo-waterfall.

One day recently, as two convicts stood near the edge admiring the fish, another convict walked up, did a shallow dive into the pond, and began doing a backstroke while singing softly.

Two lieutenants rushed over and nabbed him. They took him to their office in handcuffs and gave him a Breathalyzer test, which he passed. They then summoned a psychologist, who took him to the hospital, where he was given medication to calm him down.

His name is Paul Swanson. He said he dove into the fish pond in an attempt to get medical attention. According to Swanson, he had visited the prison psychologist earlier that day and told him he was about to "go crazy" and needed help

The psychologist was aware that Swanson had been diagnosed as suffering from, among other things, a bipolar affective disorder, rapid cycling type—which, in layman's terms, would probably define a manic-depressive.

"The psychologist had helped me get a pass from work and told me the medicine would be waiting for me at the hospital. When I got there, a nurse asked me what I was doing there. I told her the psychologist had sent me to be medicated.

"She told me that wasn't the way things were done and to get out of there and come back at sick call the following day.

"I didn't have a day to spare," he says, "so I dived into the fish pond."

Swanson is forty-eight years old and a veteran of the armed services. His desperate search for treatment of his mental problems began a long time before he dove into the fish pond.

On January 20, 1989, he says, he visited a social services office in Glendale, Arizona, and told them he was severely disturbed and needed help. They were unable to help or advise him and referred him to the Salvation Army, where he was referred to a veterans' center. There he drew a blank also. The irony was that these agencies said they could help him only if he had an alcohol or drug problem, which he didn't.

Finally, in desperation, he walked into a Methodist church and told the minister he would commit a crime if he couldn't get help any other way. Swanson says the minister replied, "I can't help you. There's the door."

After leaving the church, Swanson noticed an abandoned metal box filled with concrete and protruding electrical wires. It weighed fifty or sixty pounds. He put the box on his shoulder and walked into a nearby bank. Depositing the box on the floor, he yelled, "This is a robbery! This is a bomb! It's filled with C-5 compound."

He walked out of the bank with $6,000 and fled to Las Vegas. Several days later, he turned himself in. "I didn't want to commit any more crimes or victimize society," he says. "I only wanted help."

He picked a bad crime to get help for a mental disturbance. The government classifies bank robbery as a crime of "general intent," and insanity pleas are not allowed.

No matter how deranged a person may be, the question boils down to whether he or she robbed or attempted to rob the bank. The legal loopholes on insanity pleas are so tight that even an outright madman accused of bank robbery could not enter a plea of "not guilty by reason of insanity."

Under the new sentencing guidelines, Swanson was sentenced to fifteen years in prison. The judge wanted to give him a lesser sentence, but the prosecutor demanded fifteen years and the judge was forced to go along. Swanson will have to serve twelve and a half years before his release.

"I wish I'd have thought of it outside—I'd have jumped into someone's fish pond," he says. "Seems like I get more help that way, and they probably wouldn't have given me fifteen years for that."

In all fairness, a small minority of the PAs and nurses in here are decent, caring people who try to help convicts obtain treatment. But as one of them said the other day:

"You people are at our mercy, and I feel bad about that. But you wouldn't believe how much bullshit we have to put up with from our superiors when we try to do our best for convicts. I really don't have much energy left after that for my patients."

Recently, I was trying to get a flu shot. People come to this prison from all over the world and bring with them every kind of flu there is. The PA said I didn't meet the criteria for a flu shot. "You must be over sixty-five years of age or have a long history of respiratory problems," he said.

The cough I've had for five months from my last flu doesn't count as a "respiratory problem." I couldn't even buy a flu shot. The only treatment I'm allowed is what the government gives me.

I finally badgered someone into giving me that flu shot, and not a moment too soon. The warden's fish pond was beginning to look pretty good to me also.

---

In Dannie's next article, he showed his eye for a good story on an unexpected subject.

---

## BARS ARE NO PRISON FOR THESE CONTENTED CONS

*PHOENIX, ARIZ. (DEC. 30, 1990)*—Pablo, I'll call him, is from the high mountains of Peru. He's undergone a metamorphosis from hardscrabble peasant farmer in Peru to captured cocaine smuggler and federal prison convict.

To veteran observers of the drug wars, his story may sound like old hat. But Pablo is very happy in his new environment—the prison—and pleased with the changes in his life, and that is news to me.

He's a small, middle-aged man whom I met one day when we shared a table at lunch. I was complaining about a chicken patty by alleging they were made from chicken feet, chicken combs, toenails, and everything else. In labored English he said to me:

"My friend, this food is excellent. I do not understand why you complain when we are treated so well here."

I thought he was being sarcastic, but his expression was wide open and showed the utmost sincerity. My curiosity led me to befriend him, and our daily talks have revealed to me a new dimension of the drug wars.

Pablo describes himself as a mestizo—the son of a native Indian and a Peruvian mother of European ancestry. Until a few years ago, he'd lived with his wife and four children on a plot of land in a high valley in Peru.

"We were near starving. For ten years I tried to save enough for an old pickup, but something always happen with my kids or wife, and I can't save it," he says.

Pablo had a neighbor who, on the surface, seemed just as poor. But members of Pablo's family would stand and stare when a new Mercedes or Range Rover drove the packed dirt road to his neighbor's house. The neighbor hired Pablo to watch an old shed in back of his home for the equivalent of $2 a day.

"I thought it had tools or something. Then one day his son came in a camper, and we began loading paper-wrapped packages from the shed into his truck. The packages were the size of an adobe brick but much lighter.

"The paper on a package I picked up tore on a nail, and I saw that they were tightly packed bundles of American hundred-dollar bills. He had a whole shed full of them!"

The neighbor was a coca-paste broker, and soon Pablo was doing other odd jobs for him. A few months later, he was affiliated with a band of coke smugglers who hired people like Pablo to walk cocaine across the Mexican border in barren areas near Tucson, Arizona. "They pay me five hundred dollars a kilo, and I walk usually five kilos a time," he says.

He was caught after only two trips and sentenced to ten years in federal prison. Soon after his arrival here, he went to work for UNICOR, the Federal Prison Industries, and began sending money home to his family in Peru.

"At first, I could only send them fifty or a hundred dollars, but I make raises and now I send two hundred dollars a month and still have some left for my needs," he says. (Pablo earns about $1.15 an hour.)

"My family have moved to a much nicer place with electricity, and my wife has already bought a pickup," he says.

As we talk, Pablo proudly shows me teeth that were bridged into his mouth by a prison dentist. He also wears eyeglasses that he obtained free through the prison hospital.

"I couldn't have done these things at home. I don't like to admit this to American prisoners because they get mad at me, but coming to prison here has been a blessing for me and my family."

He says that his homesickness and the loss of sex or a beer on weekends are far overshadowed by the knowledge that his family is thriving and his paycheck is secure and growing every year. He assures me that there are many convicts like him here and introduces me to his friend Tawala, who is a Guajira Indian from the Guajira Peninsula in Colombia. Tawala's story is even more dramatic than Pablo's.

Tawala, forty-two, was a part-time fisherman who hired out on boats around the Guajira. Like Pablo, he's a small, polite man. He has a wife and four children in Colombia. He speaks very little English and works in the same factory as Pablo, and he also has no complaints about his confinement. But the way he got here is strange indeed.

Tawala is a full-blooded Indian who lived in the jungle of the Guajira with his family. Before his arrival a few years ago at a U.S. prison, he'd never seen a television, a telephone, or an indoor toilet and had never owned a pair of store-bought shoes. Shoes to him were huaraches, usually made from pieces of rubber car tires.

Talking through an interpreter, he tells me that in 1987 he was approached by a recruiter for the Dutch captain of a tramp steamer who asked if he wanted to work as a deckhand on a ship bound for Saba Island in the Dutch Antilles. The recruiter, who made frequent trips to Tawala's village to gather crews for various types of craft, said the pay for the Saba voyage was to be the equivalent of $3.50 a day for a run of more than two months.

Tawala needed the money, and he signed on as a crewman with five other Indians. They left the Guajira with a load of marijuana bound for Saba. Tawala says the captain later told him that marijuana is legal in the Antilles and that there should have been no problems.

About forty miles off the coast of Colombia, their plans were changed when a U.S. Navy ship approached, fired three shots across their bow, ordered them to "heave to," and boarded.

Tawala says that Navy crewmen accompanied by two Coast Guardsmen boarded their ship, found the marijuana, and placed them all, including the captain, under arrest. The crew was locked in the brig aboard the Navy ship, and a Navy crew was put aboard the drug vessel. The ships then traveled in tandem to Puerto Rico, where the captain and his crew were jailed and indicted for conspiracy to smuggle marijuana. Tawala says the trip to Puerto Rico took five days.

They remained in jail there for five months until their trial, at which time the Indians were appointed an attorney who spoke very little English. The captain retained his own attorney, and, as all the proceedings were in English, the captain's lawyer spent much of his court time translating the testimony for Tawala's lawyer.

All of them were convicted, including the captain. Their explanation that they'd never intended to come to the United States, much less bring anything here, was ignored. The captain told the court that he had recruited these Indians from Colombian fishing boats and that they bore minimal culpability.

The judge sentenced all seven of them to fifteen years in federal prison. Although the entire matter was riddled with serious legal questions, no appeal was filed to a higher court. Tawala says the attorney never told them that they were entitled to an appeal, and none of the Indians knew there was such a thing. The entire crew came to Phoenix while the captain went to a prison in the Midwest. So they lost the benefit of even his admittedly questionable guidance.

Tawala is a nickname given to him here by fellow Guajira Indian convicts. They call him Tawala Wayuu, which means "Indian brother" in the Guajira dialect. His tribe is the Hipuana.

Tawala sends $150 a month home to his family from his 92-cents-an-hour earnings in the prison cable factory. That is 50 percent more than he made as a crew member of a smuggling ship. There is no post office in their area of the Guajira, so he has to send the money to a niece in Venezuela who has a post office box.

His wife spends nine days each month making the round trip to pick up the money. Leaving her oldest child to watch their home, she takes the other three along. They walk long distances through the jungle and ride the bus the rest of the way. She doesn't view the trip as an inconvenience. The money is a godsend.

There's a safety inspection here in each cellblock every week. The cleanest cell in our building is awarded a small TV to keep in the cell and watch for a week. Tawala has the cleanest cell I've ever seen, and I've seen my share. To him, his own TV for a week is the epitome of luxury.

He takes me inside his cell as we try to work out in my street-slang Spanish what Tawala Wayuu means. There's not a speck of dust or lint anywhere, and his cement floor is waxed to a mirror finish.

On his locker shelves are pictures of his family, a rosary, and a drawing of the Virgin Mary. A tortured Jesus gazes benevolently at them from across the locker.

Tawala smiles and lights up like a light bulb as he points out a picture of his wife standing in a schoolyard with a teacher and two of their children. *"Mi esposa y niños,"* my wife and kids, he says with a big smile.

His wife is dressed in the flowing robes of Indian women, but the garment is new and stylish. She's well groomed, and the kids are neat and well dressed. He's obviously very proud of them.

I later talked about Tawala with a convict who does legal work for other cons and is quite proficient in legal matters, especially drug law. He is familiar with Tawala and his co-defendants and how they arrived here.

"I don't understand these people," he says. "They have good grounds for an appeal because the Navy forced them and their ship here. They had no plan to bring anything to the United States, and they were in international waters.

"I typed up a writ for Tawala, even gave him a stamped, addressed envelope. He never sent it off. When I told him it might get him out, he lost interest in the whole thing."

But another convict who speaks Spanish told me that he recently filed a habeas corpus petition in their case, and the court appointed counsel to represent them.

Tawala admits that although he misses his family, they are better off than they ever were.

Another Colombian told me that many Guajira Indians are trying to hire out with smugglers who target the United States. "There's nothing to lose," he says. "If they get away with it, they make good money. If they get caught and come to American prison, they still make good money."

As I talk with Central and South Americans here it becomes clear that there's a caste system down there that is every bit as ineluctable as the prejudice toward minorities in the United States.

When Indians marry into the mainstream, their children are known as mestizos, and so are the children of the children and on down the line. Indian blood is an anchor that holds individuals at the lower echelons of their society. Yet living in the shadow of the United States, they share that dream of better times. Even prison is not too high a price to pay.

The Cubans among us are, for the most part, black Cubans. Many of them are doing time in limbo, awaiting a deportation that never happens. Most of them admit they like it better here in prison than they ever liked Cuba.

By the time I asked them, their response didn't surprise me. After getting to know Pablo and Tawala, I know there's another way of looking at a prison.

I thought that all convicts were miserable like me when they lost their freedom. But they made me understand they didn't lose theirs. They traded some of it in on a piece of the American Dream.

---

Dannie then turned his attention to a problem tormenting all convicts—sex and the forms that primal urge takes in the distorted environment of prison. The subject was suggested by a reader.

## PRISONERS OF LONGING

*PHOENIX, ARIZ. (JAN. 27, 1991)*—A few years ago in Lompoc penitentiary, I had a friend I'll call Jim. We'd go to the recreation yard every weekday for some handball and a workout on the parallel bars. Our conversations were mainly about women, freedom, and the sad state of affairs in U.S. prisons.

Jim was a very masculine man who often spoke in a derogatory fashion about homosexuals—or "faggots," as he called them. His swaggering manner suggested machismo at its best, or worst, depending on who made the judgment.

One morning he was late for our recreation, and I walked down the tier to his cell. He was sitting on his bunk with his legs crossed, looking into a little vanity mirror that was propped on a chair next to the bed. He was busy doing something to his eyes, and the vision that assaulted my own eyes was a scene from *The Twilight Zone* or *The Hitchhiker*.

He had on a pink robe of silky material, parted to reveal his legs, and a pair of fluffy pink bedroom slippers. His formerly hairy legs had been shaved until they shined like polished marble. The brown, medium-long hair was done up in large pink curlers, and he was applying mascara beneath newly plucked eyebrows. I felt like yelling:

"Et tu, Jim?"

When he gazed up at me with softly feminine, mascaraed eyes that the day before had held nothing but malice aforethought, I remembered all the tales I'd heard about men in prison who had made the sudden transformation. But I was still reluctant to believe this one.

"Hey, Jim, is this some kind of a joke? What the hell are you doing?" I demanded.

"It's not a joke," he replied as his eyes slid back to the mirror. "Like the man said, I've decided to be all that I can be."

Although shocking to his friends, Jim's metamorphosis is a phenomenon that occurs quite often in prison. Contrary to the stereotyped image in the public mind, he didn't become a pariah among his fellow cons. He did suffer a lot of ribbing for a few weeks, but even that died down eventually.

Homophobia is no more prevalent in prison than it is outside. Indeed, the gay haters and baiters behind these walls are usually more circumspect than their counterparts outside. They must be careful not to offend some tough jocker's "old lady."

In prisons, the word "queer" is still used to denote effeminate homosexuality, and it is not in general considered a derogatory term. "Sissy" is also used quite frequently. Gays in prison will often refer to themselves by the terms "queer" and "sissy." The word "punk," however, is always used with malice. A punk is someone who submits to a sex act under physical pressure or out of fear. Punks are the low men of our society, just a notch above informers.

Most effeminate homosexuals who come to prison find an "old man" right away. We call the old man a "jocker," and he's usually a tougher-than-average convict who is able to demand and get respect from his contemporaries. A sissy with no jocker is constantly besieged, cajoled, and sometimes threatened for sex. The demand is much too intense for any degree of comfort.

When a man makes a change as drastic as Jim's, he becomes a caricature of his former self. All his alliances and friendships are realigned in light of his new image. His entire routine changes as old friends shun him and new ones seek him out. It's a difficult situation.

It's made more difficult by the fact that sex behind bars is serious business. There is nothing more serious in a prison.

In the two- or three-year period before I left Lompoc penitentiary in central California, there were five murders. Three of them were the most brutal and vicious that I've ever heard about in a prison setting. All five of those killings were said to be the result of homosexual-related incidents.

The most intense race riot that I've ever witnessed was at Soledad State Prison in California in 1963. Before it was over, rioting had spread to several other prisons, and more than a few convicts were killed or maimed. The whole affair began when a white and a black convict argued over the "ownership" of a homosexual.

The old myth about drugs and prison gangs being the source of most of our violence is just that—a myth. Nothing inflames the violence and passion of confined men more than homosexual love affairs. Those who remain strictly heterosexual watch in awe as the drama unfolds and are often caught up in the maelstrom of violence, hate, and revenge.

Nowadays, the potential for violence is enhanced because many homosexuals in prison have undergone partial sex-change procedures, such as breast implants and female hormone treatments.

They grow their hair long and walk like women, talk like women, and look like women. To some convicts, especially those serving long sentences, they are women. As a new one strolled down the sidewalk here one day, a convict took a good long look and said: "Man, that sissy is bound to cause four or five killings around here."

In our world, that is a compliment. A five-killing sissy has to be extra fine.

The most power that I've ever seen a convict accumulate in a prison setting was wielded by an effeminate homosexual in California's Folsom State Prison in the late 1960s. His jocker became the richest convict I've ever known and the epitome of a King Rat, as played by George Segal in the movie of the same name.

The sissy—Bill, I'll call him—was very intelligent and devised a way to help ignorant guards pass civil-service tests for higher rank.

Thus, we had several sergeants and lieutenants at Folsom who were functionally illiterate.

These higher staff members were so appreciative of Bill's help that they turned a blind eye to the activities of his jocker—a convict whose enterprises ran the gamut from smuggling drugs to loan-sharking and bookmaking.

The power those two held in that prison was awesome. They were virtually untouchable by guards and convicts. From where I sat, it looked as if they ran the prison.

The alienation from sex or even the sight, smell, or touch of a woman is the most brutal aspect of incarceration for most male convicts. In the past ten years, I've probably spent 50 percent of my mental energy thinking about sex, and I'm not the only one.

It's a constant, torturous longing that gives no quarter. I quit watching TV a long time ago when Roseanne Barr began to look more sexy than funny to me.

With the advent of female guards in the mid-'70s, what we thought would be refreshing has only exacerbated the problem. Just lately here at Phoenix, a female guard said to me after another woman officer had been harassed until she left the cellblock:

"Why do you guys pick on some of us female officers so much? Why do you harass some of us so much more than others? We're just here trying to do a job."

The answer seemed clear in my mind, but I didn't even attempt to respond. The problem is complex.

When female guards come to work in male prisons, most of them do everything they can to deny and suppress their femininity. They dress like men, walk like men, act like men, and even try to talk like men.

It has probably been drilled into them by male guards in orientation sessions that things like makeup, gentle manners, and femininity are dangerous in a prison environment. In the federal system, women guards aren't even allowed to work in maximum-security prisons such as Lompoc, Marion, and Leavenworth.

Convicts are very sensitive to that process. When we see a woman deny her own personality under pressure from her male superiors, to us she is like a punk losing his manhood under threat of physical harm. Once she gains "punk" status in our eyes, all respect is gone, and we peck at her like a flock of vicious chickens.

The rare woman guards who manage to retain their femininity—

indeed, use it to their advantage—often become effective officers and enjoy a high degree of respect from convicts, more so because we know they have to be strong to do it.

Now and then a love affair develops between a staff member and a love-starved convict. But when the affair is discovered—and it usually is—by officials, it's curtains for them both.

The woman is summarily dismissed, and the convict is transferred—usually to a maximum-security prison. A friend of mine was found out in his relationship with a female nurse here at Phoenix a few years ago. She was fired, and he was shuttled off to Lompoc. She still hasn't been able to visit him there.

The warden at Lompoc remarked that he viewed her actions as a betrayal, and that she is a traitor to the Bureau of Prisons.

These rare affairs are fraught with danger. Since I've been here at Phoenix, several convicts have been put in Isolation and transferred for writing love letters to female employees.

There are also occasional affairs that develop between male guards and convicts, but the stuff most of those affairs are made of belongs in an X-rated bondage magazine. When a new guard wants more than a job, he can easily find it in here.

Sex, or the lack of it, is the overriding concern of confined men. And the deforming aspect of that longing is an awesome thing to behold.

Jim made himself into a pretty nice sissy, although he wasn't fine enough to cause any killings. Two months before he went home, he got a short haircut and began growing hair back on his legs and eyebrows.

His family outside probably wouldn't have understood. I doubt that he understood it himself.

———

Despite the fact that sex is a volatile and sensitive subject among prisoners, Dannie received no negative reactions from fellow convicts to his circumspect story. His next article, however, prompted an outraged response from the government. It is short but informative, and it would probably not have merited reprinting here were it not for the extremity of the response.

This account was published in the *Chronicle*'s news section, where it ran inconspicuously toward the bottom of a page, a sidebar to the far more important events then unfolding in the Persian Gulf area. It was, once again, published under the name "a federal prisoner," and it was accompanied by the usual box explaining the unconventional format.

# U.S. INMATE-WORKERS GO ON OVERTIME FOR WAR

*PHOENIX, ARIZ. (FEB. 9, 1991)*—The spirit of "Rosie the Riveter" has returned in the form of a long line of convicts trudging to and from the connector-cable factory here in the federal prison at Phoenix. Operation Desert Storm has kicked the factory into overtime, and no one is complaining about the extra work.

The convicts who work in the factory make connector cables for the military—everything from plug-ins for field kitchens to cables for tanks and fiber-optic devices for more complex military ordnance.

On January 5, the factory here at Phoenix went into extensive overtime, and some one hundred convicts are now working up to fourteen-hour days, including Saturdays and Sundays. Overtime pays double, and the first-grade workers who normally get $1.30 per hour are raking in pretty good money for convicts.

"Almost every purchase order that comes in now is stamped 'Desert Storm,' and all those have top priority. Everything else is put aside to be done last," said a convict who works as a clerk in the factory business office.

A convict worker in the testing lab where the cables are subjected to a final once-over said cables are leaving the lab ahead of the paperwork.

"They say, 'Come on! Get 'em out of here!' That seems kind of weird because this bureaucracy always insists on the paperwork first. Now they're saying: 'Send the cables and we'll get the paperwork later.' "

There are eleven other cable factories operating throughout the federal prison system, and the clerk said he doesn't know if they are all on overtime now. An educated guess is that they are.

Surprisingly, most of the workers—even the confirmed "government haters"—show a high degree of concern and support for our troops in the Persian Gulf.

"I'm glad to be doing something to help," one bank robber said. But even he admits to feelings of ambivalence about how long the conflict should continue.

"I want us to win, but I also hope it drags on for a while. They are spending a lot of money on this war, and I'm hoping they will have to use some of that money they've put aside to build prisons with."

Another convict said he knows nothing about the war or anything else outside this prison.

"There's a hundred of us working night overtime now. That's three times more than there ever has been on overtime at this factory. I'm just doing what I'm told while counting my days and my money. If the war lasts awhile I'll have a pretty good bankroll," he says.

---

**B**OP Director J. Michael Quinlan faxed to the publisher of the *Chronicle* a letter protesting the publication of that article. Specifically, Quinlan objected to the *Chronicle*'s placement of the anonymous article:

My concern stems from the fact that the article appeared in the news section of your paper, something which I believe violates the spirit, if not the letter, of the recent decision by District Judge Charles A. Legge. . . .

While we remain very concerned about the publication of submissions by Dannie Martin in the "Sunday Punch" section and believe such publication violates the spirit of Judge Legges' [sic] decision, we believe publication in the news section is of greater concern in light of Judge Legges' [sic] decision.

Quinlan did not elaborate on his reasoning, but apparently he felt that the news section was just too "newsy" or "factual" a place for convict writing, and that therefore Dannie was "acting as a reporter" if we published anything by him in that section. The implication was that Legge's ruling governed the section of the newspaper in which editors could present writings by federal prisoners.

The acting-as-a-reporter prohibition was the undefined provision that had most troubled us when we resumed publication of Dannie's writing after the court ruling.

But Quinlan went further. In a statement that drew fire from *New York Times* columnist Anthony Lewis and other prominent journalists, the federal official "request[ed] that you [the newspaper] reconsider your decision to continue publication of submissions by Dannie Martin. . . ." He added a request that "you [not] publish this letter in your paper, and in fact [I] ask that this letter remain a private communication."

That last request was also unusual. Not only did the federal official ask a major mainstream newspaper not to publish anything further by its most popular free-lance writer, but he requested secrecy in the midst of a public legal battle over that very issue. The request did not seem to conform with Judge Legge's view that "this is not a so-called 'prior restraint' case. That is, no attempt is made to edit, restrain or prevent written material from going out of the prison or from being published."

There was no disturbance, nor any other apparent inmate reaction, attributable to publication of the news-section article.

The Bureau of Prisons has always been tight-lipped about its prison industries, and officials are especially vigilant about industries paperwork that is spirited out of the work area. Monopolistic ventures that rely on high secrecy provoke questions of malfeasance and favoritism in any institution, and indeed, convicts mutter darkly of doctored books and suspicious fires in prison industries file cabinets. Nothing untoward has been discovered in several media inquiries that I am aware of, but that has not stopped the suspicions. One can only speculate whether the BOP's exaggerated response to this short article was occasioned by defensive concerns specifically related to prison industries.

So far as I know, the *Chronicle* never replied to Quinlan's letter directly. But the letter did make my job more difficult. Not only was I not to compensate or give bylines to federal convicts, but I now apparently had to refrain from handing their writings to the news section to run with related material. Indeed, the suggestion was clear in Quinlan's letter that I was risking violation of the rule by publishing *anything* from a federal prisoner.

No one from the *Chronicle* told me to pull back in response to the letter of warning. As a result, Dannie was able in his remaining six months of imprisonment to continue to illuminate his environment despite the high-level efforts to silence him. But we will never know how many other prisoners and newspapers refrained from similar exposure of prison issues because of our well-publicized difficulties.

■

One of Dannie's next "Sunday Punch" essays again demonstrated the importance of having an observer behind bars. He disclosed an injustice of the legal system that traps powerless people for years in a maddening technicality. Rarely do such injustices from the secretive world of prisons receive a public airing.

## PLEA BARGAINS THAT AREN'T MUCH OF A DEAL

PHOENIX, ARIZ. *(MAY 5, 1991)*—Anthony Del Guzzi, forty-nine, fell into a wide crack between two prison systems. He thought his predicament was unique, but he has a lot of company. Like many other convicts doing time in state and federal prisons, he bought a deal and never got what he bargained for.

As a result, Del Guzzi will spend five more years in prison than his sentencing judge intended.

Del Guzzi was arrested in April 1985 on a charge of transferring counterfeit currency. He pleaded guilty and was sentenced to five years in a federal prison. The judge ordered him to surrender on September 16, 1985, to begin serving the sentence. A week earlier, on September 9, the state of California arrested him on a methamphetamine conspiracy charge. Now he was facing time in two separate jurisdictions, state and federal.

Del Guzzi, a balding, bespectacled man with an even temper, swears he wasn't guilty of the meth conspiracy, and convicts tell him: "Yeah, sure, Tony, we're all innocent. We were all framed by crooked judges and evil juries."

But while some of us are skeptical of his claims of innocence, we all agree that he was ill-treated by the criminal justice system.

A day or two after his arrest by the state, his lawyer came to the jail and told him he could plead guilty for a seven-year sentence to run at the same time as his federal sentence.

"I felt that I had to take that deal," he insists. "I have a daughter in medical school, and the expense of another trial would have forced her to quit. My lawyer pointed out that California allows more good time than the feds and I would be out about the same time anyway, so I took the plea bargain."

On October 28, 1985, Judge Everett Ricks of Los Angeles superior court sentenced Del Guzzi to seven years in prison, to run concurrently with his federal sentence. He told Del Guzzi that the time would be served in federal prison.

A few days after sentencing, he was picked up and driven to the California state prison at Chino. After some orientation there, he was transferred to Soledad state prison near Salinas.

"I began to smell a rat when I got to Soledad," he says. "I had the records officer at Soledad write the federal Bureau of Prisons to ask when they were coming to get me. They replied that I would be picked up "upon completion of my state sentence.""

In November 1985, Del Guzzi wrote his attorney in Los Angeles, asking him to straighten things out so that he could serve the concurrent sentences that the plea bargain called for. The lawyer replied that he "trusted the court would see that the sentence was applied as given." Del Guzzi says that thereafter the lawyer refused to accept his phone calls and wouldn't reply to his letters.

He served the entire state sentence and was brought here to Phoenix last year to begin serving the five-year sentence consecutively. He's filed several motions and a lawsuit in an attempt to get the deal that he originally bargained for. His chances of success appear to be very slim.

Del Guzzi was the victim of a bait-and-switch game that convicts believe has been going on for years in state courts. These bogus "plea agreements" cause massive amounts of litigation in appellate courts once the convicts realize they have been hoodwinked.

It turns out that most of these convicts have run up against an obscure technicality in federal law—Title 18, U.S. Code Section 3568—that requires federal sentences to be computed from the time the convicted person arrives at a federal prison. If he or she is sent to a state prison first, all bets are off, no matter what promises were made to Del Guzzi and countless others in the plea bargain.

In short, the convict is literally getting more than he bargained for—years more—because of ignorance or incompetence on the part of lawyers or judges. The official scam has gone on so long that many prisoners have become convinced that courts and attorneys involved must know at the time the deals are made that they aren't worth the paper they are written on.

Charles Smith is another federal prisoner who went for the same kind of deal.

Smith pleaded guilty on robbery charges in 1981 and was sentenced to eleven years in a California state prison. The eleven-year sentence was ordered to run concurrently with time Smith owed the federal Bureau of Prisons. He, too, wound up serving the sentences consecutively after he had plea-bargained for a concurrent sentence.

In the past ten years, Smith has filed numerous legal motions and has had several lawyers appointed at taxpayer expense to argue them. He's been to the Ninth Circuit court of appeals twice and all the way to the California supreme court.

In January 1991, the California court of appeal, first appellate district, agreed that Smith's rights were violated, and it set the stage for the voiding of his California conviction. On March 8, the case was returned to the trial court, which formally dismissed all state charges against Smith; the convictions for which he was sent to prison were nullified.

"The feds had a detainer on me at the time of my state convictions," said Smith, a slender, scholarly-looking man in his mid-forties. "By removing the state charges, all that time [spent in prison], by law, now has to be applied to my federal sentence."

According to Smith, this means that his federal sentence was fully served more than six months ago and he should be released. The Bureau of Prisons doesn't agree, and Smith was told by a caseworker here at Phoenix that he could "talk to the parole board about it in June."

On Tuesday, April 16, Smith refused to work at his prison job assignment and declined to follow other orders from staff members. "I'm not even supposed to be here. I'm being held illegally, and I'm not following any further orders," Smith said.

He was escorted to the isolation unit and locked up. An older convict remarked after they took him away, "It looks like old Smitty finally won the battle and still lost the war."

Convicts believe that courts make these shady deals in an attempt to obtain guilty pleas and clear crowded court dockets. It's hard for us to believe that lawyers and judges don't know by now that the Bureau of Prisons won't honor those agreements—because of the federal statute or, in some cases, BOP policy.

The practice gives rise to much litigation and is one big reason why people outside often complain that convicts are "tying up the courts with frivolous writs."

After a huge success in the Gulf War, President Bush called for a renewal of the war on crime. One of his stated goals in the crime strategy is to "stop the endless frivolous appeals clogging the courts." To people like Del Guzzi and Smith—who feel they have been scammed by the government—the motions are far from frivolous.

"I don't mind doing the time that I bargained for, but the deal they gave me on the record was more counterfeit than the money I got caught with," Del Guzzi says.

Adding to the frustration and litigation over these broken deals is the extremely low probability these days of obtaining any relief from appellate courts. The way we see it from in here, the courts are bending over backward to rule in favor of the government.

A few years ago, citizens would complain that courts were "coddling convicts," or that we were getting off on "mere technicalities." Those technicalities could be called by another name; they are basic legal rights.

Now that the worm has turned, there's no one to yell that they are "coddling prosecutors." When we get bludgeoned by a technicality—as Del Guzzi and Smith did—our voices don't carry well beyond these walls.

---

Anthony Del Guzzi's suit protesting his double sentence was turned down in both the district court and on appeal. One of those concurring in the ruling against him, Ninth Circuit court of appeals Judge William A. Norris, summed up: "I see this as one of those deeply troubling cases in which the law dictates an unjust result."

■

A month and a half after publication of that essay, I was back at the Federal Correctional Institution at Phoenix for my third and last appearance before Dannie's parole board. Once again, I was there primarily to see that he wasn't penalized for his journalism.

Dannie's previous target parole date was reaffirmed at that hearing.

He was not given back time he had lost for infractions before he began to write for the *Chronicle*—time that he and I had been led to expect would be restored if he kept up his good work. Nevertheless, he was not penalized further for his writing.

The parole hearing did not go as smoothly as his previous two, primarily because of the moralizing of the panel's chairman. He showed that Dannie's writing was very much on his mind by comparing him with Jack Abbott and urging him to beware of a similar fate. The implication was that because Dannie was a convict-writer, he, too, was a potential murderer . . . and he'd better behave himself.

Dannie somehow managed to explain politely the obvious differences between his background and Abbott's, but we both emerged seething over the baseless browbeating.

With his release on parole scheduled for February 1992, Dannie could expect to reach a San Francisco halfway house in October or November. Convicts call that "being short," and Dannie took to saying, "I'm so short I could sleep in a matchbox." Indeed, the next time I saw him in person was when I met his plane at San Francisco International Airport and drove with him to the halfway house.

Perhaps to keep his mind off the transition ahead, Dannie kept writing up to his release. For his next essay, he took another look at the world of paper that imprisoned him and his fellow convicts as effectively as any fences could.

---

# THE PRISON THICKET OF RULES
# AND POLICIES

*PHOENIX, ARIZ. (JULY 7, 1991)*—In the beginning was the Rule, and the Rule was good. That Rule begat another Rule that begat a Policy that begat more Rules, and they all have eternal life. Federal convicts today labor under more rules and policies than it is possible to memorize.

New ones are formulated daily, and the old ones never go away. The way most of us old-timers handle the situation is just to assume that everything we do or say is in violation of some rule or other.

For more than a year, a friend of mine in San Francisco sent me newspapers and magazines regularly. The rules say that we may receive softcover books and magazines in the mail.

She gathered *S.F. Weeklys*, *Bernal Journals*, *Bay Guardians*, and sections from the *Chronicle* and *Examiner* and sent them along. One evening at mail call, when the guard handed me her envelope it was empty. There was a yellow form inside that said the contents had been returned. At the bottom of the form was the message:

"Newspapers must be sent directly from the publishers."

It was signed "G. Popour, G. Popour." I was never able to determine if that was one or two G. Popours, but the message was clear. My newspaper-receiving days were over.

The incident didn't upset me that much, as I've long since resigned myself to the fact that whatever I may be doing in here is probably against some rule or other. But many convicts get highly upset under similar circumstances. They believe that if they are allowed to do something for a long period of time, then the practice creates a status quo that should be maintained. The sad truth is that there is no status quo in a federal prison.

The reason for these sudden and apparently arbitrary changes is not—as many think—some evil design on the part of our keepers. It's more simple than that. There are so many rules and regulations that the staff can't possibly learn them all, any more than we can. What happened to me is probably that G. Popour, G. Popour replaced someone else in the mailroom who hadn't been aware of the newspaper rule.

Louie Hatton, fifty-two, a well-seasoned convict from Modesto, California, just endured a maddening experience over a piece of cardboard.

It began when he ordered a Norton anthology of essays through the mail and the publisher sent him the wrong book. Louie decided to return it and began looking for a piece of cardboard to help construct a mailing package. He located a piece in a garbage can in the prison factory testing lab where he works. As convicts leave the factory here, they pass through a metal detector while a group of factory foremen and guards stand nearby.

Hatton made it through the metal detector and past the foremen with the piece of cardboard in his hand. But standing near the end was a new assistant factory superintendent who stopped him with the query: "Hold it there! Where are you going with that piece of cardboard?" Hatton explained to him that he had taken it from a garbage can to mail a package with.

"Nothing leaves this factory without permission from your foreman," the new man told him, and he confiscated the cardboard.

The following morning, Hatton went to his foreman and explained the situation. He then retrieved another piece of cardboard from the garbage can, and his foreman wrote on it: "Louie Hatton is authorized to take this piece of cardboard from the factory," and signed his name.

That evening, as he negotiated the metal detector and line of guards, he noticed the factory superintendent himself at the end of the line.

"Hold it!" the superintendent asked as he walked by. "Where are you going with that cardboard?" Hatton showed him the signed note on the cardboard. The factory manager took the cardboard anyway and told him the rules say that nothing leaves the factory. At that point, Hatton finally decided to look elsewhere for a piece of cardboard.

Living in a land of regulations, where it takes two days to find out you can't take a piece of cardboard from a garbage can, can have a devastating effect on the emotions of prisoners. What happened to Lenny Beasecker last year is an example.

On May 5, 1990, Beasecker's wife, Cindy, was killed when a motorcycle that she was a passenger on left the road in Byron, California. Funeral arrangements were made, and Lenny wanted to attend the service. Bureau of Prisons rules state that an inmate may attend the funeral of an immediate family member but is required to pay the expenses of the escorting guards to and from the destination.

Beasecker was told by the chaplain here and also by a unit manager that he would be allowed to attend the funeral. He had the money for the trip sent to the appropriate official, and at that point things began to go sour.

A case manager called him in and told him that they had found some association in his background with the Hells Angels motorcycle club. The unit manager told him that his original prosecutor said he would be a danger to the community and a danger to the guards escorting him.

Beasecker had his attorney call the prosecutor, only to discover that the man no longer worked in the U.S. Attorney's office and had made no such statements. Beasecker says prison officials later admitted that the statements were made by a U.S. parole officer in Oakland. The warden here said that due to the parole officer's comments, he would have to deny the trip.

Beasecker was stunned by the denial. He had been on bail before his conviction. His record has been spotless for four and a half years, and he is due to be paroled in eighteen months. In addition, there was no violence associated with his crime. Hardly a portrait of a danger to the community.

What Beasecker did not realize was that since President Bush rode the Willie Horton furlough on the campaign trail, escorted trips to funerals are becoming a thing of the past. Rules and policies governing those events are about as meaningful now as bus graffiti.

While it's understood around here that presidential politics can shift the sands of bureaucracy quicker than anything else, those of us who saw Beasecker with tears in his eyes know it's extremely raw to deny a biker a trip to a loved one's funeral because he's a biker.

One of the main traditions of motorcycle enthusiasts is paying their final respects to departed friends and lovers. They give their deceased a seat of honor in a joyous wake and pray the spirit rides free into eternity. The rites are conducted as if the person were still alive and beginning another journey.

To Beasecker, the denial became a gross personal insult. But prison officials were never known for their diplomacy or social finesse.

Often, these denials are even more complicated and hurtful. Evan Hodge, thirty-four, a convict from San Francisco, found that out the hard way last March when his father, Evan Hodge, Sr., was given three weeks to live.

Hodge Jr.—who had only eighteen months left to serve on his sentence—put in for a bedside visit. After he sent the money to prison officials, the trip was approved all the way up to the warden. His unit manager then called him in and told him that the Bureau of Prisons' regional office had denied the visit because he walked away from a halfway house years ago.

Shortly thereafter, when Hodge Sr. died, his son put in for an escorted visit to his funeral. According to Bureau of Prisons policy, the regional office doesn't act on funeral visits; that's done by the warden. So the warden denied the trip this time around.

"It's obvious no one is going anywhere on any kind of escorted trip, so why don't they just tell us that instead of putting us through all these changes before they deny everything anyway?" Hodge asked.

Hodge and Beasecker were not the victims of any rule change, but they were victimized by changes in the way age-old rules are reinterpreted at will by prison officials. Funeral visits, which used to be routine after proper precautions were taken, are now almost always denied. It seems as if you've got to be a stool pigeon to be able to attend a loved one's funeral, but you won't find that written in any book of rules and regulations.

There's another cycle in the enforcement of rules and requirements that's connected to the exigencies of everyday life in the prison.

Soon after my arrival here at Phoenix three years ago, a friend and I were walking toward the recreation yard. My companion dropped a cigarette into the dirt beside the walkway. As we entered the yard, a voice behind us yelled:

"Hey you!"

We turned around to see the warden standing there crooking his finger in a come-here sign to my friend. The warden marched him back to the cigarette butt, made him pick it up, and said:

"Don't you ever throw another cigarette butt on my yard."

The rules were very strict on littering in those days. The rules themselves haven't changed, but now we have a new warden, along with a severe overcrowding problem. There aren't enough jobs to go around, and a new evening crew has been created to clean up litter.

So now we nonchalantly flip cigarette butts in every direction. People drop food wrappers everywhere. It's a handy way to create work for someone. It may be as illegal as it ever was, but no one says anything about it these days.

A convict approached me the other day with an official Bureau of Prisons policy statement in his hand. "Look here," he said. "By their own policy I'm supposed to go to a halfway house at the end of my sentence, and the warden denied it. How can he do that?" he asked.

The paper in his hand said in part:

The Bureau of Prisons shall, to the extent practicable, assure that a prisoner serving a term of imprisonment spends a reasonable part, not to exceed six months of the last ten percentum of the term to be served under conditions that will afford the prisoner a reasonable opportunity to adjust to and prepare for his re-entry into the community.

A fifty-nine-word sentence that laid out the guidelines for our referral to a halfway house. But the warden had denied this convict because of the violent nature of his crime, a bank robbery.

"How can he go against official policy like that?" he asked me.

"He's probably following his own policy, which supersedes the official policy," I told him.

"Well, if they don't follow their own rules, how in the hell are we supposed to learn to follow rules?" he asked.

I didn't attempt to answer that, nor did he expect a reply. He's done as much time as I have.

An eighty-six-year-old convict once gave me the formula for survival and sanity in prison. It went something like this:

"Keep the head cool, the feet warm, the bowels open, the mouth shut, obey orders, and never let the mind wander out into an impenetrable thicket of rules and policies from where it may never return."

Early this morning, as I entered the mess hall for breakfast, I could hear the guards standing outside the door yelling at convicts: "Tuck in that shirt! Take that cap off! Put that cup down; you can't take it in there!"

None of them said a word to me. I was tucked in, capless, and cupless. I know enough rules to go to chow and back without getting myself in trouble. Beyond those simple rules lies the thicket that the old con warned me about all those years ago, and his rule—which he never changed on me midstream—may just be the key to rehabilitation.

Anyone out there who ever had to deal with a building inspector or an internal revenue agent would probably understand.

---

Shortly before publication of his next essay, Dannie got definite word of his halfway house placement: He was going to San Francisco on October 23, a little more than two months later.

In the meantime, he sent me a reminiscence of another old-timer with a legendary reputation in all the worst places.

# A WAGERING FOOL WHO WON
# TILL THE END

*PHOENIX, ARIZ. (AUG. 25, 1991)*—Not long ago, in the dead of winter, an old man died alone on a Greyhound bus near Louisville, Kentucky. Whoever checked his pockets for identification found the name Grady Halcomb. But to all his friends, his name was Dragline.

His passing reminded me of the Kenny Rogers song about a man dying on a Greyhound. The song's title is "The Gambler," and Dragline was a gambler. He wasn't much besides a wagering fool.

Cards and dice were his stock in trade, but he also loved what he called "proposition gambling." His propositions ran from the cliché'd—such as which bird on the wall would fly first—to the bizarre. I once heard him challenge a man to a game of "head-up" (one-on-one) baseball.

He spent most of his life in federal and California prisons, where men build reputations and become notorious by running prison gangs and killing people. Dragline became famous just by being himself, and there was no violence in his act. His reputation by far outstrips the tough guys'.

He was born in Norman, Oklahoma, in either 1912 or 1916, depending on whom you ask. Any time Dragline was asked how old he was he'd reply: "I'm not as old as I look or as young as I feel." Then he might ask a youthful inquisitor if he'd care to bet that Dragline couldn't guess his age within a year or his weight within four pounds. Many, including myself, took both bets, and lost.

I first ran into him at Folsom Prison in the late '60s. He was a lanky man, about six feet four, with pale blue eyes and an abundant mop of silver hair.

His demise reminded me of one song, but in life he reminded me of "Mr. Bojangles," because when moving he seemed to unfold and swoop like a tall crane. He appeared to dance through life.

His hands were large, with long fingers, and were endowed with pure magic. He first gained legendary status making small objects of contraband disappear during shakedowns by prison guards.

As a gambler he used those quick hands efficiently, but he didn't call it cheating; he called it "taking an edge."

Dominoes is a big game at Folsom Prison, and on that yard some of the best players in the country can be found. In a two- or four-handed game, each player shuffles the dominoes in turn. Convicts call it "shaking the bones." Dragline could play, but he wasn't allowed to shake the bones when his turn came.

Someone asked an old convict why they wouldn't let Dragline shake the bones when his turn came.

"Son," he replied, "if you let Dragline shake them bones, you may as well pay him, because you done lost the game right there."

Marbles was the favorite gambling game at Folsom in those days. We used plastic roll-on deodorant balls for "woods" and steel ball bearings for "shooters." The object was to knock five woods from the ring. But if you had a wood and your shooter was hit by another's shooter, you had to put the wood back in the ring. If your shooter got hit when you had no woods, you were "dead"—end of game.

Dragline could pop another shooter consistently from ten to fifteen feet away. He was the most awesome marble shooter who ever played in Folsom and would spot the best players a couple of woods and still win.

Besides being a well-known convict, Dragline never amounted to much in his life. He entered a California prison in the early '40s, and the first chance he got, he escaped. While on the run he committed more crimes, and not long after he was captured and put back in prison, he escaped again.

While on his second or third escape, he robbed a bank in central California and was sentenced to twenty-five years in federal prison in addition to the time he still owed California. The forty-odd years that Dragline spent in prison were more or less one long continuous sentence alleviated by an escape here and there.

He was a heavy smoker and drank a lot of prison-made wine. He built a still at San Quentin Prison where he cooked off a batch of white lightning a couple times a week. He did the same thing at Folsom, and it took the guards more than a year of constant searching to find his cooker.

By the time he reached the maximum federal lockup at Marion, Dragline was well into his sixties and riddled with emphysema. He quit smoking and spent his days in the yard trying to get his breath back.

There wasn't much to do in Marion besides time, so a few cons ran the track almost continuously. One of the runners was a man everyone called Easy. He was recognized as the best runner in Marion at any distance and was fanatic about training.

"Hey, man!" Dragline would yell as Easy jogged by. "You look like you are running in molasses!"

Or he would shout out something like: "Hey, Easy, you trying to lose some of that fat?" This to a man in perfect condition.

Easy belonged to a prison gang and wasn't a very talkative or sociable fellow. But Dragline finally pulled his chain when he told him he'd been watching him run for five years and he appeared to be getting slower.

"When I was your age, my backdraft stirred up tornadoes," Dragline told him.

After some lively conversation, a bet was arranged. Easy was to spot Dragline fifteen yards on a hundred-yard dash. There has never been a sporting event at Marion penitentiary that was bet on more than that footrace. Not even a Super Bowl.

The older convicts were betting heavily on Dragline while the younger crowd was backing Easy. Those who were broke were betting push-ups or months of desserts. Some of the guards were betting among themselves.

On the day of the race, everyone who could get to the yard was there to see it. The flag went down, and they were off on a good clean start. Drag hit the finish line a good twenty yards in front of Easy, beating him by five yards more than he was spotted.

The only negative aspect of the race was that Easy got so mad he never spoke to Dragline again. But it was a race that convicts still talk about more than ten years later. Those who were there recount it again and again. That event has gained near-mythological proportions behind prison walls.

It's often said that those who live by the gun will die by the gun. A more certain bet is that those who spend most of their lives in prison are likely to die there.

Dragline was a good candidate to die in prison. I asked him once about his future, and he said: "Hell, I don't know how to do much of anything except time, and I'm running short on that."

But he had an old, reformed convict friend who had other plans. Joe Turk quit the outlaw life in the early '60s. He hung up his gun after a long stretch for robbery and bought himself a café by the ocean in Hermosa Beach, California, and married a lovely woman named Frannie.

Joe was determined that upon his release Dragline would live with him and Frannie and not return to prison.

In the late '80s, one year before Dragline was scheduled for release, Joe's liver turned into something that resembled a chunk of cool lava rock, and he passed away. But his hope that Drag would live with him and Frannie stayed alive in her. She was here at Phoenix to pick him up when he walked out the gate after a seventeen-year stretch in federal prison.

When Dragline went out the gate, Sam, an old con who worked as a gardener, handed him a dozen red roses to give Frannie in the parking lot.

They stopped down the road for some steak and a glass of red wine. Frannie told him there was definitely life after prison and that she could prove it beyond a reasonable doubt, and she did.

Frannie and Dragline never returned near his old haunts. Instead she took him to the beach, the arboretum, the zoo, the carnival, Disneyland, and most of all the warmth and comfort of a well-lived-in house.

Before long, neighborhood kids were knocking on her door, wanting Dragline to pull more quarters from their ears or make something else vanish in those big, mysterious hands.

He lived with her for eight months and told friends it was the most beautiful and important time of his life. One morning he got up and told her that he needed to visit some long-lost family members he'd located in Kentucky.

"Maybe he knew he was dying, but I had no idea. I just helped him prepare for the journey," Frannie says.

Two days after seeing him off, she received notification by phone of his death on the bus. Old Dragline had made his last bet and done his last time in this world.

Those of us who bet he'd be back in prison lost, but we didn't mind paying off. We didn't even mind the irony that while dying he beat us one more time.

Someone said the other day that the devil likes to make propositions to people, and in that regard he and Dragline have a lot in common, as well as something to talk about.

Even as I write this, I can see them setting up the domino tables down there. Hell may never be the same again.

---

It was vintage Dannie—a quiet, human-scale memorial to a giant of the "dying tribe." No excuses, no apologies, no glorification. I think he loved that kind of writing more than all the significant essays he published out of a sense of social obligation.

Dannie was glad to get that story in under the wire, for his time was growing very short. With the anticipation of release had come a simultaneous retreat into memories of the old days in the joint. There was a security in the memories that didn't exist in the anticipation.

For his final story from prison, at my suggestion he again got personal. It was the story I think his readers were waiting to read, published ten days before his release.

---

# AFTER 11 YEARS, A CONVICT IS COUNTING DAYS

*PHOENIX, ARIZ. (OCT. 13, 1991)*—On Wednesday, October 23, I'll be getting out of prison again after eleven years, one month, and thirteen days. A lot of things have changed since September 10, 1980—both in here and on the outside.

Someone asked me how it feels to be getting out after all that time, and I replied truthfully that I don't know. I'm not very familiar with my feelings anymore because I've had to suppress and regulate them for more than a decade. In this environment, feelings are mainly viewed as weakness.

Breakfast is at 6:30 A.M., lunch is at 11:00 A.M., and dinner is at 5:00 P.M. There's no use feeling hungry at any other time. Anger or emotional verbosity earns a stay in Isolation, so we learn to suppress all that.

Sexual longing leads only to self-gratification in the dead of night. There's a time and place for everything, but not in the biblical sense of seasons. To us convicts, it's more like the treadmill of Hades.

I've had my share of recreation in here, but only at certain times on certain days and in the same place. When the bell rings and the herd moves, I move with it. When the herd stops, I stop. Individualism is a serious crime here.

It seems strange that soon I'll walk out the gate and leave the herd behind. They will probably be watching me as a cow raises her head and marvels at one of her calves who trampled the fence and struck out for greener pastures.

And I suppose I'll be looking back over my shoulder, feeling the trepidation that comes with the loss of total security, yet overcome with passion for the greener hills.

I like to think that maybe I'm no longer one of the herd. I'm no longer a drug addict, and I'm learning the ropes of journalism. When my feelings return, I'll be a lucky ex-convict if I feel like a journalist.

Fear is one emotion that never was totally suppressed or regulated. It's hooked firmly into the survival instinct, and that's something we dare not lose in here. I feel a certain fear about my impending freedom. Not the same type of panic I felt when another convict attempted to stab me in the throat but definitely an apprehension.

People in the "free world" drive big, noisy steel machines that hurtle by at breathtaking speed. Sometimes within inches of pedestrians. One misstep and I'll be looking like road kill. Sneaky little cowardly punks out there carry guns that fire thirty shells a second, so I'll need to brush up on my manners.

I'll be able to eat when I feel hungry, but I'll have to pay for the food with money I work for. Work is one of the main components of living in a free society. It's also an alien concept to me. My criminal past never prepared me for labor, and free-lance journalism is the nearest I've come to learning a trade. I've always had a job in prison, but never a job that required any work.

But I know I will have to work if I am to remain on the outside. The thought brings up a certain amount of fear, because I'll have to do something I've never done, without being sure I can do it.

But my grandfather used to say that all it takes is a strong back and a weak mind. So at the least, I'm fully qualified.

There isn't much of a work ethic in here to serve as an example. Staff members sit around behind desks computing sick leave, vacation pay, and retirement credits. The surest way to get myself in trouble is to cause one of them to have to do some work. That type of behavior is totally taboo.

Thank God for that small minority of convicts who are hyperactive and need to be busy all the time. Those who enjoy working at difficult menial tasks. Without them, a prison would go belly up and sink into its own filth and lethargy.

People often say to me that convicts never had it so good. We get free meals, free rent, and laundry service. That is true, but they don't add that convicts—the industrious minority of us, anyhow—cook, serve, and clean up after all those meals, perform all the maintenance on those free rooms, and wash and dry all that laundry. Their wages wouldn't keep a Chihuahua in dog food.

As I prepare to leave here in a few days, I notice another new attitude taking hold in the prison. I believe eleven years was too much time for the crime I committed. But all around me now I see men doing thirty and forty years with no chance of parole for lesser crimes than mine. Their fate is the result of recent drug wars and tough-on-crime legislation.

Many of them are giving up and refusing to do any work at all. Even the hyperactive ones. They are saying to their friends:

"Man, why are you working? There's nothing else to gain from it. Let the police do all the work."

I hear that sentiment more and more these days, and it is a thought-provoking one. If convicts quit working, the staff would have to be doubled or tripled. That would be one expensive mess.

Another surprising change taking place has to do with the confinement of so many drug dealers. Prisons are now awash in hard drugs. Dope is becoming much cheaper in here now because of the competition—it's always available. Aside from the hundreds of casual users, a few cons here have serious heroin habits, and they do get their daily fix.

A sad aspect of the burgeoning dope business in here is that many convicts who never used drugs in their lives are becoming serious drug addicts. "It makes my time a lot easier," a bank embezzler turned heroin user told me one day.

Recently, nineteen people here were called in for random urinalysis. A friend told me that fifteen of them tested positive for heroin, methamphetamine, or marijuana. Lately, the authorities have been

296 COMMITTING JOURNALISM

testing convicts who never used drugs, and everyone knows they don't use drugs. That procedure looks like an effort to bring the numbers down a bit.

With the drugs came problems and arguments over payoffs and quality. So the violence is escalating accordingly. I feel very fortunate to be leaving instead of arriving at this time.

The main question on my mind right now is who I will talk to out there—and what in the world will we talk about? With the exception of a few phone calls and visits, I've talked to no one but convicts for the past eleven years. We no longer talk out the sides of our mouths, but we sort of talk out the sides of our minds.

I've made some friends and pen pals due to my writing for "Sunday Punch." We've built a pretty nice bridge from my world to theirs. Maybe we'll find plenty to talk about eyeball to eyeball.

My friend Jack and I were engrossed in a horseshoe game this evening when an electric lightning storm began zapping the sky to the north of us. Jack abruptly put his horseshoes down and headed for the track around the exercise yard. When I caught up and asked why he'd quit like that he said:

"Man, what if that lightning was to strike one of those horseshoe stakes?"

It made me wonder how a man that cautious ever got into prison. Yet the logic was impeccable. I will miss these eccentric characters. They are my peer group, and I know I will find myself feeling lonely and wondering what they are up to.

But I have twenty-two years of parole to do, and the main condition of that parole is that I can't associate with convicts or ex-convicts. That's kind of like telling a crow he can hang out only with pink flamingos.

I'm grateful to all who read my pieces regularly. Even to those who consistently write letters to the editor informing the newspaper that I'm a con man and a skulking, conniving convict. A sniveler in bank robber's garb.

They keep reminding me that published opinion and public people are subject to rigid scrutiny and considered criticism. I wish the Bureau of Prisons understood that.

How do I feel about the past eleven years? One of Shakespeare's characters said in *Macbeth*:

"All our yesterdays have lighted fools the way to dusty death."

I can escape part of that trap by not being a fool anymore. My yesterdays in prison have led me to the written word. I'm going to be a writer.

These remarks about my getting out aren't meant as a farewell. I'm going to San Francisco, where I will continue to write. I must confess that right now, I feel like I'm going home.

# VI

---

# LIFE WITH THE
# FLAMINGOS
# OCTOBER 1991 —

Dear Peter: Our journey through the labyrinth of prison journalism is coming to an end. There are many adjectives that could be used to describe what we've been through, but I think you would agree that "interesting" would fit best of all. Even the lowest of the lows were interesting.

I'm not sure where we will go from here, but other than the business end of it, our friendship has meant a lot to me, and for sure that isn't coming to an end.

Also I believe we've drawn a blueprint for [prison] journalism . . . and I hope other convicts will build on it. But all we can do now is leave it here for them.

I felt good the other day when a convict I didn't even know walked up to me, shook my hand, and said, "Man, I wish you a lot of luck. You've done more for people in prison than anyone I know of."

I hope whatever I do or become out there will be as satisfying as hearing that sentiment from a convict . . . or the message in all the mail from readers out there that I've been getting. . . .

I feel like I'm taking something valuable out the gate with

me this time, and I hope I'll have enough sense to utilize it. One of my favorite writers, Robertson Davies, said:

"Experience is not what happens to a man, it's what a man does with what happens to him."

I can't help but feel he was talking to me when he said that.

We've been through a sometimes tortuous journey, but I'm a much less tortured man than I was when it all began. Things in here that used to wound me deeply don't hurt so much anymore because I found a voice to tell the world about them.

That maddening grip of awesome, tyrannical power that prison officials had on me has been loosened a lot, and just a tiny bit of grudging respect has entered into their attitude toward me. They've been forced to recognize my humanity, and I can't tell you how much that small victory means to me and a legion of other imprisoned souls.

I just wanted to write this last letter to let you know how good I feel about myself and what we've accomplished. It also feels good to have a future that may not include jails and prisons.

I've sure made some nice friends, and if I don't accomplish much else, that is reward enough.

It will be good to see you out there in your natural habitat. I do look forward to it. . . .

Right now, I'm pretty sure my keepers will slam the gate as hard as they can when I walk out. The feeling will be deeply mutual.

*Your pal,*
*Red Hog*

■

The letter was dated October 20, 1991. Three days later, I was waiting at Gate 62 to greet Dannie when United flight 1036 arrived from Phoenix. It was a moment I had never expected. When our association began five and a half years earlier, I never even dreamed of Dannie being out in the free world. There was something very final about saying, as I had done so often in print, "a prisoner serving a thirty-three-year sentence for bank robbery."

Earlier on that morning of his release, a Phoenix TV crew had captured Dannie's first moments of freedom. The crew was waiting as he walked slowly out the front door of the prison, a slight smirk flickering across his face and a sack of belongings slung over his shoulder. KPNX reporter Cary Pfeffer interviewed him just feet from the door of the prison. "I feel like it's been a long trip," Dannie told him. "I feel like I've just been over the Oregon Trail or something. I feel good. It's a beautiful day."

Then, as he walked slowly toward the AAA cab waiting to take him to the airport, Dannie glanced to his right and gave a brief, almost offhand wave of recognition in the direction of the rolled razor wire. The TV crew's microphones picked up whistles and hoots from behind the wire and the fences, but no individual was distinguishable when the camera panned in that direction. A few days later, I received a handwritten letter that began:

Dear Mr. Sussman: Today, Wednesday, October 23, 1991, there are thirty-one inmates of assorted color and ethnic background near the northeast turn on the prison yard jogging track. It is the closest point to the main gate of the federal jail an inmate can be without getting into trouble. We are watching and waving as our fellow prisoner and friend Dannie Martin heads for Freedom.

My thoughts are, there goes one of the great lights of hope and inspiration that was among us. . . .

I, along with many others you have helped, want to thank you, Dannie, "Sunday Punch," and the *San Francisco Chronicle* for putting prisoner problems on public view. . . . We prisoners call it "good looking out" for your fellow human beings, even though we are cast out of society.

Some of us will be coming out much like Dannie, with high expectations, wanting to be good citizens. Some of us will be coming out looking to get even for some rotten thing someone in the justice system did to us while we are being punished by being here. All of us need a helping hand.

The help we need is reform by the public that is almost totally misinformed about prisoners.

No First Amendment award could mean as much to me as that letter.

■

Awaiting Dannie at the *Chronicle* offices were piles of mail from readers that had accumulated since publication of his last prison essay.

Some contained cash and checks to help him get settled. (One woman earmarked her contribution for "a fresh cup of good coffee and a muffin as you breathe in your free air.") Boxes of clothing and a carton of donated sundries were stacked on the floor around my desk.

The letters gave some measure of the impact the convict had had on the world to which he was returning, thanking him for his courage, for his insights, and "for still feeling some outrage." Almost universally his fans expressed confidence in Dannie's ability to "make it" in the free world, and they cheered him on. Said one: "Don't you give up, Dannie M. Martin. Don't you do it."

A number of the correspondents looked to the writer for some insights beyond the prison: "Please keep showing us that part of our world that we'd rather not examine—hopefully it'll move us to change, to prevent, to understand."

Dannie would learn, however, that not all of the public wished him well. The convict who prided himself on portraying his fellow prisoners as individuals had to fight off powerful negative stereotypes from some who seemed to be rooting for his failure. I recall the shock I felt when a man who said he was "in law enforcement" phoned me and asked sneeringly if we would print it in the paper when Dannie committed his next crime and was hauled back to prison.

■

Some letter writers had been in Dannie's position and foresaw much of what he was to go through in the following months. One correspondent who was active in a support network for ex-cons was uncommonly perceptive in anticipating Dannie's own needs and feelings:

> Getting out is a weird and alien experience. So many things that you might think would be simple will have their complexities. And other things, just the opposite. Some people will understand what you are feeling, and others won't have a clue. . . .
>
> Almost seven years ago I was released from prison. . . . I felt like a freak and unsure of myself. Prison has a way of eating at your self-esteem. Upon release into the "normal" world, you find yourself feeling less and less normal every day. If anything is normal, it is that feeling.

Other ex-convicts, in calls and letters, spoke of various forms of unease that they had felt on emerging. They told of nightmares and paranoia, financial panic, a paralyzing lack of self-confidence.

One mentioned the overwhelming fatigue—"the kind of fatigue people commit suicide to avoid." He said he had seen men so exhausted by the strain of adjusting to life outside that they would show up at the prison gates in the middle of the night, begging to be allowed back in.

Those former convicts didn't have to face the added blessing-cum-burden that Dannie encountered—the incessant demands for lectures, articles, favors, audiences, speeches, TV and radio and classroom appearances. However well-intentioned, it was a heavy and confusing load to lay on a man who had been told what to do and where to be for every minute of the previous eleven years.

He had never seen a fax or an answering machine and now was inundated by the messages they spat out at him. He had never worked at a steady job in his life, but now everyone expected him to do just that.

He wanted above all else to be a writer, a notoriously difficult calling. He was coming from the most structured of institutions but hoped to make a living in the most unstructured of professions. He had never organized a desk, much less a career. Indeed, he seemed to operate largely on impulse. And he was incapable of budgeting what meager funds he had.

Terry Anderson, the journalist held hostage in Lebanon for six and a half years, was by all accounts a remarkably disciplined prisoner. He organized mental games and classes to sharpen his intellect and to sustain his fellow captives. Yet when he was released, he wrote that no amount of foresight could have prepared him for freedom. He said that he "never seemed to catch up with everything." He added:

> The first few weeks found me late for every single appointment, and incredibly disorganized. I'd lost the skill of managing all the small things that make up a day—when to shave, where I put my wallet, what I'm supposed to do next.

It is an apt description of what Dannie was feeling, but he had never had many of those organizational skills *before* his imprisonment—and he had four and a half more years than Anderson to lose what simple coping abilities he had once had.

For many months after his release, Dannie swung unpredictably between elation and bewilderment. The same man who could tell one interviewer, "Everything is uncertain," told another, "This is the light at the end of the tunnel. I'm standing in it now."

Aiding him immeasurably through the transition was his developing personal relationship with Jan Sluizer, a radio reporter who had interviewed him in prison and later began corresponding with him. Her apartment became his daytime writing retreat and later his home. Sluizer's solidity and inexhaustible patience helped Dannie to maintain his balance through the uncertainties of his early days on the outside.

■

**I** had got my introduction to his new institutional home, the halfway house, a few weeks before Dannie's arrival. I phoned the institution, Eclectic Communications Inc. (ECI), and spoke to Yolanda Lewis, the director. Friends had contributed funds to buy Dannie a desperately needed hearing aid, and I wanted to set up an appointment for him in advance, so that he could get the device as soon as possible. He would need it to seek work, among other things.

How soon after his release, I asked Lewis, would he be free to keep such an appointment?

"We don't even know if he'll show," she replied. "Many of them don't, you know."

I tried again, more cautiously:

"Oh, he'll be there. But all I really need to know is how long your orientation is. How soon before he is free to keep an appointment?"

"Look," she replied, "I don't know anything. I don't even have his file."

The conversation sputtered out after a few more uncommunicative exchanges. I gambled and made Dannie an appointment for two days after his arrival, but as it turned out he could have kept the appointment almost anytime. There was no orientation to speak of.

At the halfway house in San Francisco's Tenderloin district— approached by way of a urine-soaked street frequented by crack addicts, winos, and prostitutes—Dannie was thrown in with men and women whose situations were far more precarious than his own. Many, like Dannie, emerged with $50 in gate money, which they were dribbling away in dimes, making fruitless phone calls to potential employers. One man was looking desperately for a gun, which was about the only thing he could think of to buy with his $50 that would help him survive on the outside.

For most, first and last month's rent on a decent apartment seemed an impossible goal, not to mention a few changes of clothing or the medical care that years of neglect had made necessary. In Dannie's case, donated services and gifts of money helped him to secure some of what he needed: hearing aid, clothes, reading glasses, extensive dental and periodontal work, other medical tests and treatment. Making connections, purchasing necessities, and getting treatment—and simply negotiating his way around on public transit—consumed a good deal of his early weeks in the halfway house.

The workday routine at ECI involves an endless round of job searches, with curfews and other privileges liberalized over time. Dannie was frustrated by the constant demands that kept him from writing. He told me once, "I'm not even sure I can write out here. I may have to build myself a little cell in my room and crawl in there to write."

Dannie's admiring public also exerted a subtle if unintended pressure. So high was his visibility that his absence from print for a period of time could not go unnoticed. One letter to the editor published in the *Chronicle* asked:

How about laying a frame on Dannie Martin so he can be reincarcerated back into the slammer from whence he used to write those great articles that appeared in the "Sunday Punch"? Since he was sprung, we hardly ever get a chance to see his name above an article.

Finally, he was granted permission to spend his days writing at Sluizer's house. There, hesitantly, he tried to jump-start his free-lance "career" with infrequent articles.

Dannie's first two "Sunday Punch" stories told of his initial impressions of his half-free world. With the authorization of ECI and the BOP, they were written for pay, and they appeared under his own byline.

# ALL THE WAY HOME AND HALFWAY
# TO FREEDOM

*SAN FRANCISCO, CALIF. (DEC. 1, 1991)*—I sat up with a start in the middle of the night. From somewhere came the realization that I'd been mailing my letters unsealed for the previous two weeks. The recognition shocked me awake. For the past eleven years in prison I'd been putting letters in the mail box unsealed, so that the night guard could censor them.

I lay back down in my little hotel-like room at the halfway house here on Taylor Street, and my thoughts drifted over the events since my release a few weeks ago. It's been a strange trip indeed.

When I left the prison in Phoenix, a TV camera met me at the gate, and as I stood there smiling and commenting about my past and future, I had $50 in my pocket and only a vague idea of what lay ahead. I don't know what the Bureau of Prisons thought I could do on $50.

They also gave me a golf shirt, polyester slacks, and a pair of plastic slip-on loafers, which I declined. So there I stood in my handmade moccasins in front of a TV camera, feeling like a Rip Van Winkle who woke up broke and untutored in an expensive, complicated world.

I hadn't been in town but a day or two when the $50 expired on a few cans of orange juice, a pack of Camels, and several phone calls. (The phones in the halfway house, which we must use in our job searches, are all pay phones.)

That $50 sounded like a lot more to me when I was back in the prison. I was totally unprepared for the ravages of inflation during the time I'd been away.

The first cup of coffee I bought cost $1. Coffee was 10 cents a cup when I left town. It costs $1.25 to wash a load of clothes now, whereas the charge was 25 cents when I went away.

If I hadn't had friends who wanted to help me out here, I don't know what I would have done. I wouldn't even have had a change of clothes.

A man I talked with in the yard before I left the prison at Phoenix seems to me now to be Exhibit A of that $50 predicament. "Joe" had just returned to prison after being paroled to the Phoenix area. He was beginning a ten-year nonparolable sentence for a bank robbery.

"I was broke and getting ready to leave the halfway house," he told me. "I had a job that was to begin in two weeks, but I was broke and didn't have rent or grocery money. I figured I could just rob one bank and get enough to tide me over until my job began."

He figured wrong, and as we stood there looking at two high fences, I remember thinking he must be a little stupid. But now that I'm out here, his tale makes a little more sense.

After eleven years of inactivity, the hustle and bustle of society hit me like a ton of bricks.

A decade-plus of being told what to do and when and how to do it has conditioned me to the point where I'm like Pavlov's dog. It's a real shock being out here where I must make appointments, find a means to get there, then get there on time and get back again. The whole process is made more difficult by the time constraints of the halfway house.

Doing things on your own initiative is not what they teach you in prison. There, the entire day is spent waiting for everything to happen. Out here, I feel like I'm buffeted by a storm of activities. At times, getting back to the halfway house at night—drinking a cup of coffee, with no people to call and no appointments to make—is almost a luxury. Then I get caught up in one of the halfway house's prisonlike regulations, and I realize I'm better off out there in the storm.

On the streets, heading for this or that appointment, I often find myself stopping and looking around, marveling that I'm alone and free, acting on my own—and with no guard watching me. In prison, there is no place to escape observation; there is someone watching our every move.

And the people I'd been living with day in and day out have had two things in common: They're all grown-ups and they're all male. Having women and children around—friends and even passersby on the street—is an unbelievable wonder. It's one of the many impressions that crowd around me and even stop me on the street in mid-thought.

For a week or so after my release to the halfway house, I ran around with phone numbers stuffed into every pocket. I'd pull them out and ask myself, "Now, who gave me this and why was I supposed to call this person?"

A good friend finally gave me an appointment book complete with reminder calendars, address blanks, and a notebook. I'm glad he was thoughtful enough to give me one; I'd have never thought to ask for something I didn't even know I needed.

Nor did prison prepare me for the bewildering array of gadgets and systems that were installed during my eleven years of somnambulance.

I was raised in the San Joaquin Valley, where there was no subway, so there was nothing in my experience to prepare me for a ride to Oakland on the Bay Area Rapid Transit system. It was pure adventure.

In the underground station it took me a good ten minutes and the help of an agent just to get through the turnstile. Standing there on the platform looking at the tracks and waiting for whatever was supposed to arrive, I began feeling strange.

A lone woman stood at the next boarding space, and as I looked toward her, I heard a rumbling sound. Simultaneously, a tunnel door seemed to open somewhere, and a strong wind blew down the platform.

The woman's hair began blowing and weaving as if she were underwater, and as the sleek train came hurtling down the tracks, I felt as if I'd stepped onto the set of a science fiction movie. It was as though we were on Mars awaiting the arrival of the giant worm in Frank Herbert's book *Dune*.

The ride was like a benevolent roller coaster. When I returned to San Francisco, the exit gate wouldn't let me out, and another agent had to rescue me. At least BART isn't using robots yet like the phone company, which seems to have gone totally berserk.

I keep getting robots on the line that tell me I've dialed my number wrong. They refer to other robots who tell me how to dial correctly. There's still a real person on the 411 information line, but once you ask for the number a robot comes on line to finish the conversation.

Almost everyone I call has either voice mail or an answering machine, so there are times already when I feel downright lonely in the midst of a crowded city. My hearing problem doesn't make it any easier when talking to machines and robots. They won't raise their voices for anyone.

Fax machines are an incredible development in this new world of wonders. I spent almost a week calling fax numbers that I saw on business cards that people had given me. All I got was mechanical shrieks, but the machine never had sense enough to tell me that I was calling a fax number.

It's also beyond my imagination how someone can place sheets of paper in a machine in San Francisco and have them reproduced in New York in a few seconds. I can only visualize a line of robots passing the information hand to hand, faster than the speed of light.

Many of the new ideas and ways of life out here seem to have left ex-convicts like myself by the wayside. I'm finding it very difficult to plug myself back into the free world. One example of that process is a check I received lately.

About the time my $50 ran out, the Bureau of Prisons sent me a check for $10.50. The sum was to close out my canteen account, and I was glad to get it. But having no driver's license or ID, I couldn't cash it.

A friend took it to her bank of fifteen years, a neighborhood branch of the Bank of America. A teller told her she couldn't cash a third-party check because I had no identification. My friend asked to see the manager, who told her she would cash the $10.50 check for a fee of $8, which made her so mad she ended up withdrawing all her accounts from Bank of America.

I still haven't been able to cash the check, but at least my friend got an inkling of the trauma convicts undergo on this side of the prison gate.

And this former bank robber has not even begun yet to figure out how to get a bank to give him a checking account.

The halfway house is where I do my time nowadays. It is run under contract to the Bureau of Prisons. I get out daily to work between the hours of 8:00 A.M. and 5:00 P.M., but otherwise I'm treated like the convict I still am. So I'm only halfway to freedom.

Yesterday I noticed a fellow convict sitting at a table in the day-room. He's been out of prison almost two weeks and is still wearing the clothes that were given him when he left the penitentiary.

He bummed a cigarette and sat there smoking while gazing out the window at Turk Street with a troubled look on his face. I hope he makes it out here, but I couldn't help but wonder if he wasn't thinking . . .

"Maybe I can just rob one bank to tide me over until I find a job."

---

## . . . AND HALFWAY TO SLEEP

SAN FRANCISCO, CALIF. (DEC. 1, 1991)—Last night I went to bed at 9:00. At 9:30, someone knocked on the door of my small room in the halfway house. Half awake, I grunted:

"Come in!"

The door opened and my light came on. I sleep on the top bed of a double bunk with the light directly above me, and it's like a floodlight in my eyes. A man entered with a clipboard in his hand and said:

"Mr. Martin?"

"Yes, that's me," I replied.

"Okay, I'm just taking a board count here," he said. He then turned my light off and left.

At 10:30 P.M., another knock at my door, and the same exact process was repeated. When he knocked and entered again at 11:30, I asked him:

"Say, buddy, are you going to do this all night?"

"Just doing my job," he replied and left, only to return periodically the rest of the night.

This counting procedure is part of the halfway house routine. It happens every night, although some of the "turnkeys" are more discreet and just shine a flashlight at these escape-prone sleeping bodies.

I can't figure the logic of it. They let me sign out at 8:00 A.M. and return at 5:00 P.M. If I wanted to escape, I could leave at 8:00 and be in Canada before they missed me at 5:00.

Why in the world would they think I'd come in at 5:00 only to sneak out a fire escape between hourly bed checks? It must be some Bureau of Prisons conspiracy to drive convicts crazier than we already are.

Maybe they just want me to sleep on my own time. It looks like that's what I'm going to have to do.

---

Dannie was on an increasingly longer leash at the halfway house, but the people who run that institution seemed determined to yank the leash every once in a while to let him know he still had a collar around his neck.

On New Year's Eve—his first in the free world in seventeen years—Dannie had arranged a holiday pass and had plans to entertain friends for a roast beef dinner at Sluizer's apartment. He had been informed earlier that day by his caseworker that he was not following the proper call-in procedures, but the problem was apparently resolved when Dannie told her he hadn't been aware of the requirement and would comply in the future.

With dinner in the oven, he headed to the halfway house at the required 4:00 P.M. to pick up his weekend pass. When he got there, he was informed that he wasn't going anywhere, that his pass had been denied. An hour later, director Yolanda Lewis gave him the reason: "You broke the rules."

Dannie asked why she hadn't called him earlier in the day, at the number where they knew he was working, so that he could cancel his holiday plans.

"It's not my job to tell you you've broken the rules. It's your job not to break them," Lewis replied.

She told Dannie he could bring his dinner to the halfway house, so his guests were invited to meet him there instead. The holiday feast was ferried from Sluizer's apartment in several trips. But when the guests arrived, Dannie was informed that he could visit with his friends briefly but that they couldn't eat there.

In another uncomfortable episode, Dannie's caseworker scheduled a home visit to the apartment where he was working. Dannie waited for her there, but she never showed up. She apparently was unable to find the door, which was down a driveway and behind a gate. Later, the caseworker accused Dannie of lying when he told her he'd been waiting there for her at the agreed time.

These were just two of the several misunderstandings in which Dannie became ensnared, but the pattern was always the same. The people who were supposed to help convicts through their transition seemed to react first with suspicion and sanctions. As a result of similar experiences, other convicts rarely went to the staff for the help they so desperately needed.

Indeed, at times the halfway house seemed a halfway prison, operating with all the illogic of that system. It took its toll on Dannie.

███

**M**eanwhile, our legal case limped on through the appeals court, with several new developments as the judges were deliberating.

In December 1991, the U.S. Supreme Court unanimously struck down New York's so-called Son of Sam law, designed to prevent criminals from profiting from books and movies about their crimes. The court found that the law infringed on the rights of both the convict and the publisher. Although no such law applied in Dannie's case, the government and Judge Legge had cited Son of Sam statutes as an indication that, in Legge's words, "neither the public nor legislatures want prisoners to benefit financially from their criminal activities or from their detention in prison."

The Court's opinion undercut Legge's argument. It seemed to bolster the *Chronicle*'s position that a prohibition on compensation inhibits speech. And the ruling reaffirmed that a publisher's own rights are violated when it is prohibited from paying an author for published material.

We brought that decision to the attention of the appeals court, but the Justice Department was active as well. It argued that the entire case was moot because Dannie had been released to the halfway house, where rule 540.20(b) didn't apply. The government renewed its request for a "mootness" ruling when Dannie was released on parole in February 1992.

Our attorneys responded that Dannie's release in no way affected the grievances of the *Chronicle,* which was also a plaintiff in the case. Our rights would continue to be violated when other federal convicts wanted to write for the newspaper. Additionally, the attorneys argued, if the case was thrown out of court, Dannie and the *Chronicle* would be denied the monetary damages that were dependent on the outcome of the constitutional case.

Nevertheless, the appeals court did indeed declare the case moot, although it had had six months to decide the issue after the oral arguments and before Dannie's release on parole. The decision wiped Legge's ruling off the books and left the regulation in force.

The technical "mootness" issue was appealed to the Supreme Court, which refused to hear the case. We were left with nothing to show for the years-long legal battle except Dannie's safety during the time he was writing under protection of a preliminary injunction. Unless 540.20(b) is modified by the administration or by Congress, any future prison writers—or their publishers—will have to go through a similar costly and uncertain crusade before federal convicts gain the unambiguous right to publish anything more than a letter to the editor in the news media.

In the meantime, the risk of punishment will doubtless still other voices and impoverish the national debate over criminal justice.

**D**annie wrote one more story for the *Chronicle* during his four-month stay in the halfway house. His account of one young man's plight is typical of the state of the justice system since the advent of the little-understood sentencing guidelines and mandatory minimums.

## HARD TIME FOR HEAVY PAPER

*SAN FRANCISCO, CALIF. (FEB. 9, 1992)*—With his shoulder-length golden tresses, Christian Martensen looks like a cherubic hippie. But in the eyes of the law, the lanky twenty-two-year-old is a convicted felon who conspired to sell a large amount of LSD. The prospective buyer, as it happens, was a federal agent.

Martensen, who had no prior criminal record, has been moved from jail to a federal halfway house here while he awaits sentencing. If the government has its way, he'll be sentenced to many years in prison. It all depends on the weight of some cardboard.

Martensen is a Grateful Dead camp follower, a hard-core member of the group's fans, known as Deadheads. He says his father and mother are Deadheads. As a babe in arms, he floated through concerts where, between Bob Weir riffs, hawkers extolled the wonders of LSD, and the smell of marijuana and incense clung to the air like that of newly mown hay.

He's no stranger to what some call soft drugs—psychedelics like LSD, mushrooms, mescaline, and peyote. But he's about to learn a harsh lesson. Nowadays soft drugs can get you hard time, and lots of it.

In the spring of 1989, Martensen says, he met a man named Gary at a Jerry Garcia concert in Maryland. The fellow told Martensen he wanted some LSD, and it was only years later that Martensen learned he was a stool pigeon. Martensen couldn't find Gary any LSD in 1989, but they stayed in touch.

Martensen says he ran into Gary at several more concerts in places like East Rutherford, New Jersey, and Philadelphia, and always, he says, the guy asked for LSD. Martensen never had any. He made his own spending money by stir-frying vegetables and selling them at concerts. He also hawked T-shirts.

In April 1991, Martensen's luck ran out.

"I needed money to fix my car. Gary called again, and I told him

I'd find some LSD. He said he'd be bringing his boss along. I was going to make five hundred dollars out of the deal. Only problem was I couldn't find any. It took me three days to find a guy who knew another guy who had some."

Gary's "boss," it turns out, worked for the Drug Enforcement Administration. He was posing as a fellow Deadhead.

"As I look back on it, it was so obvious he was a cop," Martensen says. "He didn't know anything about music, he was very obnoxious and loud, and didn't even smoke pot."

Martensen brought his two acid contacts to a meeting with Gary and the DEA agent in a hotel near San Francisco airport. Martensen had begun having some doubts about Gary, but he says he went ahead with the meeting because he had promised Gary he would.

Martensen says the sources of the acid, Jeff Penkala and Glen Forbes, counted out the drug for the agent in front of a hidden video camera. Right after the deal went down, Martensen, Penkala, and Forbes were arrested and jailed.

The three later pleaded guilty to selling 1.56 grams of LSD. But Martensen says it had been dripped onto blotter paper in an effort to represent it as twenty thousand hits. That was stretching a gram and a half pretty far, and by doing so they may have done irreparable harm to themselves.

The new federal sentencing guidelines enacted by Congress in 1987 specify that the amount of nonparolable time a drug dealer receives is relative to the weight or amount of drugs involved. The more drugs, the more prison time.

So the prosecution is asking the judge to weigh the blotter paper also—and thereby increase the length of the sentences the three will receive. A previous court ruling appears to favor the prosecutor, but so far U.S. district court Judge Vaughn Walker has refused to go along.

On October 11, Judge Walker sentenced Martensen's co-defendant, Forbes, to six and a half years in federal prison. The U.S. attorney appealed that sentence, and if he prevails on the appeal, Forbes can be resentenced to as much as twenty-one nonparolable years in prison.

On the same day, John Runfola, Martensen's attorney, argued a motion on his behalf. He presented scientific evidence that LSD and blotter paper are not a mixture and said the paper's weight should not be used to extend the length of the sentence.

"If we win that argument, I get about five years," Martensen said. "But if we lose, I get from twelve to fifteen years."

Martensen's motion not to include the weight of the blotting paper was granted by the judge, but because the government appealed that ruling, Martensen's sentence remains in limbo pending outcome of the appeal.

While he is waiting out the judicial process in the halfway house, Martensen is spending his days—and some nights—as a full-time student at City College of San Francisco, studying history, writing, and music.

William McGivern, the U.S. attorney for Northern California, said of the Forbes appeal:

"We think the guy should have gotten more time. We also feel we are right according to the law, although the judge didn't agree. It wasn't the first time that defendant Forbes had been involved in an LSD case, and we feel that these defendants are a danger to society."

I asked McGivern if it wasn't more of a danger to society to lock up young people for fifteen years or so and have them return as hardened criminals.

"Congress must have considered that. Congress passes the laws, and we just uphold them," he replied.

I also asked him if there were provisions in these laws for men like Martensen who have no previous criminal record—or for some dumb flake who just gets in over his head.

"There are downward departures from these sentencing guidelines for minimal involvement," he said.

But Martensen's lawyer, Runfola, says these downward departures are very minor. "Essentially, the co-conspirator will get as much time under these guidelines as the main guy," he said.

Christian Martensen reminds me of one of those legendary gooney birds of the Pacific islands during World War II, the ones that flew wide-eyed into airplane propellers. I can't help but wonder how many other young kids are out there passing LSD around like chocolate chip cookies, totally unaware of the many years they would have to spend in prison.

A seasoned criminal would have smelled cop and stool pigeon all over the deal Martensen was involved in. But the three young men apparently had no idea of the seriousness of the game they were playing. Twelve to fifteen years in a violent prison may change all that.

Ever loyal to his roots, Martensen recited a verse from the Grateful Dead song "Truckin' " when I asked how he feels:

> Busted down on Bourbon Street,
> Set up like a bowling pin.
> Knocked down, it gets to wearing thin.
> They just won't let you be.

Martensen might sound flippant, but he is now fully aware of the seriousness of his predicament, and he is disturbed both by his own situation and the broader implications.

"I feel my life is getting sucked right from underneath me. I don't think justice is being served by giving me that much time. Not for me, not for society, not for anyone."

---

A little over a month and a half later, the other shoe was dropped on Christian Martensen. A three-judge panel of the court of appeals ruled against the young man, and he entered a federal prison for a term that could last as long as seventeen years. It is hard to imagine what good is served by the decade and a half that the U.S. government will have to feed and house this gentle and naive twenty-two-year-old.

The injustice of Martensen's sentence troubled all of us who met him, but we could not linger long on his travails, for within weeks after Dannie's story on Martensen ran in "Sunday Punch"—and days before Dannie's own scheduled release from the halfway house—the author himself was in deep trouble. His anxious stay at the halfway house ended in bitterness and a kind of slow-motion panic. He told the Kafkaesque story a few days later in the *Chronicle*'s news section.

---

# THE TOOTH SHALL SET YOU FREE

*SAN FRANCISCO, CALIF. (FEB. 22, 1992)*—Valentine's Day—a week ago yesterday—began as a great day for me, and I felt wonderful.

Little did I know that before the day was over I would be the victim of a Valentine's Day massacre of sorts.

I was taken hostage and terrorized by unthinking bureaucrats. Even the tooth fairy apparently was a witness against me.

At Eclectic Communications Inc., the federal prison halfway house in San Francisco, I was about to sign out for my holiday weekend pass. The following Wednesday morning, February 19, after eleven and a half years in custody, I would be officially out on parole.

I already had permission from my parole officer to travel to Texas when I was released, to visit my daughter, my four grandchildren—three of whom I'd never met—and my ailing father, who had promised me he wouldn't die before I got there.

As I approached the desk to sign out for the weekend, a halfway house worker said to me, "You aren't going anywhere, Martin. You've been restricted to this facility."

He handed me an official form, outlining charges against me. It stated that a "hard rocklike yellow substance, approximately one-quarter inch in diameter" had been discovered during a shakedown in my room and "field tested" (with a kit) at the federal prison in Pleasanton.

The "contraband," I was informed, was "found to be positive for amphetamines." The BOP form further stated that the substance had been found "in resident room #301, specifically, in a cardboard box on a wall shelf." I had been sharing room 301 with a roommate.

I looked up in terror. That report could add many months to my time in custody, and I had no idea what it was all about.

I asked the halfway house worker to show me the "attached memorandum" that the document referred to. "No," he said. "You can't see anything!"

My roommate had been given a similar incident report. Under BOP rules, any illegal substance found in a common area is charged to everyone in that area.

My roommate and I assured each other that neither of us had stashed any drugs in that room. We returned to our room, which was a shambles.

Back at the desk, I asked Yolanda Lewis, the supervisor, what the "contraband" looked like. "I can't talk to you about that," she said. "You'll have a hearing Tuesday."

When I persisted, she became extremely agitated. "Martin," she said, "you've been in the system forever. You know what's going on, and that's it."

I then demanded a urine test. I'd passed all the urinalyses in the four months I'd been at the halfway house, including two that week. But I wanted a new one. "We give tests when we feel like it," said Lewis, "not when you want it."

I retreated to a day room and sat smoking, staring at a cockroach and dreading the fate I saw unfolding before me: a routine hearing and a return to prison.

That's when the Cough Drop Theory hit me. I'd had pneumonia when I got out of prison, so I must have left a yellow cough drop in my box of personal possessions.

I went to a pay phone and called Peter Sussman, my editor at the *Chronicle,* and told him that I thought I was being shafted on a cough drop. He reassured me and promised to round up legal help.

That night I received a call from Alan Ellis, an attorney who is an expert on Bureau of Prisons rules and who had agreed to represent me pro bono, with assistance from attorney Kim Kruglick and investigator Barry Simon.

The next day, in the elevator, I chanced into one of the men who had helped shake down my room. I asked him if what they found looked like a yellow cough drop.

"I can't talk to you about that," he said. "I can't talk to you about anything."

It was the same story with my caseworker. No one could tell me anything.

By Tuesday, my roommate and I were both wrecks. He waived his right to witnesses and was tried immediately. I refused to follow suit, and my hearing was set for the next day.

Lewis, the supervisor who had denied me a urinalysis, and Pat Williamson, another employee, presided at both hearings. My roommate was summarily convicted of narcotics possession, and the recommended sentence (which had to be confirmed by the BOP) was return to prison, but that penalty was suspended provided he spent thirty extra days in the halfway house and received additional drug counseling.

On the form my roommate received after his hearing was the notation that "confidential information . . . not provided to resident" was used in reaching the verdict. It was the first we had heard of this.

After a heated argument with a halfway house employee, I was allowed to call as witnesses the two men who had conducted the search.

Last Wednesday, my hearing began at noon, four hours after I had been scheduled for release. The happiest day of my life had turned dreadful.

I was informed that the "contraband" had three times "field-tested" positive for amphetamines, but my attorney had been denied confirmation in a lab test.

The two men who had searched the room came in one at a time. I showed my cough drop, and they said no, "the substance" didn't look like that. "It looked like crack cocaine and was wrapped in a napkin with a rubber band around it," said the man who had found it.

So much for my Cough Drop Theory.

Steve Hubert, a staff psychologist who represented me at the hearing (I was not permitted to have an attorney present), argued forcefully in my behalf.

It took the two hearing officers about five minutes of deliberation to find me guilty. My recommended sentence was prison (suspended) and thirty more days in the halfway house. That sentence could have been lengthened by years once my case went back before the parole commission.

Afterward, as the psychologist tried to console me in the hallway, a picture suddenly entered my mind.

I recalled sitting in a dental chair two months earlier, having a tooth replaced. "Here, I've brought you the one that fell out," I told the dentist, handing him the tooth wrapped in a napkin with a rubber band around it.

"My God, man," I nearly shouted to the psychologist, "they have my tooth."

Ellis somehow persuaded BOP lawyers to have one of their dentists look at the "contraband." One look and the bureau's dentist confirmed that the illegal substance was my own tooth.

The bureau informed Ellis that I was free to pick up my parole papers. I later learned that my roommate was informed when he returned from work that his charges had been dropped, too. He said he was told that the substance had been tested a *fourth* time and come up negative. He was not told that the substance was my tooth.

As I signed the release forms Thursday night, it dawned on me that the "confidential information" that the BOP said was used to convict my roommate and me must have come from the tooth fairy. No one else could have known.

I was overjoyed to be released after my six-day nightmare on Taylor Street, but my joy was dampened by thoughts of all the convicts I've known over the years who received extra time over some substance—things like pencil erasers and Top Ramen soup—testing positive in a field test. Men who were badly wronged but had no money or access to a newspaper editor or a lawyer.

---

Beneath that story, the *Chronicle* ran the following line: "No one from the Bureau of Prisons was available to respond to Dannie Martin's story." But a persistent *Chronicle* editorial writer, Michael Harris, finally wrested an official reaction from BOP spokeswoman Monica Wetzel:

"He was exonerated. It shows our system works."

"It shows no such thing," Harris added in his editorial.

Even with continuous outside assistance, Dannie's new crisis was resolved only because of an unorthodox demand on the BOP. Ellis's hands were essentially tied because attorneys were not allowed at the hearing. When Ellis requested a lab test of the seized substance, he was informed that the field test is what all convicts get, and "Dannie Martin will have to be treated like everyone else."

Meanwhile, I conferred with Dr. David Smith, a prominent San Francisco specialist in addiction medicine who regularly consults with major corporations on employee drug testing. Dr. Smith told me that the field test for amphetamines is notoriously unreliable, showing frequent false positives for substances with no psychoactive properties—things like Vicks over-the-counter inhalers. "If they're using that test for forensic purposes, without a lab confirmation and a clear chain of control," he said, "it's totally irresponsible."

On the evening of Dannie's conviction, Ellis and I plotted strategy by phone. I was concerned about Dannie's mood. He had gone sleepless for days, and he was worried that someone at the halfway house could plant a gun in his room as easily as whatever it was that did appear to have been planted there. It's the kind of tactic he was used to in prison. Indeed, Dannie was again talking about returning to prison, where he could identify his enemies more easily.

Ellis had been laying the groundwork for an administrative appeal and a court challenge later. Because of my concern about Dannie's depressed mood, I argued for a bolder confrontation immediately. We had nothing to lose. I spent the rest of the evening calling dentists.

When we demanded the next morning that the BOP let our dentist inspect the "contraband," bureau attorneys were apparently startled enough by the novel proposition to agree to send a prison dentist to check the object. Soon after the inspection, a BOP attorney called Ellis to say, "Tell your client to come pick up his parole papers—it was his tooth." No other hearing or procedure was necessary.

As disturbing as the incident itself was what it revealed about the ways of the prison system. Most obvious was the issue of convicting on the basis of unreliable field tests. But I learned some other startling lessons about the standards by which convicts are judged at disciplinary hearings in prison or at halfway houses.

Not only are both inhabitants of a room held guilty for any contraband found in the room, but the standard of proof needed to establish their guilt is neither "beyond a reasonable doubt" nor "preponderance of evidence." All that was necessary to retard Dannie's parole was "*some* evidence," and the prison system had that in the field test results, however unreliable.

Also troubling was the fact that the chairperson of the discipline committee was an involved party. Yolanda Lewis had had frequent run-ins with Dannie, and now she was presiding at a hearing that could have resulted in his serving years more in prison.

Such was the suspicion with which Dannie was viewed by the prison system that even after the "contraband" in his room was identified as a broken tooth and Dannie was released, one BOP official maintained that he must have been *chewing* amphetamines, traces of which remained on his tooth (but somehow didn't register on his frequent urine tests).

███

So, bitter about his final days at the halfway house and uncertain about his future as a writer, Dannie began his parole. He needed at least part-time employment to supplement his nascent writing career, and in Ellis he seemed to find just what he was looking for.

The attorney, who specializes in post-conviction law, is besieged by prisoners' requests for representation. It is not easy to evaluate the merits of those potential cases in collect calls from prison, and Ellis needed someone who knew his way around prisoners and the prison system to assist him as a case analyst. Dannie had all the necessary skills—he had been using just such talents when he checked out prisoner grievances for his articles—and Ellis offered him a part-time position as a consultant. "No one," Ellis told one reporter, "can decipher a con man like an ex-con."

The catch was that under his parole conditions, Dannie was forbidden to "associate" with convicts. Dannie's parole officer and the U.S. Parole Commission ruled that it would be a violation of that provision for him to talk with convicts by phone as part of his job with the prominent national law firm. They refused to make an exception, as had sometimes been done for other ex-cons with similar job offers.

In a newspaper interview Dannie asked caustically, "If I worked at McDonald's and a con came in, couldn't I sell him a hamburger? To say I'd be associating with convicts is chickenshit." He speculated that prison authorities "don't want me to know what goes on inside" the prisons.

---

With problems of halfway house and parole dogging him, Dannie had little leisure to evaluate the personal pressures that bore in on him in the free world. And nothing that happened to him in prison had prepared him for coming back to himself.

That part of Dannie's story is still developing—his book is being written as his life is being lived—but the man who wrote with refreshing honesty of his prison experiences for newspaper readers feels a similar responsibility to the readers of this book to explore candidly his sometimes troubled personal transition to "civilian" life. Dannie sums up those experiences and his future prospects in a previously unpublished essay.

## A TASTE OF FREEDOM

My writing for a mainstream newspaper was an escape plot. It was a way to escape the black hole in which all prisoners are placed by society and it was a way to escape from the tedium of the place—the day-in, day-out routine.

In 1986, I was six years into a thirty-three-year sentence. My prison drug record was abysmal. There was talk of forcing me to serve until my mandatory release date, which would have put me out in 2002. My counselor first raised the possibility of taking away my parole date, and his words hit home because the same thing was happening to other convicts at Lompoc.

In 1985 my mother died, and there's no way to describe the loneliness that settled upon me after her death. To a convict on the prison treadmill, a mother means more than anything. She's the one calm and steady force in a troubled, tortured life. Ask any convict what Mom means to him or her.

So in a sense, I also needed to escape that gaping hole of loneliness her memory left in my spirit. That's hard to do in prison, but I solved the problem by reaching beyond the fence. Many of the things I wrote about were things my mother had asked me over the years about prisons—things I'd never got around to explaining to her. I'm glad I still had enough sense to realize her curiosity was probably universal.

When I submitted my first article on AIDS in prison to the *San Francisco Chronicle* in the summer of 1986, luck happened to be riding on my shoulder. The article reached an editor who had as much curiosity about prisons as my mother. It was largely through him nudging me that I began to understand that I could define the prison experience in a mainstream newspaper. It was something that had never been done. More than fifty articles later, when I was released on parole, after sharing numerous journalism awards with my editor, I was proud of the body of work that we had done.

And yet, when I finally walked out the gate in 1991, I felt more like a fugitive than a writer.

My jail stuff is done for this book. I can't feed on that carcass any longer. It's time now to talk about Alice when she got to Wonderland, which is how I felt getting back to the free world.

I moved into a nice apartment with a woman friend. I was swept up in rounds of interviews, talk shows, parties, dinners, and a speech here and there. Some very good people had donated money, so I got nice clothes and other necessities. It was a wonderful time. I was a lot better off than most guys coming out the gate. I had developed many friends through my writing who helped me financially and otherwise. I had a cushion.

But even with all the attention, in my heart of hearts I still felt more like an escapee than a writer. In the halfway house I'd been treated like a prisoner on a brief outing. I kept feeling that I had to do and experience everything I could before they took me back.

That eleven and a half years had driven my spirit into concrete and iron as if it had been shot there with a stud gun.

It is only lately that I realized I never expected—maybe never even wanted—more than about ninety days out here in the free world. After all those years, all I really wanted was a break, some rest and recuperation before returning to duty. Women, oysters, peace, freeways, alcohol, drugs, and haute cuisine. Just a good taste of freedom. I figured ninety days should just about wrap it up.

The parole commission had denied me a consulting job with an attorney because I would come into contact with convicts and ex-cons through my duties there. Instead, I was running into all kinds of ex-cons through the drug testing I am required to do at least three times a week. I also go to counseling once a week with a room full of ex-convicts, and almost daily, as I walk the streets of this city, I meet someone I've known in prison. All those people are potential sources of drugs and constant reminders of the dilemma I'm trying to escape.

The only ex-cons I'm not supposed to hang out with are the ones who could do me some good—the people I might talk to on the phone in the course of earning a legitimate living; also, old friends who have found a way to stay straight and are eager to help me remain out here.

Although my writing has changed me somewhat, much of the change was in the public perception of me. Inside, I really hadn't changed that much. At some point I got a legitimate prescription for codeine and was soon taking a lot more of the pills than had been prescribed.

I thought I would use opiates the way rich people do—legally. It didn't work, of course. My candle began burning at both ends. I could feel the undertow gently sucking at my feet from behind prison walls.

I began missing appointments and deadlines. My parole officer was saying things like "Now, Martin, you're taking a lot of codeine." My candle began burning hotter and dropping wax.

My life was being lived in two worlds, on two levels. I was a drug addict rapidly burning up his freedom and I was the writer with some projects going—nothing very definite yet, but some things in the works. In fact, pencil wasn't touching paper much anymore, and it's hard to be a writer unless you take care of that part of it.

Between these two worlds, I still had an overriding sense of lone-liness. I believe I was lonely for the tribe that over the years had become my family.

My daughter and granddaughter visited me from Texas. I nodded and mumbled the entire month they were here. My daughter pulled me aside one evening and said:

"Dad, you've got to quit that shit."

It wasn't only my daughter and family. I could see pain in the eyes of friends I was letting down—people I didn't have time for now that opiates had entered my life again. I began to feel like the same old tortured fool I'd been twelve years ago. It wasn't a feeling I wanted back in my life ever again, but there it was.

Then I began a cycle of trying to clean up. It was the first time I had ever tried to get on top of my habit before it led me by the nose right back to prison.

I had never done or even attempted to do a parole in my life. I'd always begun using drugs and running right from the gate. One time it took them two and a half years to apprehend me. Whenever they caught me, I'd kick another habit in jail and go back to prison on a parole violation, usually with a new charge or two.

This time, I began to realize, it wouldn't work again. I can't run anymore. I'm too wrapped up in my writing and my family and the friends I've made along the way.

Cleaning up after this lapse has made me feel much stronger and more confident than I've ever felt before. I know now that I can live without a cage around me, and it's a wonderful feeling.

Drugs left a hole in my spirit, but they haven't done near the damage that the cage has done to me. It's difficult to admit to myself that my deepest goal in life was to get beyond a razor-wire fence and spend ninety days in the free world. Prison time will do that to a man or woman—reduce goals and horizons to seeming absurdi-ties. It warps a person.

I think about these young people now doing twenty and thirty years—with no parole—for first-time drug involvement. If eleven years made me yearn for ninety days, would twenty years cause one of them to long for six weeks? The minor orgy I had would be an April shower compared to what they will have to cram into six weeks after twenty or thirty years.

If we keep stuffing people willy-nilly into prisons at the rate we have been, we had damn sure better find out all that those places do other than hold felons and provide jobs for failed military types. Prisons propagate the ways of life that we're most concerned about doing away with. They deform minds and kill spirits.

Not long after I cleaned up, I began to realize that nowadays I identify more as a writer than a dope fiend, a convict, a bank robber, or anything else. The thing that helped me the most to understand this was rereading hundreds of letters from my readers and meeting people on the street who recognize me and comment on my work.

Many of them tell me what an important contribution I've made to society by interpreting issues in human terms that heretofore had never been defined by a convict or anyone else.

I decided not to repay their gratitude by falling back into my own self-destructive trap. I decided it was time for personal bookkeeping, some assets and liabilities. I was winning awards and making speeches at Rotary clubs and lawyers' conferences. I have prided myself on the honesty of my prison journalism, and now I don't want my awards or my speeches to be a lie. I don't want my life to be a lie. I am determined to try my best to live the life of a writer.

I've made some friends on this writing journey, people that I dearly love. Most of them aren't aware of how it's been with me. They think I was "sleepy." The ones who are aware of how it's been have gladly gone that last mile for me. Those are people like Peter Sussman, and Jan, my roommate.

I have always been aware of the chasm between the way prisons are run and operated and the way the public thinks they are. Most convicts are maddened by that recognition sometime or other because they see it so vividly.

I feel very fortunate for the opportunity to attempt a bridge across that gap in a mainstream newspaper. The progress I and my editor made was sort of like rock climbing—feeling for a ledge or a foothold wherever we could find one. It was dicey at times but always exciting and a hell of an adventure for an old, tired, and lonely convict.

When my release finally arrived and the adventure ended, I suffered a loss of confidence in my ability to write in a totally new environment. That subtle feeling of inadequacy took hold and grew. I reacted in familiar old ways. Self-sabotage is another word for it.

Time now to climb the rock.

Living with the flamingos isn't bad at all. They're set in their ways and don't take a lot of foolish chances. They'd rather endure pain than tempt the madness that lurks in painkillers. They do have their little eccentricities, but at night in their homes they are comfortable. They don't fear that knock on the door.

On city streets in daylight, they don't look over their shoulder. It's not a bad life-style, and it surprises me to find that I may be able to adapt and fit right in with the flock.

I have the taste of writing in my mouth again, and it's sweet on the palate. Today, I took two old friends to a train station and a man sitting there on a bench said to me:

"Aren't you Dannie Martin, the writer?"

He went on to say how much he enjoyed my "dispatches from the dungeon," and talked about some of the insights I'd given him about prison life.

I felt grateful toward the man not because of his praise about my writing but because to him I was Dannie Martin the writer, not Dannie Martin the ex-con. I begin to think I can live the image that man has of me instead of the one I brought out of prison with me.

I can now begin scraping off these old self-destructive tendencies like barnacles from the bottom of a ship. It's not easy, because their roots run deep and have been nurtured for years by institutional accommodations.

I'm beginning to understand that my roots as a writer run just as deep. I'm fortunate that they never withered and died in the parched and unfeeling environment where I spent so many years.

The old fugitive has escaped the trap that lay just beyond the wall, and I've got my next caper planned out well.

I'm going to commit some big-time journalism.

# EPILOGUE: DUNGEONS AND DRAGONS

"She is an opium-eating dragon from the land beyond the Great Wall. The vilest sort of dragon ever known. How she got here I know not. . . . She must be dispatched. It's either her or us."

"I believe this was once the dungeon where the most evil prisoners were kept. . . . I don't like it because the gate is made of iron. . . . The presence of iron has weakened our ancient lands."

Sixtoes left the broom in his bedroom and would not use it. He had been heard to say, "Why should I sweep away my footprints. If they cling to the mother earth, do not they belong there as well as I belong to the world? I have nothing to hide."

—From Dannie's fairy tale,
"Sixtoes and the Lonely Isle"

The lonely isle of Dannie's beloved fairy tale contains twin evils that are never fully distinguished—the dungeon and the dragon. The man who created that magical place has been haunted by both, has wrestled with both. But he has refused to surrender finally to either, even when he was in its thrall. To have given in would have destroyed what he cherished most—every person's right to leave his own individual footprint on this earth.

"I pretty well caged my dragons in that area," Dannie once wrote hopefully to Mike Schwab, speaking of drugs. In the end, though, he brought his dragons out with him when he left the dungeon. It is not surprising.

Prisons and drugs are inseparable. First, of course, drugs are widely available in prison. And this country has used prisons increasingly as places to isolate those of us with drug problems—often for decades, in some states even for life. Yet what happens to such people in prison generally has little positive effect on the drug problems that helped to send them there.

As Dannie wrote once, speaking of the prison building boom:

Sowing prisons means reaping convicts. It's another form of deficit spending. If the authorities can't control drugs with existing prisons, I wonder why they say that building more will help solve the drug problem. That's like saying that building more hospitals will stop disease. Prisons are results, not preventive measures.

Prisons not only don't prevent drug problems, they may actually exacerbate them. The heroin dragon feeds on low self-esteem. It digs its claws into people who, for whatever reason, crave dependency. Prison, in turn, fosters submission and habitual dependency. It further *de*personalizes people whose overwhelming need is to *re*personalize. "Prison *is* an addiction," says one former inmate.

Sending people to prison punishes them, as it should. But except in rare circumstances, we are not helping people survive in this society by taking them out of it. Learning how to be controlled, often harshly, in prison does not teach one to make reasoned individual decisions on the outside.

Dannie wrote often in his "Sunday Punch" essays of the toll prison exacts of its inhabitants—the self-hatred, the "rage, frustration, and alienation," and, beyond that, the "impotence, futility, and resignation." For those serving long sentences, he wrote, "the future is totally devoid of hope, and people without any hope are dangerous—either to themselves or others." And he confessed how, with violence all around him, he watched as his own feelings disengaged from his senses.

Years earlier, he wrote in a letter from prison to his friend Diane Osland, "I know that I can't get even or regain anything I lost in here. All I can hope now is that it doesn't take more than I can afford to pay."

In Dannie's case, the question now is not how much he can afford to pay but how much he has already paid—to both the dungeon and the dragon. And it was not until he left prison that he could begin to separate the two.

---

**P**risons are necessary. Some people belong there (as Dannie did in 1980), although perhaps far fewer than we now send there. But because prisons affect the people placed there in ways that often reinforce the very behavior they are designed to punish, it is essential that outsiders learn what goes on behind bars.

For the public to get the perspective it is missing on those places, we will have to rely on the kind of people who live there. We have been lucky to find an observer with the honesty and the humanity of Dannie Martin.

Over time, and not of his own volition, his personal fate became a part of the story he was telling. Partly that was because of the prison's response to his writing. But also, the American way is to focus on personality, not issues. Dannie's is an engaging personality. But it does come with all the flaws that one finds in the places where he has spent most of his life.

Dannie is not a Jack Abbott, a killer, a violently paranoid and dangerous man, a bitter writer. But he has been an addict and a criminal and a dependent of the state for most of his life. He has never claimed otherwise.

---

**I**s he rehabilitated now?

"Rehabilitated?" Dannie once asked me. "Hell, I've never been *habi-litated*."

"Rehabilitation" is a useful concept in penology. But the word often carries simplistic, moralizing connotations. In common usage, it is based on a criminal stereotype that rarely fits actual people. It is as if everyone is labeled, by some immutable law of nature, either "criminal" or "noncriminal," without the grays of real life. (Remember the recent "law and order" president who violated both the penal codes and the Constitution itself, yet declared, "I am not a crook"? He could find refuge in that contradictory assertion because of just such faulty stereotypes of criminality.)

Well, then, can Dannie at least make it out here this time? Can he find an accommodation that works?

Dannie's writing experience has given him tools that he did not previously have at his disposal—and not just in a narrow vocational sense. The habit of writing and the dialogue he established with me and with his readership have, over time, given him new, less impulsive ways of evaluating his experiences. In the act of communicating with the straight world, he began to adopt both its terms of reference and even some of its values.

He emerged from prison with a stake in society that he'd never had before. He had a body of work of which he is justly proud. He had writing projects on which he was eager to embark. And, for the first time in thirty-five years, according to an old friend, Dannie had "a group of friends he likes a lot and who like him who are *not* junkies. He had the camaraderie he always thought he'd have to give up if he were straight. As his support system grew, he seemed more certain of his ability to stay clean."

But he was still an ex-con adrift in a scary world.

The longest he had been out as an adult was thirty months—and never during those brief sojourns was he drug-free. Cumulatively, he had spent about twenty-six years behind bars.

It took American society years to appreciate the panic of many Vietnam veterans returning by plane from the barbarism of that jungle war to the deceptive comfort of our consumer society. The public has yet to understand the feelings of an ex-con released from a far longer tour of duty in a world every bit as alien as a Southeast Asian jungle at war.

Like the Vietnam vet, Dannie can anticipate years of flashbacks and cultural readjustment. As a recovering alcohol abuser and heroin addict, he faces a lifetime struggle. He plans to stay off drugs, but as he once told a friend, "I have never met a junkie in my life who planned to be one."

The story we have told does not and cannot have the tidy ending of a fairy tale. Dannie's frailties speak for themselves. But so do his achievements and his newfound potential. As Herman Melville wrote in "Billy Budd," "Truth uncompromisingly told will always have its ragged edges."

■

Dannie and I over our years of working together have gone from strangers to colleagues to friends. Ours is not a friendship based on similar upbringings or social and educational status. Rather, we are like war buddies who have fought side by side through so many battles that we have come to share a common history and a mutual respect and trust. We have had to rely on each other, and we have.

As his editor and the one who shared his experiences most intimately these past seven years, I have been changed by the experience, too, and there may be a lesson for the journalism community in my own experiences: that the most enlightening journalism does not end on the printed page. The same risk of personal involvement that in some circumstances results in unacceptable bias can also bring invaluable journalistic insights that would otherwise be unavailable.

That is especially true when, as in this case, the considerable forces of government are mobilized to cover up places that manifestly need uncovering. Prisons are the most secretive of public institutions. To open up those hidden places demands a commitment, if not a crusade.

Such personal involvement can also be a useful and refreshing antidote to the slick corporate journalism and the hyperkinetic public-relations machinery that often compromise the profession, robbing it of much of its initiative, its spontaneity, its honesty, and, in the end, its significance.

In his court testimony, Warden Rison referred to Dannie and me and "the activities they were involved in, whatever that was." Well, it's called journalism.

■

In the United States today, one of journalism's most urgent callings is to explore the roots of our out-of-control crime problems. We cannot hope to solve those crippling problems without understanding them from all perspectives—perpetrator as well as victim, police officer, prison guard, warden, judge, government policymaker, and academic expert. Of those perspectives, perhaps the least understood and the least available is that of the criminal.

Understanding other viewpoints does not mean condoning them.

But without such understanding, our crime-and-punishment dialogue will be impoverished by the same clichés that have perpetuated this muddle: "crime in the streets," "law and order," "throw away the key," "country-club prison," "teach 'em a lesson," "drug-crazed punks," and so many more. Those are emotion-bearing clichés, but there are others that are more neutral and that also mask real experiences—terms like "recidivism" and "security." Such terms are the common coinage of reporting in newspapers, which generally pay scant attention to events inside prisons.

Social problems appear manageable when the words are familiar. But the comforting terms disguise the complexity of our problems, and our social options are limited to repeats of past failures. We cannot hope to hide every malefactor behind either bars or clichés. There are simply too many criminals and not enough bars or clichés.

Feature journalism offers the reader another lens—a way of looking at real, particularized experiences. It's especially useful in inaccessible places like prisons. On complex issues like crime and punishment, it's an important supplement to deskbound reporting. And, of course, it offers a depth that is impossible in the letter-to-the-editor sound bites permitted by federal prison regulations. Done well—as Dannie did them—such stories help us to bypass the gridlock of conventional attitudes. As James Baldwin wrote in another context, in *Notes of a Native Son,* ". . . one is doomed to remain inarticulate about anything which one hasn't by an act of the imagination made one's own."

Dannie and I never expected to become entangled in a years-long First Amendment dispute, but in retrospect we should not have been surprised. The people whose fragile voices need constitutional protection are rarely pillars of the community; they are more likely pariahs of the moment—eccentrics, protesters, outlaws. But they have much to teach us.

Public dialogue thrives on diversity. When we are all in agreement, no one is offended, but no one is enlightened either. It is the business of journalists to further public dialogue, so it is our duty as well as our right to publish without restriction these divergent voices.

We half expect First Amendment issues to come to us written on parchment, but it doesn't happen that way. They are as likely to emerge from a telephone message slip or a hand-printed letter from a prison cell: "Peter: I'm in Isolation. They won't give me *anything*. Not even a pencil or paper. I borrowed this stub from the man next door."

The Bureau of Prisons' exaggerated response to Dannie's writing was as revealing as the stories he set out to tell. If our legal challenge proved nothing else, it at least assured that the issues of prison accountability and accessibility would be aired in the retelling.

No government bureaucracy is more isolated from public scrutiny than prison management, partly because the public is happy to leave to the prisons a job for which it has no stomach. Former state correctional official Patrick McManus, in a declaration to the court in our case, said:

> Prisons are not self-healing institutions. Because legitimate power is so unevenly distributed between the keepers and the kept, left to its own inertia abuses of that power will inevitably creep into any prison without diligent and sensitive oversight. Prisons generally are tucked away, off the main thoroughfares of social criticism. In my experience, they can readily become places where constitutionally intolerable practices become accepted, and hence have drawn the vigilant scrutiny of the courts.

Too frequently, prison administrators less enlightened than McManus take advantage of their isolation and autonomy by assuming total control of prison information, suppressing what they don't want the public to hear. In the final arguments of our lawsuit, Assistant U.S. Attorney Mark St. Angelo argued: "The issue here, your honor, is communication with the public . . . and the Bureau of Prisons can make sure that information gets to the public."

But control of information is not a neutral, managerial function. "The prisons want their own voice coming out," Dannie once told an interviewer. "I guess they don't like mine."

St. Angelo maintained throughout the trial that information must be controlled because what goes out to the public can then return to the prison in the newspaper and undermine security, to which McManus, a member of the correctional hierarchy, replied in his testimony:

> The fundamental issue with publishing in general-circulation periodicals is not to let the inmates inside know what they already know; it's to let the folks on the outside know what they may not know.

Isolated and secretive though they may be, prisons are public institutions whose policies have important consequences for the public welfare and safety. How felons are treated within prisons has a direct bearing on their behavior when they emerge to live among us again. We must examine all aspects of incarceration before the increasing reliance on long prison terms, with little judicial discretion, creates an irreversible social tragedy and a fiscal nightmare.

The role of the news media is not limited to policy issues. They act as a kind of constitutionally protected ombudsman. They provide a forum for prisoner grievances and a safety valve for the abuses that are bound to flourish in closed, authoritarian institutions. Dannie's own best protections from retribution were the unremitting interest of the news media and the popularity of his own writing. They probably did more to protect him from unjust punishment than the courts did.

■

The governmental elites that control access to public information are also likely to be the people shaping our stereotypes, such as those we have attached to criminals. Indeed, they often owe their tenure to those simplistic attitudes. The 1988 George Bush campaign's Willie Horton ads served such a purpose.

In America today, we are all frightened by crime, and government officials have stoked our anxieties. In our confusion we have allowed our fears to dictate new crime policies, and we have cast prisoners as simple projections of our worst fears. But fear makes bad law.

It is almost axiomatic that depersonalized people are capable of barbaric acts. If we continue to assume that every lawbreaker—or every lawbreaker who doesn't wear a white collar—is Jack the Ripper, then we can expect to find many more criminals acting out the roles to which we have relegated them.

The prisoners who succeed are the ones who are able to find new identities besides heroin addict or criminal.

In the reactive and predatory environment of prison, says one ex-con, prisoners become self-destructive. They survive by reflex, at whatever cost. Dannie's writing, says this former convict, has shown his fellow prisoners ways to evaluate their own environment. "If they can understand it," he says, "they can survive it as human beings."

■

In an interview once, Dannie was asked, "Do you consider writing work?" He replied:

> Yeah, but it's work I enjoy doing. Writing is the only thing I've found that I'm good at. It's the only thing I ever tried that I didn't fail at. And even if I fail as a writer, it wouldn't be nearly as bad as failing in another bank job.

Before 1986, society defined Dannie Martin. When he began to define himself—as a writer—the government tried to take away his name and stop his writing. That action jeopardized society's interests, and it threatened the hope he represented for other convicts.

In his dispatches from prison, Dannie did not exonerate his fellow prisoners. But he gave them back their names and personalities and families and the same vulnerable emotions we all have. He restored their human complexity. That may be the first step out of our quagmire of crime and punishment.

■

> The dream then took him back to the Fairy Wood, and he could see his mother, Cleo, standing over one of his footprints in the glade while saying to some other fairies that stood about, "No! You will not sweep away this footprint. It belongs to my son, Sixtoes, and it was meant to be here."

# ACKNOWLEDGMENTS

The events chronicled in this book, as well as the writing of the book itself, required an expenditure of time and a single-mindedness of purpose that would try the patience of the most devoted of friends and family members. Foremost among those who have shown us more patience and support than we have any right to expect are Pat Sussman and Jan Sluizer. They have made our cause their own and stood by us through the high moments and the low, with humor, with ideas, with energy and solace and perseverance, and with unconditional love. They are the hidden heroes of this story.

Countless others have contributed much and endured much during the six-plus years of our saga. They include family members who often were due more of our time than we were able to give them in the heat of battle—Stephanie Sussman and Katherine Sussman; Deborah Woodbury and her children, Nathaniel and Linaea; Julie Carpenter and her children, Star, Thomas Jordan, Jonathan, and Linda René; and our surviving parents, Ann Rosenberg and Roy Martin. (Roy Martin died just prior to publication of this book.) Jerry Martin and Peggy Frost were helpful in sharing their family recollections for this book.

Colleagues, too, got caught up in the vortex of this demanding venture and had to cope with less guidance and assistance than we owed them. They did so cheerfully. Thank you, Leslie Guttman; also Teresa Castle, Alice Kahn, Wendy Sheanin, Tom Meyer, Margot Doss, Mike Bigelow, and so many others at the *San Francisco Chronicle*—not to mention the many colleagues whose words of support at the water cooler made the discouraging moments more bearable. And to Regan McMahon, kudos for her "guest headline": "The Tooth Shall Set You Free."

When our otherwise successful efforts ran into a fusillade of opposition from prison authorities, higher editors at the *Chronicle* backed our efforts without hesitation. Assistant Managing Editor Rosalie Wright was encouraging from the start. Executive Editor William German and Managing Editor Matthew Wilson gave us enough rein to commit our unprecedented brand of journalism and enough legal support to protect us when those journalistic efforts drove us into dangerous territory. And Editor and Publisher Richard Thieriot, with nary a word of complaint, provided the generous financial backing without which this thin voice from the prisons would have been stilled.

City Editor Dan Rosenheim and his editors and reporters willingly and skillfully investigated both the abuses we uncovered and the abuses to which we were subjected.

Of necessity, our legal case became at times as much a crusade as a "job." Without many attorneys' vigilance, creativity, and doggedness—and inordinate amounts of time—we would have been lost in the judicial never-never land that has swallowed up so many otherwise worthy causes. Many of our attorneys worked virtually around the clock with little hope of recompense—none more persistently than Jeff Leon. Others who at one time or another worked with selfless dedication on our behalf and, in the process, redeemed in our minds and hearts a much-maligned profession include John Hagar, Bill Turner, Ron Ingram, Lisa Zinkan, Marty Kassman, Jim Wagstaffe, Neil Shapiro, Mark Tuft, Alan Ellis, Joseph Kennedy, George Harris, Bruce Sanford, Bob Lystad, Doug Lee, Carol Sobel, Debbie Leon, Donna Brorby, and Elizabeth Laporte. Our thanks, too, to the ACLU Foundation of Southern California for its backing.

Many personal friends were continuously supportive, never flinching when the going got rough. People like Mike Schwab, Diane Osland, Barbara Bliss, Paul Allen, Rev. Victor Carpenter and Cathe Carpenter, Janet and Rudy Hurwich, Ed Bender, Sandy Pyer, Kathy and Ed Dieden, and so many more.

Drs. Arlan Cohn, Don Brown, Bruce Bothwell, and David Bradshaw generously donated their time and professional services. Bob Madory and the San Francisco Hearing and Speech Center were also most supportive. We are indebted, too, to Dr. Mary Ann Barr for her thoughtfulness and insight.

Readers of the *San Francisco Chronicle* "Sunday Punch" section responded with hundreds of stirring letters that gave us the heart to forge ahead against often maddening obstacles. They became our allies and our friends. Many rolled up their sleeves and provided special assistance—monetary, legal, emotional, secretarial. We cannot acknowledge them all, but it would be a great injustice not to thank publicly Ed LeClair, "Rosebud," Nancy Hoffman, Connie Lurie, Gerald M. "Evil Roy" Martin, Laurie and Jake Rohrer, Leni Miller, Terry Pearce, Dr. James Harris, Bruce Roy, Melissa Snyder, Mary Straus, Gloria Snyder, Stephen Townsend, Matilda Kunin, Joyce Leopardo, Sandra Sears, and Carmine DelaBarre.

Others, in the legal, political, and journalistic communities, offered valuable counsel and went out on a limb to give our endeavors legitimacy through public and private endorsement. They risked their good names to defend us. We are grateful to Supervisor Terence Hallinan and Sheriff Michael Hennessey of San Francisco; also, Jessica Mitford, Justice William Newsom, Judi Epstein, Terry Francke, Betty Medsger, Tom Goldstein, Olive Talley, Judy Rowcliffe, Micha Peled and Dan Kalb and Nell Bernstein and the other dedicated people at Media Alliance, Sandy Close, Loren Ghiglione and Craig Klugman of the American Society of Newspaper Editors, Michael Rosenthal, Mel Opotowsky, Don Specter and his associates at the Prison Law Office, Ben Bagdikian, Sara Miles, Luke Janusz and his associate, Dorothy Walsh, of the prison magazine *Odyssey,* Wilbert Rideau of *The Angolite* at Louisiana State Prison at Angola, Dennis Riordan, Donna Rosenthal, and the many conscientious people at the Society of Professional Journalists both locally and nationally—far too numerous to mention, but including most prominently Bruce Brugmann, Carolyn Carlson, Reginald Stuart, Paul McMasters, and Fred Talbott. It is gratifying to be part of a profession that has such people in it.

Mark Mauer of the Sentencing Project in Washington, D.C., provided many of the imprisonment statistics that we have included in this book. The project itself provides an essential public service in assembling such statistics.

In addition to its other assistance, the Society of Professional Journalists helped to organize and finance the amici curiae brief that gave national stature to our legal appeal. Other organizations that stood up to be counted in the appeal are the American Society of Newspaper Editors, the Associated Press, the California First Amendment Coalition, the California Society of Newspaper Editors, McClatchy Newspapers, the Press Enterprise Co., the Reporters' Committee for Freedom of the Press, and the *Stockton Record.*

The Scripps Howard Foundation, the Playboy Foundation, the California Freedom of Information Committee, The Newspaper Guild, the James Aronson Award jurors at Hunter College, the Brechner Center for Freedom of Information, the Media Alliance, the California Society of Newspaper Editors, the Society of Professional Journalists, PEN American Center and Newman's Own, Inc., and the Prison Law Office have all recognized our efforts, several of them before it was "safe" to do so. With such invaluable institutional backing, our small voices were amplified considerably.

Miles Corwin, John Roemer, Craig McLaughlin, Lisa De Merritt, Joel Simon, and Alex Sokoloff have all written penetrating profiles of Dannie for various periodicals, and we have made use of several of their observations and the quotations they elicited. Eric Spillman generously went back through his records to confirm years-old memories.

It may not be proper to acknowledge by name the work of all the journalists to whom we are indebted. Their efforts were dictated by professional responsibility, not personal allegiance or conviction. But their even-handed attention to our quandary and our legal case gave us a measure of credibility that was vital to our cause. Almost uniformly, they probed beyond official press releases. We are grateful for their dedication. It is their professional fate to remain unnamed, but we know who they are and we hope they recognize themselves in this description.

Our thanks to literary agent Fred Hill for his skilled and energetic assistance and to Gerry Howard, our editor, and the others at W. W. Norton who took a gamble on a journalist and an ex-con with no previous book-writing experience.

And finally, we have been the beneficiaries of truly heart-warming support from prisoners throughout the country. They have sent us glowing letters of support and provided legal research and valuable inside-the-prison information, often at great risk to themselves. To name them might further jeopardize their already precarious positions, but we are ever mindful of their courage, and it is our hope that this book will help to put prison issues back on the public agenda and in some way improve the conditions and the lives of our necessarily anonymous benefactors.